The Other Side:

Closing the Door

by

Donna Girouard

Front Cover design by Brandon Coley
Back Cover design by Donna Girouard

"The Old Front Porch" appeared in the February 2014 issue of *Gravel Magazine*.

"Adopted" appeared in the August 2013 issue of *Sugar Mule*.

An excerpt of "The Fat Tree" appeared as "Guerilla Baptism" in the Fall 2014 issue of *The Riding Light Review*.

"Doppelgangers" appeared in the Fall 2013 issue of *Border Crossing* and was nominated for The Pushcart Prize.

"Vincie" appeared in the May 2013 issue of *Apeiron Review*.

"The Most Important Thing in the World" appeared in the Spring 2013 issue of *The Oklahoma Review*.

"Your Father's Children" appeared in the 2013 issue of *Florida Literary Magazine*.

"Going Home" appeared in the anthology *t(here): Writings on Returnings*. Ed. Brandi Dawn Henderson. Copyright 2014 by Martelet & Mare.

The author has made every effort to recreate the incidents and conversations recorded n this book as accurately as possible but acknowledges that others' memories may differ somewhat from hers. A couple of the names in this memoir have been changed to protect the privacy of those individuals and their families.

ISBN-10: 0996424903
ISBN-13: 978-0-9964249-0-5
Printed in the United States.

To Scott, who encouraged me;

to Chloe, who inspired me;

and, most of all,

to my mother, who never stopped believing in me.

1921—1996

Table of Contents

2008: A CROW FLIES OVER NORTH BROOKFIELD

THE DRIZZLE IS FRIGID FOR EARLY MAY, AND THE TENDER NEW SHOOTS JUST BE-
GINNING TO BUD HANG LIMP IN THE MORNING FOG, BUT THE OLD CROW DOESN'T NOTICE.
MOST CROWS LIVE ONLY INTO THEIR TWENTIES, ALTHOUGH SOME HAVE BEEN REPORTED TO
LIVE MUCH LONGER. SHE DOESN'T KNOW IT, BUT THIS CROW IS WELL INTO HER THIRTIES.
SHE DOES KNOW THAT SHE HAS SPENT MOST OF HER LIFE ROOSTING HERE IN THE LOOKOUT
TOWER OF THE ABANDONED BATES OBSERVATORY ON BELL HILL. IN 1893, T. C. BATES DO-
NATED THE TOWER TO THE TOWN OF NORTH BROOKFIELD AFTER BUILDING THE RESERVOIR
THAT PUMPED WATER FROM HORSE POND FOR ITS RESIDENTS AND SPEARHEADING THE IN-
STALLATION OF THE UNDERGROUND WATER SYSTEM. LOCAL LORE HAS IT THAT BEFORE THE
SURROUNDING TREES MATURED, THE MASTS IN BOSTON HARBOR COULD BE SEEN FROM BELL
TOWER, BUT, DESPITE THEIR SHARP EYESIGHT, NO CROW HERE CAN SEE THAT FAR, EVEN ON
A CLEAR DAY, BECAUSE OF ALL THE OVERGROWTH. THE OLD CROW DOESN'T REMEMBER A
TIME WHEN THE OBSERVATORY WASN'T EMPTY - BOARDED UP AND FORLORN, THE RESERVOIR
DRY.

THE CROW PERCHES ON THE EDGE OF THE CRUMBLING BRICK AND STRETCHES HER
WINGS, PREPARING FOR FLIGHT. SHE HEARS THE OTHERS IN THE MURDER CALLING OUT TO
EACH OTHER IN THEIR SEARCH FOR FOOD. THE ACREAGE AROUND THE TOWER PROVIDES AM-
PLE UNDISTURBED AREA FOR FEEDING, BREEDING, AND PLAYING BIRD-GAMES, BUT THIS CROW
PREFERS THE CEMETERY AT THE END OF BELL STREET FOR HER BREAKFAST. WITHIN SEC-
ONDS, SHE REACHES ST. JOSEPH'S CEMETERY AND PERCHES ON TOP OF THE STATELY
WROUGHT IRON GATE. SHE SEES NO ONE AND HEARS ONLY THE TWITTERING OF THE MUCH
SMALLER BIRDS, CHICKADEES AND ROBINS LOOKING FOR WORMS. SHE CALLS OUT, WARNING
THEM TO MOVE ASIDE FOR HER, AND FLIES OVER THE GRAVESTONES IN THE PART OF THE
CEMETERY WHERE NO ONE PLACES FLOWERS ANYMORE, THE OLD SECTION WHERE LIE THE
IRISH IMMIGRANTS AND THEIR OFFSPRING: "RYAN," "O'BRIEN," "SULLIVAN," ROW AFTER ROW
OF FORGOTTEN STONES. THE OLD CROW PAUSES BEFORE ONE, "ELIZABETH KELLEY — BORN
IN IRELAND," TO EAT THE REMAINS OF A MOUSE POSSIBLY DROPPED BY AN OWL MAKING HIS
PRE-DAWN ROUNDS. SATISFIED FOR THE MOMENT, THE CROW THEN TAKES TO THE AIR. ON
HER WAY OUT OF THE CEMETERY, SHE FLIES OVER A SOMEWHAT NEWER SECTION WHERE A
HEADSTONE ALONGSIDE THE ROAD STANDS OUT BECAUSE OF ITS LARGE ST. THERESA STAT-
UE. THE NAME "MARTIN" IS ETCHED INTO THIS STONE, AND ON ITS OTHER SIDE, "ANNIE G.
KELLEY." THE SKELETONS OF LAST YEAR'S PORTULACAS CROWD THE STATUE'S BASE UN-
DER WHICH ELIZABETH KELLEY'S DAUGHTER AND HER FAMILY ARE BURIED.

1

The Old Front Porch

I sit on the step, on the hard concrete that stays cool despite the muggy July nights, and I wait for him: my prince, my white knight, the man who will drive just past my house and stop at the stop sign. He will turn his head and see me sitting here, softly illuminated by the street lamp at the intersection and be struck – LOVE AT FIRST SIGHT – such that he will be compelled to round the block. Oh, the romance of it! Though a bit shy (as am I), on his second circuit, he will speak, *must* speak, and we will both remember this moment as magical.

It can still happen, I tell myself, even after all the fruitless years of my sitting out here, waiting and watching for him. The time just wasn't right before; perhaps I was too impatient, or perhaps *he* wasn't ready. So I gave up hope and left my home for a man whose past needed running away from. We fled to the tropics and together we made a life and a child. I tried convincing myself that my life there was perfect, then good, then . . . good enough. Finally I realized that complacency isn't a substitute for joy. Joy! I wanted joy in my life. I returned home hoping to find joy and the passion I'd always promised myself would fill my heart. Now as both my child and my elderly mother sleep inside the house, I sit here and wonder if my soul mate will pass by my porch on this night.

So many hours during my early teens, I pulled down the shades, and in the half-light of my bedroom, wallowed in the pain of unspoken love, unrequited love, rejected love, lost love; expressed through the outpourings from my stereo and blasting through the yearning and pain in my own soul. Art Garfunkel's "Looking for the Right One," a repeat offender on special occasions when my aloneness felt unbearable, broke me into pieces. My mother, wise in so many ways despite her limited education, never invaded my privacy. Only when I finally emerged from my pit of despair into the daylight, ragged and tear-stained, did she approach.

"Get out," she encouraged me. "You won't meet anyone in your room. And you need to smile more."

Sometimes, when my adolescent self-pity hopelessly prophesied nothing more than a lifelong wasteland of solitude, I went to the back porch, tucked into a corner of the house and partially hidden from Forest Street's few passersby, where I continued to sulk. However, sometimes I would head for the front porch, more of a concrete stoop, because of its proximity to the traffic that passed by on North Common Street and because a spark of hope had been lit in me that IT. COULD. HAPPEN. Right here in this very spot where I now sit. I knew it then as I know it now because it *had* happened once, long ago, to my mother.

The chipped and weathered clapboards that are now covered by faded yellow aluminum siding would have been a smooth light gray in 1937 and the porch a grand wooden farmer's porch that wrapped around the Martin house's front corner, its railings surrounded by hedges and lilacs. A porch swing hung slightly off to the side, partially hidden by roll-up blinds, but directly in front were the captain's chair that belonged to my grandfather, Homer, and the rocker in which my grandmother, Annie, spent many hours overseeing the neighborhood. When my grandparents first bought the house in 1920, Annie finally pregnant with my mother after years of trying, the roads had not yet been paved, and rows of boards served as a sidewalk. As the first house in Little Canada to be converted to a single-family, in the section of North Brookfield originally built for the factory workers and their families - and the merchants too - the working class people who were immigrants or first generation Americans, the Martins' corner home had achieved a certain amount of status in the neighborhood, its matriarch herself a merchant, owner and operator of Pauline's Dry Goods, a notions store that thrived in the house's downstairs half that would later be called "the Other Side." Annie's store had a large picture window in front, shaded by a striped cloth awning and its own little porch that Homer

kept scrupulously swept. The store's private front and rear entrance indicated that the house had originally been built for just such a purpose, the large open space accessible to its owner from inside the main house by way of one door on the first floor, tucked into the end of a short hallway so as to be hidden from view of the other rooms.

At sixteen, my mother had already dropped out of school. At first, she secretly worked in the asbestos factory where Homer had been hired as soon as he'd been old enough and would work until he could work no more. He had already started to cough and had nothing good to say about the place but felt he was too old at fifty four to begin another career. Once the deception was found out, after weeks of looking over her shoulder and ducking around corners, my mother was forced to quit her job at the factory ("No daughter of mine will work in that filth," Homer had exclaimed), but she refused to return to school. Annie compromised and hired her daughter to stock shelves and wait on customers in the store that had been named after her.

The day the front porch worked its magic, Pauline had stepped out of the store to take her break, get some fresh air, perhaps sneak a cigarette. A pretty girl with her father's dark hair and eyes and her mother's fair Irish skin, my mother would have taken in everything she could see from her vantage point on the porch, the front porch, not the little store porch where Annie would be keeping watch. From here, Pauline could see all the way down North Common Street and around the Town Common, up North Common Street towards St. John, and part way down Forest Street towards the Kelley family home where her mother had grown up. Polly, as her friends called her, would have missed nothing, so she certainly saw the strange car even before it approached the house. Automobiles were not numerous in this neighborhood. The Martins themselves never owned one, and most people walked where they needed to go or paid for a ride in Mr. Bush's taxi, a real taxi now

that he'd retired his buggy and team of horses. Those few cars that did routinely pass through Little Canada, like Polly's Uncle "Bun" Martin's Ford, would have caused only a passing glance.

But this, a strange black car, driving slowly as if unsure of the area, this required Polly's full attention. She waited, watching as it rounded the corner down by the Common and headed her way. As it approached, she demurely looked down. She wouldn't be caught acting as if she cared. But the car slowed, the engine idling, and despite her resolve, she looked up.

Three young men, a bit older than she, all with thick, dark, curly hair and swarthy complexions, brothers as it turned out, Italians from Brookfield, all waved at her. She blushed, looking over her shoulder to make sure that Annie hadn't somehow seen. Annie still hadn't forgiven her older daughter Ruthie for eloping ten years earlier and would no doubt take unkindly to the impertinence of three boys from out of town approaching her younger daughter. The black car, driven by the oldest Faugno boy, continued up the street, but not before Polly got a good look at the boy in the back seat, the best looking of the three with his broad shoulders and dazzling smile.

All that afternoon in the store, Polly fantasized about the boy in the back seat. Would she ever see him again? Annie had had to raise her voice to be acknowledged, and Polly had mistakenly overcharged Mrs. Adams for her purchases, counting the buttons twice.

The next afternoon, Polly kept an eye on the clock, and at precisely the same time as the day before, she asked if she could go outside for a breath of air. She waited on the front porch, her heart pounding, hoping for, but simultaneously fearing, sight of the black car. And then, there it was, rounding the corner of North Common Street. This time, she looked off in the distance, with an expression she hoped passed for nonchalance on her face. This time, when the car slowed, the boys spoke: "Hello, hello." She smiled and waved, just a little; after all, she was a good girl.

The boy in the back seat leaned out of his window. "What's your name?" he asked. Polly looked into his deep dark eyes and fell in love, right there in front of God and the whole neighborhood. As if in a trance, she stepped off the porch onto the narrow boardwalk and up to the car. Johnny Faugno, the boy who would within the year become her husband and then the father of her son Jay, reached out for her hand and she let herself be swept up in the magic.

That's how my mother's life as an adult began, right here on this porch. Many changes have taken place in the house since that day almost sixty years ago when my mother fell in love. Pauline left home but didn't go far, only a couple of houses up the street to a second floor apartment to begin her married life. Four years later, when Annie died of pneumonia, my mother moved back home with her husband and son, having already realized the mistake of her marriage, and there she stayed, through the death of her father, her bitter divorce from Johnny, Jay's departure for the Marines, and her remarriage to the man who would be my father.

In 1962, when I was three, my mother decided to renovate the house she had bought from my grandfather in 1943 for one dollar. Keeping the deed in her name alone as she had promised Homer, she took out a mortgage, and the work began. My mother had always resisted Annie's love of the old-fashioned (along with her love of the color grey); once, as a small child, she'd been severely punished for taking one of Homer's saws to the headboard of her bed in her attempt to "make it modern." Now as the well-established owner of the house with money coming in from her new husband's job and whatever she earned by taking in children while their mothers worked, Pauline could finally afford to make the changes she'd dreamed of. Interior improvements included new appliances for the kitchen and a new full bathroom upstairs in mint green and lemon yellow. She chose yellow again for the house's exterior color, aluminum siding that the salesman promised would last forever and never need to be painted. So the weathered grey clapboards were covered up, the modern hiding the outdated.

But my mother did not stop there. The wooden farmer's porch, once the grand gathering place of the neighborhood where Homer had sat and Annie had rocked, where all the cousins had played while their mothers - Annie and her sisters and sisters-in-law - had gossiped, and where my mother had first fallen in love, now sagged in desperate need of repair. The steps came loose, the lattice rotted. Pauline decided it had to come down, along with the old store porch and the back porch. Might as well make a clean sweep of it.

Poured concrete stoops replaced all the porches and each entryway was framed by silver aluminum side scrolls that held up the silver aluminum awnings to provide some shade from the sun (though not much relief from its heat). My mother wanted a raised flowerbed, so most of the space formerly occupied by the old farmer's porch became an L-shaped garden for her portulacas and pink plastic flamingos.

The front stoop (I refuse to call it a porch) is just big enough to fit the two matching aluminum-framed chairs my mother bought, their seats and backs of plastic webbing. Chairs that fold for convenience and are still kept in the garage until needed. As a child, on those rare occasions when my parents would sit here together on a summer evening, I had to sit on the steps because there was no room for a third chair. Dad would send me three doors down to Silveo's store for ice cream cones: chocolate chip for him, chocolate for me, and frozen pudding or rum raisin on a sugar cone for my mother. I'd be proud to go, to be trusted by my father with getting this errand right, and I hurried back before the ice cream began to drip. Of course, once Dad began his second shift job at the steel factory, a third chair became unnecessary. Ma's treat for our shared nights on the front stoop was individual store-bought sponge cakes (she called them shortcake and not until much older did I learn the difference)

smothered in Birds Eye frozen strawberries and garnished with Reddi-Whip. By then, Silveo had died, and his store had become a fix-it shop.

On this summer night, long after my father's death, as my mother and daughter both sleep upstairs, I mourn the old front porch but haven't given up on its magic. The foundation is still here, only covered up by the concrete. No matter that the love she'd felt the day my mother met Johnny proved to be false, the spark had ignited right *here*, and I believe it could again. I make a promise to the house: someday, when I am the owner, I will restore its character by tearing off the faded aluminum siding grown chalky with age and give new life to the grey clapboards underneath. I will place new darker grey shutters around windows that no longer have shutters, and, most importantly, I will rebuild all the old porches, especially the grand farmer's porch, using the black and white photographs in Annie's album as my reference. I'm so busy fantasizing about the changes I will one day make that I don't notice the headlights until they've already rounded the corner of the slumbering street.

I hear the car before I see it, and the sound of the purring engine jars me back to my earlier fantasy. A lone car slowly approaching in the middle of a sultry summer night – can this be the man I've waited for? I do not turn away, as my mother did when she was sixteen. I'm divorced with a child; I don't need to be demure. At the same time, if my soul mate is rolling up the deserted street, I don't want to seem desperate despite my rapidly beating heart. I assume what I imagine is a casual posture, and I wait.

As the vehicle nears, I can see the bar across its roof. One of the cruisers just making its rounds. I no longer know who's on the force because I've been gone too long - until recently, returning only for visits. But instead of passing the house, the cruiser stops and the driver's door opens. Almost instantly, I recognize the man even after almost twenty years and despite his full uniform and the dim glow of the street light.

"Joey Hollway! I didn't know you were a cop!" Is this fate? Is Joey, a former classmate and before that a neighborhood playmate, "The One?" I stand up.

"Donna! Long time no see." He gives me a hug and I look for . . . something. In him, in me.

We start to make small talk: what we've been doing since high school mostly, and then he says he's divorced. As he speaks, I remember the Joey from junior high, curly hair, laughing eyes, a bit on the stout side but certainly not fat. Joey was one of the "nice boys," a little shy and liked by the teachers because he was always willing to help when needed. In eighth grade, we had home room together, and I noticed that only he seemed to pray during the moment of silence. Every morning right after the Pledge of Allegiance, Mrs. Lundeberg instructed us to take a moment of silence, and I'd see Joey bow his head. I knew he wasn't trying to show off because he stood in the back of the room. At the end he always crossed himself. When I told my mother, she said, "Joey's a good boy. Good family."

Now as he and I shoot the breeze on my mother's front stoop, I think I could do worse but simultaneously I realize that there's no spark here, for either of us. Just two old friends catching up.

When the small talk ends, Joey tips his hat and turns toward the cruiser. I wait a moment until the car is out of sight, then go into the house.

JUST SOUTH OF BELL STREET IS MT. PLEASANT STREET, AND, AS THE CROW FLIES OVER THE LANE-HERARD ESTATES HOUSING FOR THE ELDERLY, SHE CAN REMEMBER YEARS EARLIER WHEN ANOTHER BUILDING SAT ON THE HILL OVERLOOKING WHAT WAS THEN AN EMPTY FIELD. THE ST. JOSEPH'S SCHOOL ONCE SPRAWLED NEXT TO THE PARISH RECTORY AND ACROSS FROM THE CONVENT. LONG AGO, IN ITS HEYDAY, FATHER MCGILLICUDDY REIGNED SUPREME OVER HIS PARISHIONERS, HIS TYRANNY UNQUESTIONED DESPITE THE STORIES OF LITTLE GIRLS FORCED TO SIT ON HIS LAP AS THEY CONFESSED THEIR SINS OF IMPURITY: "TELL ME DEAR, DO YOU PLAY WITH YOUR 'NAUGHTY?'" BEFORE THE SCHOOL WAS TORN DOWN, THE CROW, THEN YOUNG, HAD FOUND HER WAY INSIDE THROUGH A BROKEN WINDOW AND WOULD SOMETIMES POKE THROUGH THE DEBRIS ON AND AROUND THE MOLDING OAK DESKS STILL BOLTED TO THE FLOORS. NOW, THE SCHOOL LONG GONE, THE ONCE LIVELY CONVENT SITTING EMPTY FOR YEARS, ONLY THE RECTORY IS STILL IN USE, ONE LONE PRIEST RATTLING AROUND ITS DRAFTY ROOMS.

2

Adopted

Biopsy. The phone felt heavy in my hand. I had not yet recovered from my mother's death, and my favorite aunt, my mother's only sister, had just called to tell me of her upcoming biopsy. For months her son Jack and I had been nagging at her to take better care of herself. Well into her eighties, Aunt Ruth had spent over a year putting aside her own needs to attend to those of her husband, Chuck, who lay in a nursing home dying of emphysema.

"She's going to kill herself for that old bastard," I angrily complained to my second husband Bob each time I returned from visiting her and seeing her so worn out. No one could convince my nearly blind aunt, who was trying to cope with her own failing health, that daily visits to see Chuck were taking too much of a toll on her. Even when she saw the bloody discharge in her underwear, she refused to see a doctor.

"I'll deal with it later," she promised me, "Chuck is my first concern." I knew better than to argue.

Upbeat and mellow about most things, Aunt Ruth always held firm in her convictions regarding her husband of over sixty years. In her eyes, he could do no wrong. Neither my mother nor I had ever let on about his attempt to molest me when I was twelve. Certain that Aunt Ruth wouldn't have believed Chuck capable of such depravity, my mother, fearing a rift between her and her only sister, had made me promise not to tell.

So, over the years, I'd gritted my teeth and pretended everything was fine. If my aunt noticed that I would no longer kiss or be kissed by her husband, she never mentioned it. When she told me last year how he no longer seemed in his right mind, how he'd begun calling her from the nursing home at all hours of the night, complaining that she hadn't been in to see him (even though she'd been in just that day) and accusing her of cheating on him with other men, her tone was conversational rather than exasperated. Nothing he did or said ever seemed to faze her. Now it would seem that my fear may be realized; her dogged devotion to him may have ended up costing her her own life.

What to say? How to answer without adding to whatever stress she may be hiding beneath her matter-of-fact tone? I decided to be just as matter-of-fact.

"Well, I'm sure there's nothing to worry about," I tried to keep my voice even. "Cancer doesn't run in our family."

"Well, that wouldn't apply to me," she didn't miss a beat, "I'm adopted."

I laughed. What a kidder. "Yeah, okay." Always smiling, so laid back, Aunt Ruth could be counted on to lighten the mood.

"I'm not kidding." Her voice was serious. "I'm adopted."

That afternoon, I sat on my mother's older cousin Flory's couch, jogging her memory over tea. I'd gotten very little information from Aunt Ruth after her startling revelation, only that she discovered the papers that verified her adoption one day when she was about fourteen. Bored and alone in the house, she'd been "snooping" in the attic. She never mentioned her discovery to my grandparents for fear of being punished. My mother, only about four years old at the time, had been too young to confide in. Even when she got older, Ruth kept her discovery to herself, telling only Chuck. She had no idea who else in the family knew.

"Oh, yes," Flory Barnes said to me on the phone, just minutes after I hung up with my aunt. "We all knew. I'm surprised your mother never told you."

"*Ma* knew?" I thought my mother had told me everything! "I'm coming over."

"Your mother found the papers after your grandmother died," Flory now picked up her teacup, tilted her head back, and looked down at me through her bifocals. "Annie had made her the executrix even though your grandfather was still alive. Homer wasn't really well, you know, even then. He'd already started coughing up the asbestos."

Flory chuckled. "Pauline came running to me first, too, just like you have. I think because I was older and had grown up next door. Of course, I hadn't been born when it happened; I was born right after." She sighed and looked off in the distance. "My mother, Molly, had her hands full with all of us kids, especially after my father died from the consumption. We spent a lot of time over at Aunt Annie's."

Trying to be polite, I cleared my throat. "So everyone knew, but no one ever talked about it?"

Flory peered down at me. "Didn't seem to be any point. Your grandmother didn't want Ruthie to know, so it was all kept quiet."

I shook my head, still trying to absorb everything I'd heard that day. "But my aunt already knew!"

"We didn't know that. Everyone was protecting her – even your mother when *she* found out. But I just assumed that she would have told you when you got older. It's quite a story." She chuckled again and sipped her tea.

* * *

Annie Martin stood alone on the platform in the biting March wind and pulled her heavy knit shawl tighter, wrapping her arms around her ample bosom. She sniffed the air, and despite the ever-present odors of rubber and asbestos from the two factories across the street from the station, thought she could smell the snow that the low gray clouds had been promising all morning. With any luck, the storm would be moving in from the west and therefore not delay the train's arrival to North Brookfield from Boston. Conscious of her rapidly beating heart, she took a deep breath and held it a moment before exhaling, at the same time silently reprimanding herself for being silly.

'Tis but a child, after all, being brought from the big city, and a wee one at that. A little girl who would be theirs, hers and Homer's, and about time too, after nearly six years of a pleasant but childless marriage. Why, Molly already had two children, and though Annie loved taking care of her nephews, her heart had nearly burst with longing both times her younger sister had announced that she was with child.

Many nights as Annie and Homer sat around their kitchen table by the soft glow of the gaslight, Homer, in his quiet way, had tried to reassure his wife that nature would eventually take its course. She was only twenty seven, a bit late to be just starting a family but still well within child bearing years. Worrying about it would do no good, he reasoned, and she agreed; nevertheless, she argued one evening, surely the time had come to face facts: five years was enough time to rely on nature, or faith, or God. The time had come for action. Homer just shook his head. He knew that when Annie made up her mind to take action, the world better step aside.

The next morning, Annie found herself in sudden need of a small screwdriver. Or maybe a hammer. Whatever would be less expensive but would require a trip to Jim Ivory's hardware store around the corner. Of course, she could just walk to the end of the street and knock on the Ivorys' door to ask about the "state" children they took in, but she didn't want to seem desperate. She had her pride. So, over bins of tools and barrels of nails, she casually asked Mr. Ivory how the children were doing, and how many lived at the house now, and how someone might go about arranging to take care of a child from the state – a baby if possible - if someone had a mind to.

That evening, the Ivorys joined the Martins around the kitchen table as contact information was exchanged: names and addresses of case workers who might be helpful. Annie wrote the letters, filled out all the forms, and waited. Finally, a letter came from one of the case workers – a little girl was available for adoption. Her mother, an unmarried medical student from Tufts, had decided she could no longer afford the time and money required to care for the toddler and wanted her to have a real home - away from the city and with two parents. A home visit was arranged. Homer met the train that day and, while Annie fussed with the last minute details at the house, he walked with the case worker from the depot up Forest Street to North Common Street, hoping his brothers-in-law would not see him and decide to stagger out of Hart's Café with too much of the drink in them.

This time, however, Annie herself would meet the train, her arms aching to hold Ruthie, the little girl the case worker was bringing to North Brookfield to her and Homer. Leaning slightly forward and into the wind, wisps of her auburn hair whipping against her forehead and pale, freckled cheeks, Annie squinted through her glasses, hoping to see the first curl of smoke over the trees.

When the train chugged into the depot, Annie barely acknowledged her brother Bob Kelley's greeting as he waited for the tourists going to the Barre Hotel. When Bob was sober, he made a bit of money driving the team for Mr. Bush, whose livery was a bit down and across from the asbestos factory. The horses stomped and huffed, their breath pluming in the frigid air, but Annie's eyes and ears focused only on the people descending from the train.

Ah, 'tis the child! And already walking, but, yes, Annie had known that. A golden-haired child of golden complexion, with a high forehead and tiny nose. Not exactly the fair skin Annie was expecting when told the mother's name was "Cadigan."

"Daughter of a Welsh woman," Annie's younger sister Lizzie Kelley had said, "should fit right in, unless her Da be English." And a big bow in her silky golden hair! Wasn't that just the most cunning thing! Annie vowed then that Ruthie's hair would always be sporting a bow.

Feeling suddenly timid, Annie did not step forward to help the case worker as she led the toddler by the hand, down the steep steps of the train's passenger car. What will Ruthie think of her? Will she cry when the train leaves her behind with a stranger? Ruthie still had not looked up. Annie's heart swelled with longing as she watched the tiny high-laced boots struggle with the steps. The child carried some variety of rag-doll that fell to the ground when her other hand reached out to grab the railing. Unable to hold back any longer, Annie sprang forward and picked up the doll just as the child's feet both touched the ground.

Uncharacteristically at a loss for words, Annie simply handed the doll to the toddler. The case worker spoke first as she transferred the tiny hand in hers to Annie's.

"Ruthie, this is your new Ma," she said.

The child looked up at Annie, and, glory be to God, she smiled.

"Hello, Ruthie," Annie said, "and, yes, I'm your new Ma."

Annie straightened from giving the bean pot a stir and closed the oven door. Her face flushed and dripping sweat, she wiped her brow with a corner of her apron and tried to ignore the little pile of wooden blocks still in the corner. Molly's boys would like those. Now that Molly will be having another baby, she'll be glad for more toys to keep the boys occupied. Now that Ruthie won't be needing them. No, 'twill do no good to think of Ruthie. Tonight Annie's brother George and his wife Florence from next door will be coming over for brew and beans. Think of that, not of Homer walking out the door and down the street with little Ruthie by the hand. Any minute now, the train from Boston will be pulling in to the depot, carrying the caseworker who will take Ruthie back to her Ma, her real Ma, the one who said Annie and Homer could have her baby but then changed her mind. Will Ruthie even remember being here in Annie's home after only a few months? Will she remember being rocked and sung to? Being kissed goodnight? Annie choked back the tears that threatened just behind her eyelids.

Without intending it, Annie found herself at the window, looking across the street at the house she eventually hoped to own. Her French-Canadian in-laws, the Martins, were good to provide the top floor of their

two-family until a proper house could be bought. Annie had already decided on the Barrett house. From her kitchen window, she could see the
wrap-around porch, perfect for a rocking chair or two and planting the
lilac bushes around. The big barn could be a workshop for Homer, and a
chicken coop and lavatory already occupied the sizeable back yard. Annie knew that, on the other side of the house, a large space ran the
house's entire length and had both a front and rear door. A space such as
that could be rented out for extra money to a shopkeeper or, perhaps
someday, she herself might like to run her own store.

The side yard of the Barrett house is ripe for a hammock, Annie
thought now, of striped fabric like the ones in the Sears and Roebuck
Catalogue. She could picture it full of laughing children, one of them a
golden child with a big bow in her hair. Annie bit her lip and turned from
the window.

"Someday, Annie," Homer had said when the bad news came last
week in a letter from Boston, "you will have your house, and we will
have our children. When God decides the time is right."

Annie sat herself at the kitchen table and looked up at the statue
of the Virgin on the shelf near the stove. The Virgin's serene expression
and open hands, palms facing out, promised help to the troubled. Annie's
Ma, Elizabeth Kelley, had raised her to pray to Mary for a heartfelt need
because Jesus never refuses His Mother.

"Please," Annie whispered to the statue, "I want to be a mother
too, like you."

As Annie stood on the platform at the depot, she wished she'd
taken her shawl. She could feel just the nip of an early fall in the air,
enough to raise the goose flesh on her bare arms. In such a hurry she was
to meet the train, she'd rushed down Forest Street oblivious to the chill
until, now, standing and waiting, waiting once again, waiting for Ruthie,
her Ruthie!

Annie had been dickering with the ragman when the letter came.
Another letter from Boston, but this one good news. The caseworker had

written to say that the woman from Tufts who had taken Ruthie back because she missed her so had again changed her mind. Medical school so expensive that she had to work, and she realized she had no time for the toddler. The caseworker had told the woman, name of Cadigan, about Annie and Homer's lovely home and couldn't she see how well taken care of Ruthie had been during those few months she lived away from the city in North Brookfield? A big family she would have, with grandparents up the stairs and down the street, aunts and uncles all around the neighborhood and lots of cousins to play with. This time, the letter had promised, the adoption would be for good. Ruthie would be coming with a paper hand written, dated and signed by Hazel D. Cadigan giving "full surrender" of the child, "Ruth D. Cadigan" to "Mrs. H. O. Martin."

The shrill whistle cut through the air, announcing the train's arrival and exciting the horses Bob Kelley kept reigned in. It being midweek, tourists to the Hotel were unlikely, but the team gave him the excuse to see the joy on his sister's face where lately only the sadness had been. Annie stepped close to the train before it even stopped and peered up into its windows.

"Annie, girl, be careful, or ye'll be sucked in," Bob called from his perch on the wagon.

"I'm fine, Robert Kelley, and you can mind yer business, thank you very much," Annie tried to sound cross at his nosiness but couldn't – not today when her prayers had been answered.

The child appeared, held by the hand of the caseworker, her other hand still holding the same rag doll from last spring's train ride. Annie stepped forward and caught up the little golden girl in her arms. She had so missed the impish little face, the mischievous sparkle in Ruthie's eyes, her tugging of the skirt when she wanted Annie's attention.

"Ruthie, d' ye remember me, your Ma?" and Annie hugged the child who would soon be Ruth D. Martin, all papers that said otherwise to be safely locked away. As Ruthie's chubby little arms reached around Annie's neck, Annie whispered her thanks to the Virgin who had brought Ruthie back home for good. Annie would see to it that no one would ever again take her Ruthie from her.

Annie Martin's hand shook with anger, disappointment, and disbelief as she reread the hastily scrawled note her older daughter, Ruthie, had left on the pillow of her unslept-in bed.

"Homer!" she bellowed.

When her husband entered Ruthie's bedroom, Annie thrust the note at him.

"She's left with him! Eloped!"

Homer silently read the note, his face sad, then looked up at Annie's red, raging scowl and waited.

"She thinks that by sneaking out like this she will get her way, does she?" Annie continued to holler, oblivious to how the voices carry on a spring morning with the windows open. "Well, 't is another thing she has got coming!"

Awakened by all the commotion, six year old Pauline, still rubbing the sleep out of her eyes, walked into her older sister's room. "What's wrong, Ma?" Then spying the still-made bed, she asked, "Where's Ruthie?"

Annie turned to her child, the miracle child she had given up all hope of ever having, finally born to her and Homer right here in this house the year she, Annie, had turned thirty five. "Pauline Ida, 't is nothing to do with you, so go get yourself some breakfast as long as you're up."

Pauline knew better than to argue when her Ma used the mad voice. She scurried towards the stairs and went part way down to where she could still hear.

"Some of her clothes are gone," Homer said in his calm, quiet way while opening drawers and the door of the closet.

"She's still but a child," Annie's voice continued to rise. "Barely sixteen and run off with that . . .that . . Hooligan saxophone player!" She

snatched back the note and headed down the stairs, almost catching Pauline darting down before her and around the corner.

When Annie entered the front room, she could hear the key turning in the lock of the other front door that led to the large space she and Homer rented out to the butcher. A bit of a smell on the slaughtering days, but fresh meat nearly at the fingertips as well as blood and the casings for the boudin that Ida, her mother-in-law, had taught her how to cook for Homer.

As a tenant, the butcher was agreeable enough, and the money he brought in helped to pay the mortgage on what used to be the Barrett house. The Martins bought the property in 1920, right after Annie had discovered she was carrying Pauline. A fair amount of work had had to be done to the house, which had been used as a two-family, but Homer proved handy with a hammer and saw, as most Canucks were. "Give a Canuck a hammer, and he's a carpenter," Annie's father-in-law, Emery Martin, was fond of saying. Homer had converted the two separate living quarters into a single-family, even cutting out walls for doors where needed.

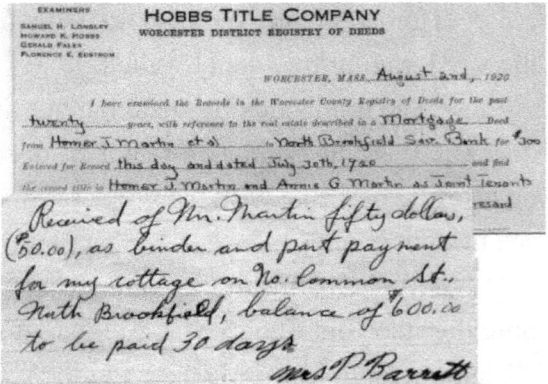

Thanks to the Virgin Mary, Annie had the proper home she always prayed for and the two children too, except that now one of them had gone and run off. Silly in the head over a dirty-minded man too old for her who didn't even have the decency to keep his hands to himself when he came courting. How many times had she caught him pawing at Ruthie's bosom, and even one of her fierce looks brought barely a blush to his impertinent face! Ruthie would be giggling and pretending to fend him off - and Pauline pretending not to see - as Annie fumed. Finally, she and Homer had put the foot down: Ruthie would not be allowed to keep company with Chuck Vernon, a Yank from Spencer. Yanks were only trouble, and what kind of a name was "Chuck" anyway? And no more

out of town dances where a young girl could be taken in by the likes of a saxophone player in a jazz band! Annie had overheard Ruthie confiding to her cousin Flory, Molly's girl, about the band members smuggling in the drink, "hooch" they called it, and the dirty songs they'd be playing, something about "with your pants off" and the whole crowd singing it. No, Annie had decided there and then, if the family dances with the old fiddler in the big barn at the end of Forest Street weren't good enough for Ruthie, then her Highness could stay home and be done with it. Ruthie had not argued (but then, she rarely did), so Annie assumed obedience. The note in her hand, however, told the real story. Ruthie had just decided to wait for the Yank to come snatch her away.

Annie picked up the receiver of the newly installed telephone and asked the operator to connect her with the police.

"But I don't understand, Ma." Pauline whined, her mouth turned down, her eyes threatening the tears, "Why does Ruthie have to go?"

"Child, 'tis my last nerve you're getting on right now!" Annie's patience nearly gone, she continued to stuff Ruthie's things in a laundry bag while Ruthie silently sat on the bed, her head down, her eyes lowered.

Barely two months had passed since the day the troopers brought Ruthie in the back door in front of Pauline and in sight of the whole neighborhood, having finally caught up with her and the Yank back at the Vernon house in Spencer where they intended to live as a married couple. Crossed the state lines, the two had, into Maine, where they had lied about Ruthie's age, and Annie had had a good mind to charge Vernon with the kidnapping, but Ruthie became hysterical, swearing she would behave if only they would let him go, she loved him so. The police let him off with a stern warning never to step foot near the Martin home and not to try to contact Ruthie who would meanwhile be seeing Father McGillicuddy about the annulment. At Annie's insistence, Homer had nailed Ruthie's bedroom windows shut so she couldn't sneak out at night since, clearly, she could not be trusted.

Then the vomiting began and Annie's badgering finally got the truth out of Ruthie. She had allowed that man to be intimate with her even before the night they ran off together, and now her monthlies had stopped.

"There, 'tis the last of it," Annie said and turned to Ruthie. "We'll be taking you there in the Uncle's car. I don't want that man of yours anywhere near this house."

"Ma?" Nearly in tears, Pauline looked from her mother to her sister and back.

"Say your goodbyes now, Pauline. Ruthie has misbehaved, and she will no longer be living in this house." Annie turned her back on the sobs and headed for the stairs.

A few minutes later, as young Emery, one of Homer's brothers, stayed behind the wheel of his idling Model T, Annie led Ruthie by the arm up the walk of the Vernon house on Ash Street in Spencer and pounded on the door with her fist. When the door opened, she did not greet the surprised older woman who stood before her but merely said, "'Tis your son I'll be wanting to see."

Almost immediately, the tall, lanky man with the quick hands and insincere eyes appeared. Annie roughly pushed Ruthie into his arms before he could even speak.

"She belongs to you now," Annie said.

Ruthie turned to face Annie. She hadn't spoken since she revealed the nature of her condition that morning, had barely spoken during the two months she'd been back home, kept nearly a prisoner in her room.

Her large, sad eyes locked on Annie's.

Annie looked at the girl she had raised as her own and remembered a golden child with a big bow in her hair, stepping down from the train nearly fifteen years ago. It was on her lips to say "No daughter of mine would ever behave in such a way!" but, no, no matter how hurt and angry Annie was, she could never tell Ruthie she was adopted. That information had stayed a secret all these years at Annie's insistence. Instead, she looked Ruthie in the eye and said, "You made your bed, I hope you're happy lying in it."

Annie would never know that, having found the adoption papers a couple of years earlier while in the attic where she didn't belong, Ruthie nearly responded with the words that were on *her* lips: "If I were your real daughter, your flesh and blood, you would not be treating me like this." Instead, Ruthie said nothing as Annie turned and walked away.

* * *

Cancer shrunk my Aunt Ruth. Despite the radiation and chemotherapy treatments, the disease ate at her body, and over the last few months of her life, I saw her grow progressively weaker, until she became bedridden in the same nursing home where she had almost daily visited her husband, Chuck, until his death.

The Ruth I knew had always been a woman who saw the bright side of even the darkest day. She rarely got angry, never scolded, and always had a joke or a warm, ready smile. Amazingly, though the cancer ravaged her body, it never broke her spirit. At least twice a month, I drove from North Brookfield to New Hampshire to see her, and every time, she was upbeat. I marveled at (but now understood) the vast difference in personality and temperament between Aunt Ruth and my mother, Pauline.

Certainly, while growing up I had noticed the disparity, especially during my teenage years when it seemed that my mother and I fought over everything. There were times when I would toss in frustration at my mother "I bet Aunt Ruth would let me." My mother's cool response would always be, "Would you like to go live with your Aunt Ruth?" As tempted as I might be at the moment, I immediately thought of the prospect of living with Chuck and kept silent. I had long since stopped spending the two weeks every summer at the Vernons' apartment in Cambridge, then at their retirement mobile home community in New Hampshire. After the uncle that I thought I knew had betrayed my trust in him, I could hardly stand to look at him let alone live there.

My aunt's perpetually sunny disposition had its drawbacks too, however, by discouraging any bad news or negativity. It forced people to feel protective of her good-natured innocence. Since she always remained positive, people around her felt a responsibility to stay positive too. Ruth was not the go-to person to vent anger or feelings of injustice, at least, not for me, nor for my mother. When a woman is angry, she wants the person to whom she vents to feel anger on her behalf, a sort of vicarious misery-loves-company attitude very common among members from both the Irish and French-Canadian sides of my family. My mother had this down to a science, sometimes even to the extreme. She and I would feed off of each other's anger over an injustice done to one of us, until it reached its crescendo, whereupon we could wind down and feel refreshed and ready to move on with our daily lives. Aunt Ruth, however, seemed to lack the ability (the genetic trait? I now wonder) to carry it off and really never even seemed to see the point in trying.

Many times over the years, Ma said to me, "I don't get my sister" and proceeded by relating her most recent attempt at a serious discussion with Ruth, who just didn't have it in her to be serious. I remember many comments my mother made about her "little" sister (referring to height rather than age) and how she wondered how they could be so different. "I don't know where she gets it," Ma said about this or that trait of Ruth's, her remarks making it even harder for me to wrap my head around the fact that Ma knew about the adoption and had kept it from me. Ma had told me so many stories about her own childhood and about my grandmother Annie that I felt almost as if I had grown up with her. Ma's detailed accounts have allowed me to crawl into the skin of this woman who died before I was born and know how she would respond in a given situation. She made Annie come alive for me. My mother had also told me about Ruth's elopement and how, though only a small child, she vividly remembered the police bringing her teenage sister through the back door, the yelling afterward, and then the cold silence that lasted for days. So why hadn't she told me about the adoption? Perhaps for the same reason Annie had never told her: to protect Ruth.

Of course, now that the adoption information was out in the open, I wanted to talk about it, to ask my aunt how she felt about it when she found out and how or whether it changed her, but she insisted the past is the past, so I stopped asking. Not trying to be stubborn, Aunt Ruth simply stayed true to her nature never to dwell on the unpleasant.

The week before she died, Ruth turned eighty nine. Because her birthday fell on a Thursday, and my daughter, Chloe, was in school, I decided to make the trip to New Hampshire on the upcoming Saturday, but I still called to wish my aunt a happy birthday. As far back as I can remember, every year on my birthday, Aunt Ruth would call me and begin singing the birthday song as soon as I picked up the phone. Somewhere along the way, I began reciprocating. This year, I struggled to sound cheerful as I sang, knowing this birthday call to her would be my last. The doctors had already informed the family that Ruth had reached the point of receiving only the drugs to keep the pain "manageable." All actual treatment for the cancer had been exhausted.

As soon as I finished the song, Aunt Ruth surprised me by beginning it again, singing it to herself: "Happy Birthday to me . . . Happy Birthday to me . . . " in a voice so weak she had to pause at the end of each line to gather the strength for the next line. Tears trickled down my cheeks, but I could not let her know that I was crying, just as I could never have shattered her trust and belief in the goodness of her husband by revealing his attempt to molest me. That kind of pain and disappointment had no place in her world, just as acknowledging the pain of cancer and a lingering death had no place in her world. Coming from anyone else, the birthday song being sung while dying and half groggy from morphine would have struck me as bitterness, but coming from my aunt, it fit as a natural response to her condition. I remembered how my mother had re-acted to her own failing health, angry and despairing over what she saw as her body's betrayal. I could understand that reaction and could see my-self behaving similarly. In contrast, however, Aunt Ruth continued to treasure and find joy in each day of her life. Once again, just as I had so many times before, I marveled at her resilience.

Two days later, I stood at the foot of her bed as she attempted co-herence through the haze of the pain killers increased to get her through the end as comfortably as possible. Before the close of the following week, Ruth would slip into a coma and quietly pass on, but now, though she recognized and greeted me, she rambled about events and people from her past, something I had never before known her to do. I only half listened until she started talking about her parents, my grandparents, An-nie and Homer Martin, and what she referred to as "the trouble."

"I'm sorry for all the trouble I caused them," she said, her eyes closed. "I didn't mean to."

I didn't know how to respond. Should I respond?

"I was in love," she continued, "*We* were in love."

I remained silent since she didn't seem to be looking for answers. In her drugged state, perhaps she was no longer aware of what she was saying.

"But it was never the same afterwards," she said. "She never for-gave me."

I assumed "she" referred to Annie, and though I'd not heard it from my mother, her older cousins had told me about the "tension" be-tween Ruth and Annie that lasted even after the birth of Ruth's first baby, second baby, and right up until Annie died of pneumonia when my moth-er was twenty one, Ruth thirty one and pregnant with her third child.

"And Poll got the house," Aunt Ruth said, referring now to my mother, "Poll got everything. I didn't get any of it."

Now I felt uncomfortable and a little guilty. My mother had told

34

me that after Annie died, she and her first husband Johnny had moved into the house with their son Jay to "take care of Pa," who arranged to sell her the family home (where I now lived with my family) for one dollar. It never occurred to me to question what my aunt had received or why my mother, as the younger sister, had been executrix of Annie's estate and had been given power of attorney over Homer's finances. Obviously, I realized now, Ruth's feelings had been hurt enough for the slight to be on her mind over fifty years later while on her death bed. Yet I had never heard her say an unkind word about either of my grandparents, nor seen or felt any resentment directed toward my mother. Even now, Ruth's tone was not bitter or angry, just sad.

"It's okay though," she said, her voice weak and breathy, her eyes still closed. "I don't blame anyone. It wasn't their fault. It was right to leave everything to Poll. She was their daughter. I was adopted."

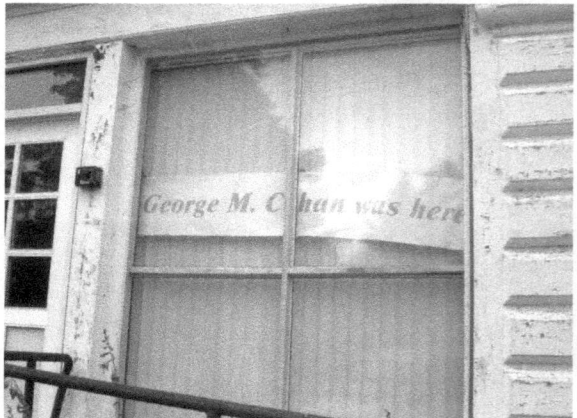

AT THE CORNER OF MT. PLEASANT AND NORTH MAIN STREETS SITS A LARGE VICTORIAN STRUCTURE, MAJESTIC IN ITS DAY AS THE ESTATE OF AMASA WALKER, WHO HID RUNAWAY SLAVES IN ITS SECLUDED ROOMS DURING THE CIVIL WAR. THE RUSTED SIGN OUTSIDE READS "MOHAWK MOTORS," AND IN THE LOT ARE A FEW LEFTOVER GAS GUZZLERS FROM THE 1970S SLOWLY SINKING INTO THE GROUND, THEIR PAINT CORRODING FROM YEARS OF EXPOSURE TO THE ELEMENTS AS WELL AS THE RESIDUE FROM THE SAND AND SALT TRUCKS WHEN THE CORNER ICES UP. THE CROW PECKS AT THE FLAKING PAINT ON THE HOOD OF AN AMBASSADOR STATION WAGON, THEN SIPS FROM THE WATER THAT HAS TRICKLED DOWN THE WINDSHIELD IN RIVULETS AND POOLED IN THE WIPER WELL.

WHEN THE CROW FLIES OVER THE CENTER OF TOWN, SHE SEES A FEW CARS STARTING TO PULL IN TO THE DIAGONAL SPACES IN FRONT OF THE CUMBERLAND FARMS AND, FARTHER DOWN, THE NEWSROOM — PEOPLE IN SEARCH OF FRESH COFFEE OR THE MORNING PAPER. SHE HEADS FOR ITS HIGHEST POINT, THE BELFRY OF THE TOWN HOUSE, AND PERCHES ON THE RAIL. FROM HERE, SHE CAN OBSERVE ALL OF MAIN STREET AND THE STREETS WITH WHICH IT INTERSECTS. THE BELL TOWER IS EMPTY AND LITTERED WITH PIGEON DROPPINGS, THE BELL REMOVED AWAITING REPLACEMENT IF THE CONDEMNED STRUCTURE IS RENOVATED, IF THE TOWN CAN AFFORD IT. BUILT IN 1864 AND LISTED IN THE NATIONAL HISTORIC REGISTER, THE TOWN HOUSE MOST RECENTLY HOUSED THE TOWN OFFICES, BUT LONG PRIOR TO THAT HAD BEEN THE GATHERING PLACE FOR TOWN DANCES, TOWN MEETINGS AND OTHER PUBLIC AFFAIRS. IN 1934, BOYHOOD-SUMMER RESIDENT GEORGE M. COHAN RETURNED TO STAGE HIS RENDITION OF AH, WILDERNESS!, WHICH HE DIRECTED AND IN WHICH HE PERFORMED FOR HIS EXTENDED FAMILY (THE KELLEYS) AND FORMER NEIGHBORS ON THE GRAND STAGE THAT ROTS THREE FLOORS BENEATH WHERE THE CROW NOW SITS.

THE CENTER OF NORTH BROOKFIELD ONCE OFFERED TO ITS RESIDENTS NEARLY EVERY CONCEIVABLE SERVICE, ALL ON OR WITHIN WALKING DISTANCE FROM MAIN STREET: DRUG STORE; HARDWARE STORE; LIQUOR STORE; FRUIT VENDOR; BUTCHER SHOP; RESTAURANT; SHOE STORE; DENTIST'S, DOCTOR'S AND ATTORNEY'S OFFICES; LIBRARY; AND MOVIE THEATER. GAS AND SERVICE STATIONS FLANKED BOTH ENDS OF TOWN. NOW NO ONE SELLS GAS IN TOWN. THE LIQUOR STORE REMAINS, AS DOES THE LIBRARY, BUT EVERYTHING ELSE FROM THAT EARLIER AGE OF PROSPERITY IS GONE, MOVED TO SOMEWHERE ELSE OR GONE OUT OF BUSINESS. THOSE BUILDINGS ON MAIN STREET STILL BEING USED OFFER A COUPLE OF VIDEO STORES, A HAIR AND NAIL SALON, THE CUMBERLAND FARMS AND THE ONLY RECENTLY REOPENED NEWSROOM. THE FORMER STAR THEATER, AFTER SITTING EMPTY FOR SEVERAL YEARS,

IS NOW HOME TO A FLORIST, AN INSURANCE AGENCY, AND A SUBWAY SANDWICH SHOP THAT GOES IN AND OUT OF BUSINESS.

3

The Other Side

Ron Murphy was never easy to get a hold of, so I always tried to make the most of his services when I could. This time, I had a list.

Since I'd had to get a mortgage anyway to pay my brother Jay the $20,000 my mother had promised him in her Will so that I would have full ownership of her house, I borrowed enough additional money to make some necessary repairs as well as some improvements. The electrician had already updated some of the electrical outlets and replaced the fuse box in the hall by the front door with a circuit breaker system. "Wow, this is right out of the 1960s," he said when he'd taken his first look.

I'd also hired a contractor to switch out all the old windows and their storms with vinyl replacements that would be easier to use and clean as well as (hopefully) save me a little on the heating bills of a house with no insulation. At the same time, he replaced the old aluminum screen doors with more solid wood-framed doors and tore down the ugly aluminum awnings my mother had picked out in 1962 after my father and Jay ripped off the sagging porches and she had the formerly gray clapboard house sided in lemon yellow aluminum. My dream was that someday I would tear down the faded and dented siding and either restore the clapboards or cover them with deep gray vinyl, but for now I would settle for rebuilding the porches over their still existing foundations. I not too patiently waited for Mike Sanford, the contractor, to return as soon as he could schedule the job. Meanwhile, I had my list for Ron, the plumber.

"I'm supposed to be retired," Ron grunted when I greeted him at the back door, "but I've got more work now than I ever had."

"That's because you're good," I said. And cheap, I thought. Too many people had figured out that Ron was not out to be a millionaire. He charged fair rates, and he didn't pull permits. If anyone asked, the owner had done the work.

I led him through the kitchen, then stopped to push aside the curtain that hung in front of a small hallway, on the other side of which could be found, on the immediate left, the door to the cellar (just a crawlspace, really) and straight ahead another door into the large space that ran the length of the house and which I was now using as my bedroom. The layout of the upstairs rooms did not suit my need for privacy from my daughter now that I'd recently remarried because the original master that had been my parents' opened directly into the bedroom that had once been mine with no separate entrance into the hall. When I was a child, I'd been forbidden to enter the master unless invited or accompanied, but Chloe lacked the fear of reprimand and punishment that I'd had at her age, so I let her have that inner room with my former bedroom serving as a place where she could entertain her friends. I decided that, with renovation, this large first floor space with its own private entrances was the obvious choice for an en suite master. Ron scratched his grizzled beard as he looked around the area that anyone could see was no ordinary spare room.

"What was this room used for?"

How many times during my life had I heard some form of that question? Elderly relatives and the town's old-timers would ask my mother, much to her annoyance, "What's where Annie's store used to be?"

Guests would sometimes sense the disproportion of the outside to what they were allowed to see of the inside and ask, "What's on the other side of the house?"

"Why are people so concerned about what's in my house?" I often heard her say during my childhood.

Visitors to the house would notice the little hallway with the door at the end on their way from the kitchen into the living room and ask, "What's in there?"

"Just storage." My mother would wave away their curiosity and try to disguise her irritation.

Finally, to hide the hallway, she hung a dark curtain at the opening, but then guests would ask, "What's on the other side of the curtain?" "I don't know why people have to be so nosy!" she'd say after they left.

"What's the big deal?" I sometimes asked. "Just show them."

"I don't want people in there," she insisted. "There's nothing to see."

And for the most part, there wasn't. Yet, perhaps more than any other room, this space on the other side of the house (referred to by my immediate family long before my birth as simply "the Other Side") has led a varied and colorful history since the property's purchase by my grandparents in 1920.

My earliest memory of the Other Side is of a massive, dingy, cobwebby area filled with boxes and old pieces of furniture such as my grandfather's favorite overstuffed chair (badly in need of reupholstering), except for the very front part where a half dozen or so ropes were strung from one wall to the opposite wall. Although the washing machine was in the kitchen, my mother hung the wet clothes on these lines in the winter and on rainy days (instead of on the outside pulley) and set up her ironing board right where Ron and I now stood. The clotheslines had been taken down after Jay bought Ma a used dryer, but Ma's ironing board still leaned off to one side. I had had my first lesson in not touching what I'd been told not to touch when I was about three years old and my mother left her iron unattended to answer the phone. I don't remember the screams that reportedly brought her running back in, but the resulting scars around the fleshy part between my left thumb and forefinger never disappeared.

A round fluorescent kitchen light (yet to be replaced) hung from the ceiling at this front end of the room, and I pulled its chain and turned to Ron.

"Well, this whole room was once my grandmother's dry goods store, but that was years ago. I want to turn it into the master bedroom slash bathroom. That's why you're here."

The first step in my grand plan was to move the washing machine out of the kitchen (replacing it with a dishwasher) to where it belonged: next to the dryer, the same one Jay had surprised Ma with one year when he'd actually remembered her birthday and not had to be reminded. Ron looked at the dryer, then walked over to the exposed plumbing that went from the upstairs bathroom down through this room and into the cellar. Whoever designed the house had had no notion of indoor plumbing when drawing up the plans in 1870, and when a "modern" bathroom was installed, all the pipes upstairs were afterwards hidden by tile work, but their lower extensions remained exposed along the ceiling and in the front far corner of the Other Side.

"Well, it will be easy to tap in over there," Ron said, pointing to that corner, "and extend the pipes to here. I see you got yourself a tub. That's an old one." He walked over to an original claw foot cast iron tub I'd just bought out of a tenement in Worcester.

"The woman I bought it from said her grandmother had had it since 1913. My parents broke apart and threw out the one they'd had the last time they renovated the bathroom upstairs in 1962 or so."

"Lots of people did that. Well, this goes with the character of the house," Ron said.

As part of my redecorating while I'd waited for my mother's Will to probate, I'd removed Annie's long gray wooden store shelves that had once displayed bolts of fabric, notions, and canisters of penny candy, and where my mother had later kept extra dishes and pans, rarely used items like my Memere's bean pot and Annie's meat grinder, and cleaners and other supplies bought ahead. I wallpapered over the plaster walls ("toxic-waste green," my daughter had called them) with what I considered an old-fashioned flower pattern of peach and rose and painted the ceiling with a matching peach. I chose a warm chocolate brown for the wainscot and door frames. I'd always wanted a claw tub like the one in my paternal grandparents' home, a deep tub for stretching out and soaking in, not like the smallish built-in mint green tub upstairs in what would soon be Chloe's bathroom.

I had never liked either the style or colors of my mother's '60s bathroom, but after the nightmares started when I was a teenager, I developed even more of a distaste. Again and again, I would be drawn to the tub, always in shadow, because I could hear the sound of a slowly dripping faucet that should not be dripping. The dreams always abruptly ended the moment I pulled aside the mint green shower curtain to reveal sludgy water just about to overflow the tub's sides. In reality, I had no actual fear of the bathroom; nevertheless, these recurring nightmares spooked me, as if there were some sort of message being sent that I was too dense to receive.

The day I arrived back from Florida to open up and live in the house that had sat unoccupied for nearly a year, I headed upstairs to the bathroom almost as soon as I unlocked the front door. As soon as I sat on the toilet, I could hear it: my daughter Chloe's voice downstairs, yes, but something else. Slowly. Dripping. Water. I looked around, trying to get a grip. Late afternoon sunlight streamed through the window next to me. My dog barked from somewhere in the house, and Chloe laughed. No dream this. I held my breath, and there it was: DRIP. Telling myself I was being silly, yet feeling a weird mixture of dread and awe, I hesitantly approached the mint green tub and slowly drew aside the matching curtain. I screamed when I saw the tubful of stagnant water nearly overflowing the edge. Had I lost my mind? Stepped into some kind of alternate reality? Was this an omen? When my ten year old daughter bolted into the room, she saw me pointing to the tub, babbling "My dream, my dream." No, Chloe was welcome to the mint green '60s bathroom.

"Also, I picked out a pedestal sink for the corner." I now pointed to the spot next to the large ceiling-to-floor drain pipe situated directly under the upstairs toilet, then to a couple of boxes that contained a new traditional-style white sink.

"All doable," said Ron,

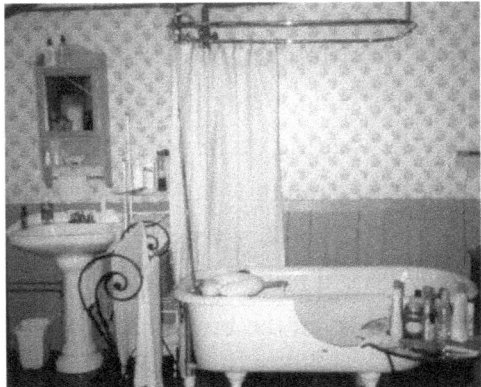

nodding. He pointed to the exposed pipes bracketed to the ceiling. "Those don't bother you?"

"The alternative would be a drop-ceiling, and those are uglier than a couple of skinny pipes," I said.

"Well, it makes things easier for me, but if you ever want to sell the house, those pipes from the upstairs plumbing could turn off buyers."

I shrugged. I had no plans to sell. I expected to live here until the far-off day that Chloe would inherit the house from me just as I had inherited it from my mother and she from Annie.

"One more thing." I'd saved the best, at least in my opinion, for last. I walked back toward the Other Side's inside entrance off the kitchen, where there was another solid wood door with a latch handle. I opened that door, pulled the string hanging from the small, round, metal overhead light fixture, and stood back for Ron to see in.

"And in here is where I want the toilet." Ron looked doubtful until he saw the capped-off pipe in the corner of the closet-sized room.

"There used to be a toilet in here?"

"Yup. My mother had one put in sometime after she inherited the house."

After Annie died, my grandfather sold the house to my mother for one dollar under the condition that she move back in with her first husband Johnny and their four year old son. Homer had already begun to show signs of asbestosis from working at Aztec Industries all of his adult life. A few years later, after his death and after her divorce from Johnny, Ma arranged to rent the Other Side to her Uncle Bob Kelley who was getting on in years but was not yet infirm enough for the nursing home.

"He had his privacy, and I still had mine." She'd told me the story when, as a child, I'd spied the broken toilet with the green seat nearly but not quite buried un-

44

der the coats and jackets hanging from a newly installed rod. "He could drink, and he could come and go as he pleased because he had his own front door."

I'd looked at what, at one time, had been the front entrance to Annie's store and tried to imagine it being used and with its glass exposed. I'd supposedly met Uncle Bob once when he was in the nursing home, but I couldn't remember it. He'd died soon after.

"That way he could sneak in Mary Fletcher, too, and I could pretend I didn't know about it," she said, smirking.

"Mary Fletcher?!" I knew Mary. She lived in an apartment in the center of East Brookfield and because she'd never gotten her license, she walked to North along the East Brookfield Road, knowing that sooner or later someone would see her and give her a ride. Little and round with snow-white hair that she kept in a bun, Mary spoke with a thick brogue and had frustrated me more than once along the way to town with her criticism of America and how it fell sadly short of "Mother Ireland." One time, after we'd dropped her off in the middle of town, I'd said to Ma, "If she misses Ireland so much, why doesn't she just go back there?" "I think sometimes they forget just how poor they were there," my mother had answered. I could not imagine Mary Fletcher as anybody's girlfriend; she had to be in her eighties at least.

"Oh, yes. My Uncle Bob would sneak her in, thinking I wouldn't hear. The next morning, he'd be off somewhere, and she'd be in there all by herself singing. 'Eye-dee-dye-dee-dye-dee-dye.'"

Nope, I couldn't picture it. "And they never got married?"

"No, that's why he snuck her in. It was a sin. She kept the place clean though."

"So what happened? How come he moved out?"

"Uncle Bob started getting a little funny. And he still drank too much. I came home from work one day, and he'd gotten into an old can of paint I had in the barn. He painted a beautiful oak buffet of my mother's that I'd let him use. Painted it yellow. And all the doorknobs too. Every single doorknob in the house. Yellow. After that, I figured it was time."

After Uncle Bob had been moved into Quaboag Nursing Home, the Other Side ended up as the catch-all for unused furniture that I remembered from my early childhood. The little room with the toilet in it became an extra closet, and after a while, since there was no reason to heat a storage room, the bowl cracked from the cold. The day I'd unexpectedly discovered it while being underfoot as my mother pulled out some item hanging overhead, I'd jumped back, scared at first. The cracked toilet with the green seat peeking out from among the coats had struck me as vaguely evil. Eventually, it was pulled out and brought to The Dump, but the pipes and the drain had merely been capped off and now could be used for the new white toilet with the oak seat that I bought.

Of course, the current downstairs toilet would be removed since there'd be no need for it with an en suite master. I walked Ron back through the Other Side door and into the main room of the downstairs living space. During my childhood, this room had been first the living room and later the dining room. Annie's ball and claw set had gone to Jay according to my mother's Will, along with the china cabinet and oak buffet. I'd donated the pictures of Jesus, the statue of the Infant of Prague, and most of the crucifixes, except for the couple I'd given to my daughter for her vampire kit. I'd gutted the horsehair plaster walls and put up sheet rock, replaced the outdated wall-to-wall with inlaid linoleum, and decided tongue-in-groove pine wainscot would give my new living room the Shaker look I wanted. Annie's cherry rocking chair had come down from the attic and snuggled into the corner by the closed door to which I now led Ron.

I turned the knob to reveal an area about two feet by three feet and again stepped aside.

Ron gaped. "A toilet! In here?"

"Yeah. I want it gone."

Ron looked back toward my living room, his eyes wide.

"This used to be a dining room," I said. "You can imagine what it was to have a toilet practically next to the dining room table. Even with the door, there was no privacy."

"I can imagine," said Ron, shaking his head. "So what was this originally? A closet?"

"It was my grandmother's pantry, but when my mother decided to use the Other Side" - I gestured - "as storage, she didn't need a pantry. She'd already taken the old broken toilet out of there and instead put one in here." I rolled my eyes. I'd always been embarrassed by having a toilet just off the dining room. You couldn't wash your hands in there because there was no room for a sink, so you had to use the sink in the kitchen. The room, if you could call it that, was barely big enough to turn around in, although my mother had hung a mirror at eye level directly opposite the toilet. In order to use it, though, you practically had to straddle the seat. There'd been plastic shelves behind the toilet, over its tank, for tissues, extra toilet paper, Q-Tips, etc, and an ashtray had been screwed into the wall within easy reach so that my father could smoke while he read the paper and did his business. Granted, we usually ate in the kitchen, but Sunday dinners and holiday meals always took place in the dining room and, invariably, instead of going upstairs to the toilet in the full bath, my father or Jay would use the closer one. The door obscured the view but did not hide the noise nor mask the odor. I could never understand why my mother, normally so image-conscious, didn't seem bothered by the lack of privacy. There wasn't even a lock on the door.

One day during one of our visits from Florida, my three year old daughter, perhaps at first not aware or perhaps not caring that my mother was using the toilet, opened the door and went right in to talk to "Gram." Ma's Cocker Spaniel, Katie, jealous and clingy by nature, immediately followed. At that point, the door to the closet-sized room could no longer close, so when I came through her dining room, I saw my mother's profile as she sat on the toilet, her slacks and underwear down around her ankles, and my daughter and the dog crowded around her legs.

"Oh, I've gotta get my camera," I announced, at which point, my mother couldn't help but laugh.

"No one but you better ever see this picture!" she yelled when the flash went off.

"Once the toilet goes," I said to Ron. "I'll be putting shelves all along these walls for a pantry."

The spring after Ron completed the plumbing work, Mike Sanford finally came through with my porches. When I showed him an old black and white photograph from Annie's album, he said he could duplicate the arrangement of the railings, posts, spokes and curlicues for the wraparound farmer's porch in the front as well as the simpler style for the porch in the back. The smaller front porch was also redone but as a roofless stoop, just as it had been for Annie's store. Once all the concrete had been covered up by the new wooden porches, I felt as though some of the earlier charm had been restored to the house, even though I couldn't yet afford to change the chalky yellow siding. I spent an entire summer painstakingly painting the new porch in the charcoal gray and white from Annie's pictures. As I worked, occasionally some of the town's elderly men drove by or strolled over from Hart's Café to comment.

"I remember when Annie used to sit out here in her rocking chair," Lionel Tebeault reminisced one day as I slathered white paint on the lattice work. "And Homer was always over there sweeping that little store porch."

"I remember Aunt Annie out here as if it were yesterday," remarked my mother's cousin Billy McCarthy who had grown up in the original Kelley homestead a few doors down on Forest Street. "She sure kept an eye on the neighborhood. I was always over here because Polly and I were closest in age. We used to call each other 'my favorite cousin.'" Billy was one of my favorites, too. In fact, he'd given me away at my second wedding. "She ever tell you about the time she pushed me through the plate glass store window?"

Some would remark on how authentic the porch looked and wonder how Mike had been able to accomplish that, whereupon I would whip out the picture he'd used. Many people stopped to chat that summer, which was no doubt why the job took so long, but I enjoyed every shared memory.

A few years passed before I noticed the buckling aluminum siding all along the patio at the rear of the house. Almost simultaneously, a brown stain appeared on the plaster ceiling of my mother's sewing room on the second floor (redecorated by me as my den), indicating a leak in the roof. Time to refinance.

After I got an estimate for a new roof, I called Jimmy Angel, a contractor referred by Lissa, a friend of mine who had bought my great-grandparents' two-family across the street where Annie and Homer had lived for the first few years of their marriage. Jimmy shook his head when he checked out the damage in the rear of the house.

"There's no real foundation for this part," he said. "The house just sits on top of the ground for at least twelve feet, so it's sinking. Was this part added on?"

"I don't think so," I said, envisioning a much larger job than I'd anticipated. Together, we crossed the patio and stepped onto the back porch. Instead of going in the back door, I turned toward the double shed doors on the right. These original solid wood doors had become misaligned over the years as the house had settled, until they'd reached a point where they would no longer latch closed. My mother had hired someone to construct a sheet of heavy plywood, painted to match the house's trim, to hang over them, with a padlock secured to the frame. This section of the Other Side had originally been part of the larger section until my father had put up a thin wall partition sometime during my childhood so that he could have a tool shed / woodworking shop without the mess getting into the rest of the house, thereby rendering this area accessible only from the outside. Once Dad built the new garage when I was around ten, he abandoned "the shed," and the following year I'd taken it over as my clubhouse, but I could still remember the sawdust and wood shavings surrounding his table saw and how particular he was about where and how he kept his tools.

One afternoon – I must have been seven or eight – I'd gone in just to breathe in the fresh smell and maybe poke around a little. The shed fascinated me. I picked up some of the tools, one by one, just examining each, then carefully putting it back exactly where I'd found it. The folding ruler lay out because Dad had been using it. I wanted to see how far it unfolded. I turned each segment, first in one direction, then the next, unfolding until I'd opened the whole ruler. As I began to fold it back up, however, one part stuck. To leave the ruler unfolded would have led to my detection, so I tried to force the segment to swivel closed, and the piece snapped off in my hand. I panicked. Now my crime was worse than simply being where I didn't belong. I couldn't just leave the broken ruler on the workbench, so I looked around for a place to hide it. Dad's rubber fishing boots seemed like a good choice. After all, when had he last gone fishing? I dropped both pieces of the ruler into one of the boots and after a while forgot all about them.

Just before supper a couple of weeks later, I heard my father's raised voice on the phone. I didn't think much of it until I again overheard him in the kitchen with my mother, and I caught the words "your son" and "my tools." Uh oh. The gist was that Dad had missed the folding ruler and thought he had set it down somewhere, so he had searched for it. As it turned out, my hiding place had not been a good one, and when he found the broken ruler, he assumed Jay had done it, so he confronted him. Jay, not knowing anything about it, denied even using it, let alone breaking it; whereupon, my father accused him of lying. My mother was protesting that Jay wouldn't lie about something like that. No one thought of me.

I could not, at that point, interrupt their heated argument to face my angry father and admit what I had done. Had I known then the hostility and disappointments that my half-brother Jay would later inflict on me, I might have kept quiet about the whole thing and let him take the blame, but my conscience bothered me. After things quieted down, I approached my mother and explained what had happened. I assume she told my father, but he never said anything to me about it, and neither did Jay.

Jimmy Angel looked around the nearly empty shed, taking in the chipped psychedelic-paint remnants of flowers and fat letters ("Groovy" and "Flower Power") on the walls, and grinned.

"Yours?"

"Yeah, whatever. I was ten."

"Well, we can either get to the problem from the outside, by breaking up the patio, or we can gut the inside and tackle it that way. You gonna miss any of this, flower child?"

I ignored the smart-ass remark; instead I pictured a brand new three-season room that would once again open up into the Other Side. "Let's do this."

"I wish I could see underneath to get an idea of how much sill rot there is." Jimmy looked down at the floor.

"Not a problem." I walked back over toward the shed's entrance and bent down to grab the edge of the once bright green and blue linoleum that my mother and I had bought at The Fair Department Store for ten bucks a roll. She and I had walked around on it until it was flattened out, then we'd hammered thumb tacks all around the outside edges and down the middle where the two pieces joined. I could easily pull up the edge now, not caring when the linoleum tore, and, as Jimmy watched, I uncovered a large trap door in the old hardwood floor underneath.

"Go for it," I said, pointing.

Jimmy pulled out a screwdriver and pried open the door to reveal a space as wide as the shed and about three feet deep. "What was this used for?"

"I don't know. This whole side of the house was a lot of things before I came along. I know that when I was a kid and one of my pets died, my mother would drop it in here. Not the dog; Pepper's buried out in the back yard. But all the birds, frogs, and turtles – they're all down here."

"Nice," said Jimmy as he lowered himself into the space.

When we walked into the Other Side a few minutes later, Jimmy immediately zeroed in on the raised floorboards about halfway into the room.

"No, it's not what you think," I said. I explained how one year, when my mother had spent the winter with me in Florida, she had asked Jay to keep an eye on the house. Although she had set the thermostat at forty degrees, Jay had turned it off, thinking he'd save her money, but he'd ended up costing her money when, during an unexpected deep freeze, a pipe had burst and the cellar that had otherwise never seen a wet day flooded. Several of the old floorboards in the Other Side buckled and even when dried out never completely flattened.

Jimmy walked over to the partition that separated the Other Side from the shed and bounced up and down on the floor until he found the place where the foundation actually began, about ten feet back from the partition.

"Okay, this whole area, from here to the back end of the house, will need to be supported. Step here. Feel how it drops down right here?"

I nodded.

"I saw rotted sills and beams underneath that shed, and I'm guessing they extend over to here. Also, there's a leak under the corner of the foundation that you can see from the outside. I'll be tearing out the shed floor to get underneath the house, but part of this floor will have to go too. While I'm at it, I might as well replace the whole floor in here. Part of it's already messed up anyway." He gestured back toward the buckled floorboards. "Wouldn't you like a brand new hardwood floor in here?'

I looked down. When I'd redecorated in here for my master bedroom, I'd pulled up the linoleum that my mother had installed years earlier and found a layer of brittle yellowed newspapers, most of them dating from the 1950s. As soon as I picked up the first few, I discovered their intended purpose: the original wide floorboards were not bare but neither were they varnished. Instead, there was some kind of oily substance on them that had soaked into the wood but that would still, even decades later, rub off. Evidently, my mother had thought that lining the floor with newspapers would prevent any seepage from discoloring the linoleum picked out once she decided to begin reusing the Other Side. I didn't know how that kind of oily floor could have been practical in a store, although I did remember my mother saying something about its never having to be washed and how just a good sweeping removed whatever anybody tracked in. After all, as a place of business, it's not like anybody would have gone barefoot in there. She'd also told me that right after Annie and Homer had bought the house, they had rented this space out to a butcher who had spread sawdust all over the floor to soak up the blood from his chopping block.

"Oh, ew! He slaughtered animals in here?"

"Right here." She'd taken me to a spot right about in the middle of the floor. "I remember it because he was still here when I was small. We had a few chickens of our own then, and my mother would chop off their heads in here."

I could only stare at her in horror.

"That's what people did back then. The women would kill, pluck, clean, and then cook their chickens." She thought for a minute. "She used to cut the dogs' tails off in here too."

"*What?*"

"We always had a little stray dog around. After one died, another one would show up. Ma always named them Tippy. I wanted the dogs to be able to come into the house, but my mother hated when their tails knocked things over. So each time we had a new dog, she'd bring it in here and chop off its tail. That way it could stay in the house."

"How could you stand that?" I shivered, nearly sick to my stomach.

"I didn't really think much of it," said my mother.

Perhaps, despite the sawdust, the bare wood of the original floor had been so stained by animal blood that only the dark oil could make it salvageable for the barber shop that followed the butcher shop, and the shoe store that followed the barber shop. The shoe store had been the enterprise of my mother's Uncle George Kelley until it became prosperous enough to be relocated to Main Street, whereupon my grandmother opened her dry goods store.

After Annie died, and my mother moved back home, she rented out the Other Side as a pool hall. Jay was still very young but became sort of a mascot in there. "John Jr.," or "Junior" for short, had never felt comfortable with his gruff and critical father, and the guys in the pool hall made a lot of him, carrying him around on their shoulders and giving him sips of beer. Before long, "John Jr." became "J.J." and, ultimately, "Jay," with only some of the elderly cousins still calling him "Junior." Aside from the nickname and Jay's happy memories, the only vestige of the pool hall that remained was the wood strip with cast iron coat hooks on the wall just inside the little front door.

Sometime between the Other Side's end as a pool hall and its beginning as Bob Kelley's love nest, my mother had spread the newspapers and laid down the linoleum. Apparently the oiled floor had been acceptable for business traffic, but certainly not for living quarters. Even decades later, it took me three coats of premium semi-gloss floor paint on those still porous boards before the floor could be useable for my bedroom.

"There are hardwood floors now, real hardwood and already finished, that snap together and will last forever," Jimmy Angel said. "Bruce makes a whole line of them. If you go to Home Depot and pick one out, I'll put it in for you after I replace everything that's rotted. You'll love it."

After we discussed installation of an additional fuse box, to be located behind the hot water heater, Jimmy walked back over to the partition.

"So . . . a doorway here?" He took out his tape measure.

"French doors." I handed him the specs for the solid wood multipaned double doors I'd ordered that would restore the Other Side to a semblance of one unified space.

Like many of the houses in the neighborhood, this one had originally been designed as a two-family with the large additional room as merchant space, either for the owner or for rental income. The little front door, just steps from busy North Common Street, gave exposure and access to the public while the back double doors, opening onto the back porch and set back from quiet Forest Street, allowed for deliveries and for the merchant to come and go without disturbing the family living in the first floor apartment of the house. The original intent of the design, however, was probably for an owner-operated business, hence the space's third entrance directly into the downstairs apartment. By modern standards, since cottage industries had largely gone out of fashion, the Other Side had the potential to be a mother-in-law apartment someday, sort of an updated version of Bob Kelley's living quarters, but, for now at least, I saw it as a grand en suite, with bedroom and full bathroom already having been installed by Ron Murphy, and now a three-season sitting room to be connected by French doors.

As Jimmy measured and made notations, I looked around the room. Big changes had taken place compared to when this area up to the partition had been my playroom. When my mother had decided she wanted a formal dining room, she relocated her living room from just off the kitchen into what had previously been a nursery where I had played with the children she took in while their mothers worked: the Plantes and the Wymans. Ma had quit her job at the Gavitt Wire & Cable in Brookfield after my birth, so having a daycare of sorts brought in pretty good money.

Once I started school, though, she went to work as a waitress in Phil's Restaurant downtown, and the nursery became the new living room. Since I was not allowed to bring playmates into my bedroom, my parents cleared a small area in the Other Side at the farthest end from the laundry area, about one third of the space left over after Dad had partitioned off his shed. Of course, the area was wide open to the rest of the space, but since only my mother came in (and primarily on laundry days) the open floor plan never bothered me. I felt very lucky to have a place to myself in the Other Side, which was, in itself, set apart from the rest of the house.

I don't know where it came from or how long it had been there, but I was still very young when I first noticed the glint of gold that turned out to be a likeness of Jay engraved in foil and tucked behind some things in the borderline area between the playroom and my mother's storage / laundry room. The large matted but unframed piece had a professional appearance, but I'd never before seen it or heard it mentioned. Why wasn't it hanging in Jay's house? Any of Jay's other things that Ma had in storage – his toys and baby things, for instance – were kept in the attic, not in the Other Side. That time, I carefully slid the engraving back where I'd found it, but for some reason it bothered me.

Days, weeks, who knows? passed, before I went back to the foil work, but I did go back and often, sometimes just to look at it, sometimes to add a line or two of my own with my fingernail or the point of a Bick. I reasoned that no one would notice another line in the cheek or forehead. After a while, I told myself that if the engraving actually meant anything to anyone, it wouldn't be here out of sight. I became reckless with my alterations. I darkened the eyebrows, giving the face a more sinister appearance. Another time, crow's feet appeared around the eyes and more lines down the cheeks. Finally, the crowning touch: pink crayon on the grinning lips. Perhaps that finishing touch scared me more than the others because I hid the ruined engraving in a different part of the storage area and vowed to leave it alone.

I was much older the day my mother found it when clearing out some things and asked me about it. I admitted my earlier vandalism, though I couldn't explain why I'd done it. Ma didn't seem upset. Several years had passed without Jay's ever asking for it, so she probably assumed he'd forgotten about it. The engraving ended up in the trash with nothing further being said.

The playroom part of the Other Side perfectly suited my childhood needs. Along one wall, metal shelves held my books and games. Storage boxes underneath held dolls and stuffed animals. My parents' old black and white television sat on a corner table with a small rocker in front of it where I watched *Flipper* and *Lassie* and, later, *Dark Shadows* and *The Wild Wild West*. Somewhere around the time I turned nine, I asked if I could redecorate the playroom because, though my friends were jealous of all the space I had, it just didn't look cool enough to suit me. The year was 1968, and I had become very conscious of "cool."

I used my allowance to buy a gallon of sunflower-gold paint (I hadn't cared for the toxic-waste green either) and a 9x12 cobalt blue shag rug that just about covered my floor space. Before Ma and I laid the rug, Dad grabbed a couple of paint rollers, brushes and a tray and, in a rare father-daughter moment, gave me a lesson in how to cut in and paint a wall. He taught me well. I painted many rooms in the years that followed and never forgot his instructions, to the extent that, years later, when my second husband Bob and I painted peach over the remaining toxic-waste green I insisted on sticking with my "Zs" over his "Ws:" "Back off. I know what I'm doing. You go paint down there."

Since, as a child, I spent more time in the Other Side than in my bedroom, a small pine desk and chair arrived one day where I could do my homework. I also picked out a neon-orange inflatable chair – great for reading in – and my old phonograph ended up in there too after I received a small console stereo for my bedroom on my birthday. Nobody cared how many thumb tacks I hammered into the walls, well, wall actually, since the metal shelves took up one of the three and the window most of another. The only wall I really had was the partition, and I made the most of it. Posters mostly, psychedelic for the black light I bought. All in all, a pretty cool "room" I thought, even after part of the storage space became a bedroom for my father a few months later.

Banished from my mother's bedroom because of his snoring and the odd hours he kept once he started his factory job at the steel plant, Dad took over the middle portion of the Other Side rearranging it to accommodate a roll-away bed and a nightstand. My end was untouched, however, and remained "cool." And now, thanks to first Ron Murphy then Jimmy Angel, it would be cool by adult standards.

New roof; new sills and foundation in the back of the house; new floor, walls, and ceiling in the former-shed-now-three-season-room; new trimmed out doorframe restoring the Other Side as one great accessible space with adjoining French doors waiting to be hung; enough extra money for blown-in insulation and new gray vinyl siding to replace the yellow aluminum; and one big, scary mortgage later, I watched Jimmy and his helper snap in the last few boards of the Bruce hardwood.

"You know," I began, and by then he knew me well enough to realize that my tone meant potentially more work for him. He paused and grinned.

"That window behind you. How hard would it be to put in a different one?"

"Not hard at all. What are you thinking?"

Early black and white photographs of the front of the house show a large store window next to the second, smaller front door. The summer I spent painting the new front porch, Cousin Billy's story about how my mother pushed him through the plate glass when they were children had not been the only reference I'd heard made to the original storefront window. Old Lionel Thibeault, who had once owned the house diagonally across the street, had remembered more about Annie than her sitting on the porch in her rocker.

"When your grandmother died, they carried her coffin out that window,' he'd said, pointing over my shoulder. "Well, not *that* window. The one that used to be there. The coffin couldn't fit through the doorways, so the whole window was taken out, and the coffin passed through. I could see it all from my porch. The whole neighborhood watched. Everyone liked Annie."

Although my mother had told me many stories about my grand-mother – enough to make me feel as though I had actually known her – she rarely spoke of her death and only when I pressed. Ma had been only twenty-one when Annie died, and the loss of a mother she'd adored had hit her hard such that only in her elderly years could she even bear to look at Annie's photographs, and even then only those of Annie in her youth rather than as Ma remembered her.

Annie's death had been unexpected. There'd been some ongoing health issues, but the details I got were sketchy. "She had a little sugar," my mother said when I'd asked, "and high blood pressure. She was a big woman." Pictures that I'd seen of Annie showed a woman who was sig-nificantly overweight, but whatever her health problems were she did not take any medication. "She didn't like doctors," Ma said.

For several days, Annie had not been feeling right. Although my mother lived with her first husband and their son in an apartment a few houses up North Common Street, she kept a close eye on her parents and often brought Jay to visit. As Annie's condition worsened, the doctor was summoned at my mother's insistence. He diagnosed pneumonia and tried to convince Annie to go to the hospital, but she refused. A cot was moved into one of the downstairs rooms, and my mother tried to take care of her.

"Then there was one night, when I came in," Ma said, the only time she could bring herself to talk about it, "and she was wheezing and unconscious. I lifted the blanket off her feet to adjust it, and they looked almost black in the dim light. I guess the blood had pooled there. I knew then that she was dying."

"But . . . if she had gone to the hospital, she might have lived," I said.

"That's not what she wanted," Ma quietly answered, the tears in her eyes reflecting the pain still there. "I had to respect her wishes."

My mother sat beside Annie, holding her hand until she died. Af-terwards, she bathed and dressed her. During the vigil, she was the one who sat up all night with her mother's body. All of this my mother had told me, but not about the coffin through the window.

"I'd like to put a picture window in there," I told Jimmy Angel. "It will let in a lot more light." And look more like the original window, I thought but didn't say.

"Well, if you're gonna do it, now's the time," he said. "Pick out what you want, and I'll make it happen before we put up the siding. Any other changes you want to make?"

"Actually, yeah." I headed toward the former closet in which Ron Murphy had installed a toilet and motioned for Jimmy to follow.

At the top of the outside wall and abutting the ceiling, a small window had long ago been nailed shut and covered over by the yellow aluminum siding. Now that this tiny room was once again a "toilet room," restoring the window would help with air flow as opposed to leaving the door open. Jimmy stood on the toilet to get a better look, and informed me that a new window would need to be purchased but could easily be fit into the wall.

"We'll just have to make a note to leave it uncovered when we side," he said.

I barely heard him. Suddenly I was fifteen again, watching my father move aside the coats and dig through the boots that used to clutter up the closet, frantically searching for random hunting or fishing items he hadn't yet sold while trying to hide his concern over finding nothing else worth selling. He'd already been through the garage.

"Just a little short on cash right now." He dismissed my questions just as he'd shrugged off all the overtime hours he'd started working. Not until after his death a few months later, when the bills started coming in, did my mother discover the extent of his gambling debt.

Once the last of the gray vinyl siding was up, the curb appeal of the house tripled. I went out through the little front door of the Other Side, now a complete en suite master bedroom with a large adjoining sitting / t.v. / game room and joined Jimmy in the front yard.

"What do you think? Love it?" Jimmy asked.

I walked around the house then returned to the front and just stood there taking it all in.

"It looks great."

"Everything you wanted, right? Back to its original integrity only even better."

"Almost," I said and reached into my pocket for the picture from Annie's album that Mike Sanford had used to rebuild the front porches. "There's only one thing missing."

"Shutters," Jimmy said when he looked at the picture.

"Dark gray vinyl shutters will complete the outside renovation."

"Then you'll have your doll house." Jimmy grinned. "You'll never want to leave."

I smiled. No, I would never want to leave.

4

The Fat Tree

The first time I pass the Fat Tree, I see a light on upstairs in the DiCesare house, so I keep driving. I glance at the dash clock: 3:30. What the hell is someone doing up so early? Frustrated, I turn onto Willow Street, throw a couple of sample papers on my way down, then bang a uey. On my way back up, I put my Tracker in park in front of Jo Powers' house and get out to deliver her paper. After almost nine years of delivering the Worcester Telegram & Gazette, I still hate this stop more than most. Up the long walk, then open the screen porch door, and carefully lay the paper up on the narrow window ledge so that it won't fall off. On Sundays, roll and rubber-band the bulky paper and stand it up against the door frame. Jo is elderly and doesn't want to bend over to pick up her paper. Quietly close the screen door so she doesn't wake up, and back to the car. Jo does tip though, I'll give her that.

After I toss another freebie onto Mary Gendron's walk, I look back up at the house that used to be the Bouchards'. No lights. Maybe one of the DiCesares had only to use the bathroom. Still, I want to be sure not to be seen, so I decide to finish the hill.

I rush through the next few stops because I can feel myself getting stressed over what I am about to do. Though I suppose any tree would suffice for a protection ritual, I'd chosen the Fat Tree as the oldest and, therefore, most powerful of trees in my neighborhood. Unfortunately, despite the darkness of the new moon, the corner street light would illuminate an interesting spectacle for anyone who might be passing by a window. I don't really know the new family living in Delia Burke's old house across the street; I'm more concerned about being seen by Mr. Bouchard's grandson, Mark DiCesare or his wife, Pam Caron (who never misses a trick) since, even though I sort of consider the Fat Tree town property, technically I will be in their yard. The DiCesares are Catholic – still practicing for all I know – and they might think it's pretty weird seeing a pagan ritual performed in their yard in the middle of the night. Wicca can easily be misinterpreted as devil-worship by the ignorant. Truth be told and property lines notwithstanding, though, I actually consider the Fat Tree more mine than my next door neighbors' anyway because the tree and I share more of a history.

I grew up at the North Common Street corner of Forest Street. One block north, at the Willow Street corner, right at the end of the sidewalk and at the outermost edge of the DiCesares' small rarely used front yard, stands the majestic old maple that someone from my childhood – I've long forgotten who – named the Fat Tree. I'm guessing one of the Searahs named the tree, or it might have been a joint decision, but even before I'd met Andrea Searah and her large family the old maple held meaning in my life. Prior to my starting kindergarten, my boundary when I played on the sidewalk unsupervised had been only to the privet hedge of my back yard. Once I started school, however, my freedom grew, and I was allowed all the way up to the end of the street as long as I stayed out of the road. After the privets of my yard ended, a straight line of maples began, marching along the sidewalk up to the grand old much larger maple on the corner that marked my new boundary.

I had almost daily been walking with Vincie Kizzle on the sidewalk up Forest Street, stopping just at the privets' far edge, for longer than I have memory. The day that my boundary changed, I waited, as I always did, at the corner of my house for him to appear from his first shift at the Rubber Shop, even more excited to see him than I normally was because I planned to surprise him with my new privilege. I still don't know what it was that drew me to this quiet man who lived alone in his little house on Willow, but every weekday when I was small I watched for his approach so that I could take his hand and accompany him up Forest Street. On this special day, as we walked by my driveway, then the first of the privets, I tried not to appear too excited so I wouldn't give away my surprise. He knew from our earlier conversations that I had just started school, so he asked what I had learned and if I liked my teacher.

"Her name is Mrs. Pease. When we got there, she was eating

lunch at her desk. We all stood around and watched her. She had a piece of tuna on her lip."

I liked talking to Vincie because he looked right at you instead of off into space the way some adults do when they're pretending to listen. Usually I talked fast because I had to get everything out before we reached the end of the privets - but not today.

When we got there, Vincie hesitated but I kept going, tugging his hand.

"Guess what? I can walk all the way up the sidewalk now," I said, "to that tree." And I pointed to the great old maple at the end of the sidewalk. Vincie smiled and his eyes crinkled at the corners when he told me what a big girl I was.

"Okay, I'll sing the high part, and you sing the low part," I said to Andrea once we reached the Fat Tree. Darkness had already fallen and though we considered ourselves brave girls, the stillness of the empty streets scared us a little.

By day, the Fat Tree was not only my boundary but now Home Base when I played tag with my friends. No one could touch you as long as you were touching its gnarled old trunk. Although we spent a lot of time on the swing set in my spacious back yard, grass is no good for running, not to mention wagon, bike, and scooter riding, so we probably spent way more time on the sidewalk that ran from my driveway all the way up to Willow Street. Although Debbie Searah was in my third grade class, I seemed to hit it off more with her sister Andrea, older by two years. There were thirteen of them, including two sets of twins, and they were crammed into their little house at the very top of Willow Street, so almost always, Andrea played at my house. Besides, I had the bikes, wagon and scooter. Up and down the sidewalk we raced. My thick glasses threw off my depth perception, so I fell a lot, but that didn't slow me down. My knees got so torn up that eventually permanent scars formed.

In the spring, Andrea and I fearlessly aimed squirt guns at the bees in the privets, and in the fall, we sneaked into Mr. Bouchard's yard that abutted mine and stole rhubarb from his garden. Whenever we heard the Hood Milk truck rumble up Willow Street and make the turn onto Forest, we ran alongside it, madly flagging down the driver until he stopped and chipped off a chunk of ice from inside for each of us to suck on. One day we accidentally discovered that the maples that lined Forest Street had patches of their trunks covered by long, skinny caterpillars and that if we squeezed their downy bodies from the right end strings of green came out. Days were long and wonderful, and each one in my memory of that year ended with mosquito bites on my arms and fresh cuts on my knees that stung in the bathtub. But before my nightly bath, I had to walk Andrea partway home in the dark.

We stood by the Fat Tree, under the glow from the nearby street light, having decided on our song for that night, and then I waited there for Andrea to cross the road. As she continued up Willow towards her house, I touched the craggy bark once more for luck and turned back down Forest towards mine.

"'I found a horse shoe. I found a HORSE shoooooooe,'" we sang as loudly as we could, as company for each other while we made our separate ways home. Mr. Sacco had taught harmony to the music classes at the Grove Street School that year, and the Horse Shoe song was our favorite.

"'I picked it up and nailed it to the doooor.'" Even though I could see the lights on in my house as I looked down Forest Street, I still kept my eyes on the road ahead and frequently looked over my shoulder at the road behind me as I sang. My body stayed tensed in case a strange car approached and slowed, the man inside asking if I wanted candy. You never knew, my mother always warned me. You had to be careful.

"'And it was rusty, and full of nail holes.'" And we were careful. We never talked to strangers, and we never played in the road. As children, how could we have known that sometimes the most dangerous things in the world are things you can't see? Years after I'd lost touch with Andrea, my first real best friend, I found out that she died of breast cancer at only forty two.

"'Good luck 'twill bring to you forevermooooore!'"

My neighborhood had no real climbing trees, a fact that frustrated me as soon as I became old enough to want such things. I considered myself a tomboy even though I had no talent for most sports because I loved playing outside and didn't mind getting dirty. I hated dresses – especially the ones with the stiff sewn-in slips that my mother forced me to wear to Mass every Sunday. While I sat in the pew, my white gloved hands clutching the little white purse (which I tended to lose) containing a hankie and a miniature white Bible (that I never opened), my black patent leather Mary Janes tapping the kneeling bench, I squirmed and scratched at the picky slip and my itchy scalp under my equally picky hat and wished I could stay home as my father did on Sunday mornings. He went to church only on Christmas and Easter, which seemed reasonable to me, but my mother insisted on weekly Mass, followed by Sunday School. So prim in her suit and stylish hat with the feather or the little veil, she got angry when I fidgeted in the pew and told me that Father Curran had a strap for children who couldn't sit still. I couldn't wait for Sunday mornings to end, to change into play clothes, except on those Sundays when David Messier walked me home. He wasn't my boyfriend but we walked the long way around and sometimes he held my hand.

As soon as I got into my jeans or shorts and orange canvas Keds, I felt like I could move around and be myself. I could swing and not worry about showing my underpants. I could play in the grass and not worry about stains on my clothes. And I just knew I could climb trees too - if there had been any to climb. The only tree in my back yard was a horse chestnut that was so old it no longer produced anything edible. Just a few hard little balls every so often that had green stuff inside. "Grandfather Tree" was very tall, and none of its branches could be reached from the ground. Still, I loved the chestnut, and I often lay under it, telling it my problems. I imagined that Grandfather Tree had an ancient spirit that lived inside it. Somehow, I felt that it listened, and when I finished talking to it, I always stood against it and wrapped my arms around it as far as they could reach.

One day, I came home from school, and there was a truck backed into the yard, and a man was sawing branches off of Grandfather Tree. I ran into the house where my mother calmly told me that she'd hired the man to remove the dead chestnut.

"But it's not dead!" I cried. I had seen a few branches fall into the yard, but how could the tree be dead when it still sprouted leaves?

"It might as well be," she insisted, "And what if it falls? It's so tall, it will fall on the new garage. Is that what you want?"

I didn't see how the old tree could be in danger of falling over, but I recognized that arguing would be pointless. I had no say over this matter and I knew it. Adults do not listen to nine year olds.

I locked myself in the attached shed that I had recently claimed as my clubhouse, turned up The Vogues on the record player, and cried. After the man and his truck had gone, I went back outside. Only the trunk and some random chunks of wood, one of which I kept, remained of the

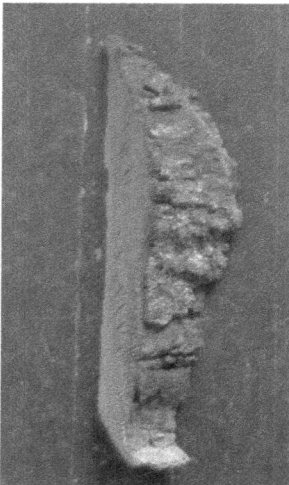

tree. I knelt by the trunk, ran my fingers over the still sticky surface of the raw wood and apologized to the now dead tree.

Eventually, the stump was removed. I planted a rose bush there in memory of the tree, but the bush never blossomed and it died the next spring. Over the years, I tried to plant other types of shrubs and once a small tree in the same spot where Grandfather Tree had stood, but nothing lived there for very long. It was as if the tree had cursed the ground when it was killed.

When the Searahs walked by one afternoon eating the "pear-apples" they'd picked from one of Vincie Kizzle's trees, I'll admit that I was jealous. I'd never even noticed the fruit trees in his overgrown yard, let alone considered climbing them. By now, I'd completed the fourth grade and rode my gold Huffy with the banana seat and streamers all over town, even as far as Hillsville Road where going down to the Fivemile River without using any brakes took my breath away and was well worth the long walk back up. I had a real boyfriend too, and Brian and I often rode double on his bike. I had no boundaries or limitations except that I had to be home by dark. Yet most of us kids practically lived on the Common just down the street from my house because there were always other Common Rats there to play kickball or dodge ball or just hang out with on the swings.

Even though Vincie's apples sounded tempting, for me it was more about climbing the trees, so the very next time I saw Vincie, I asked him if he'd mind my coming by. Debbie Searah and I had lately been spending more time together since, at twelve, Andrea had outgrown me, so it might have been Debbie – or maybe JoAnne Foster who lived at the top of North Common Street – who went with me to pick "pear-apples" that Friday afternoon at Vincie's. All I really remember was being focused on climbing as high as I could. I never even saw the vines that wound their way around the tree trunk.

That night, at The Clam Box, my legs started to itch, and I furiously and deliciously scratched back, thinking only that I'd run into some particularly aggressive mosquitoes. While I waited for my grilled cheese (prepared on round bread) and my pink lemonade, and Mom waited for her clam fritters, we talked about the vacation that just the two of us would leave for first thing in the morning. Dad had gone to Bermuda on Mr. Krock's yacht so that Mr. Krock wouldn't have to drive himself around whenever they docked. Mom didn't think "lounging on the boss's boat" sounded much like working, so she dipped into her tip jar and brought our suitcases out from the attic. She and I were excited about a week of fun without the fighting that typically occurred when we took a vacation as a family.

Jug End Resort, a "dude ranch" somewhere in the Berkshires, ad-

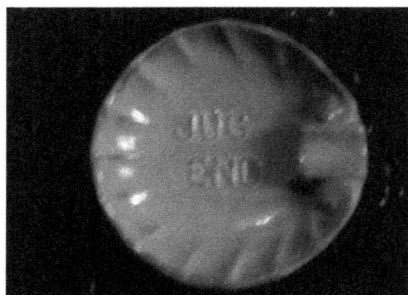

vertised all kinds of activities like horseback riding, swimming, and hiking. Mom had sent for brochures. The only time I'd been on a real horse was when Butchie St.Jacques from across the street had had a pony in his yard for some reason, and someone put me on it to take a picture. I couldn't even remember the occasion, so it didn't count anyway. I didn't know what a "dude" was, but I couldn't wait to ride a real horse instead of the succession of spring horses I'd worn out as a little kid.

The next morning, Mom and I got up early to pack the Rambler. As I put on my green flowered bell bottomed pants with the yellow sash belt, I saw the rash that had already begun to bubble. By that night, both legs were covered, from the tops of my tennis shoes to mid-thigh where the cut-offs I'd worn to Vincie's had ended. I lived in misery the entire week, my legs so stiff with Calamine Lotion and so swollen with pus-filled bubbles that I could barely walk. I had to sleep with a pillow (draped with a

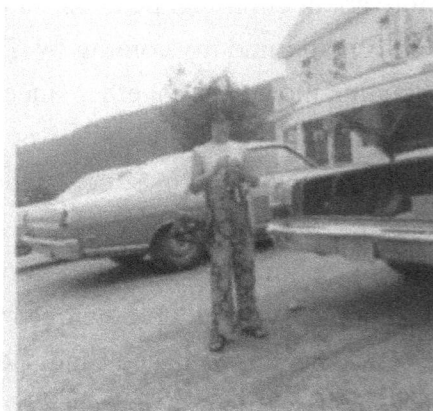

bath towel) under my knees. I couldn't go into the resort swimming pool, and the only day I did ride a horse, the itchy agony of my legs rubbing up against the insides of my jeans every time the horse took a step made me want to scream.

I took the assault personally. For some reason, Vincie's trees did not like me. I never went back.

As Mother's Day approached during the spring of my junior year of high school, I confirmed the arrangements I needed for the purchase and delivery of my present to my mother. This year's would be the best yet, better even than the terrarium I'd put together for her a couple of years earlier that still thrived in the living room window. I'd decided on a tree.

I gave a lot of thought to the type of tree I would buy at Bemis Farms Nursery – something pleasing to the eye that would stay fairly small since I planned to plant it in the side yard where Ma could see it from the kitchen window. A tree there would attract even more of the birds she fed with scraps of bread. Every morning after the dog came in, Ma went back outside in her housecoat and scuffies with crusts in a tin pie plate. She scattered the crusts around the bird bath then tapped the plate with her fingers to "call the birds."

Mother's Day morning, Theresa Coffee, one of my friends who'd already gotten her license, picked me up and drove me to the nursery, where we strolled the outermost aisles, passing by people buying their boring Mother's Day tulips and daffodils. Where is it? Where is it? Ah, there, the selection of flowering crab trees, many already showing bits of pink or white. I chose the pink flowering variety, already picturing it proudly stretching its limbs next to the back porch.

"The fruit will be inedible. Just so you know," the clerk said as he rang up my purchase.

Fruit?

We hoisted the burlap-wrapped root ball onto the floor of the passenger side of Mrs. Coffee's car and leaned the tree's thin flexible branches over the top of the front seat. When we got to my house, we hoisted it out and hauled it over to the spot in the side yard where I envisioned it would live in beauty and glory for the next hundred or so years. I then poked my head in the back door and hollered for my mother to come out, that her Mother's Day gift had arrived. Card in hand, I waited for her reaction.

When she came out onto the porch, she stopped, looked, opened her mouth, closed it, opened it again, and closed it again.

"Well?" I couldn't stand it, I was so excited. I mean, what a cool gift!

"A tree?" Ma finally was able to speak. "But . . . where will we put it?"

"Right *here*, see? Don't you *love* it?"

"But, so close to the house? Won't it interfere with the roof?"

"No, it'll stay small."

She looked doubtful. I think she mumbled "more leaves." Then she more closely peered at the tree. "Is that a crab apple tree? It's going to drop little *apples* every fall, isn't it?"

"Yeah, but it's okay," I assured her, already forming an attachment to our new addition. "The guy at Bemis' said they're inedible."

My belief that trees have spirits that live somewhere inside them was never consciously formed, but it's the only belief of any spiritual nature that for me has never wavered. I don't think of these spirits as being either "good" or "bad," just as I don't see animals in those terms, but I do think of them as being either friendly, neutral, or unfriendly. Most trees strike me as neutral; only the very old trees, wise in their years, seem almost to have personality: either friendly or unfriendly. Yet, despite my long -held convictions regarding trees, I did not, in my early years, imagine them as necessarily sacred or powerful. I'd been raised a good Irish Catholic girl.

Looking back though, I realize that the aspects of Catholicism that attracted me most were those left over from Paganism. I admired the vestments and each Sunday tried to guess which color I would see worn by the succession of priests; from Father Curran, to Father Jalbert, Father Choquette, and Father Hughes; at St. Joseph's parish. I loved the chants and the bells that rung after the refrains. I believed that the two giant candles crossed and held up to my throat by the priest as I solemnly knelt at the altar rail on St. Blaise's Day would protect me from strep. One of my favorite Masses was Palm Sunday, when I could close my eyes and breathe in the scent of burning palms from the thurible. When I got home, I tucked the palm frond I'd received behind the picture of the Sacred Heart that hung in my bedroom, burning the one from the year before in my little brass incense burner.

My very favorite Mass, though, was the Easter Vigil, avoided by many Catholics because of its length. The point of the ceremony is to simulate the faithful waiting through the night for the Resurrection of Christ at the tomb. Everyone present at the Mass is given a candle, and at the appointed time, the candles held by those parishioners at the ends of the pews are lit. Those people turn to the people next to them and light their candles, and so on down the pew until everyone's candle is lit. I couldn't explain to my mother why I had to attend this ceremony every year on Holy Saturday because at the time I didn't understand it myself. There was just something about the candles.

Although as a child I'd hated reciting my prayers before bedtime, somewhere around Junior High, I acquired a new rosary – a black one I chose for myself to replace the white one given to me for my First Holy Communion – that I used nightly (and privately) before going to sleep, finding comfort in the lulling repetition. One of my Catechism teachers (for by now, I'd outgrown Sunday School) passed out scapulas, and I wore mine under my clothes, removing it only to take a bath. At thirteen, I threw myself into preparing for my Holy Confirmation, much more enthusiastic about the actual ceremony than about what it stood for in relation to the Church. For a while, I considered becoming a nun, fig-

uring to do so would be the closest thing to performing the holy rituals myself, but realized even then that I could never pledge celibacy. Nevertheless, I fasted during Lent, avoided meat on Fridays, said my rosary, and attended Mass every week and on Holy Days, although Ma and I more often went to the church across from Webster Square in Worcester rather than to St. Joseph's in North Brookfield. Instead of listening to our own Father Hughes get all worked up every week over abortion, I preferred the young, more progressive priest in the city who often quoted literature in his sermons, and after Mass, Ma and I usually went to nearby Abdow's Big Boy for fish and chips and the hot fudge ice cream cake.

During my late teens, I recognized what I considered inconsistencies in the Catholic teachings and instead of overlooking them as my mother and many others I knew could, I picked at them until they multiplied in my head. I just could not wrap my brain around the concept of a virgin birth, nor did I agree with the Church's outdated and illogical position on birth control. Furthermore, the concepts of Limbo, Purgatory and guardian angels struck me as fairy tale-ish. I even found myself doubting the viability of a personal God, and every time I heard "the Devil" referred to as a living, functioning entity that walks among us, I had to smother a laugh. I detested the idea of "sacrifice," sneered at "penance," and decided that "worshipping" a spiritual "King" is no different in theory than kneeling before any other monarch or dictator, and I would have none of it.

I quit CCD, stopped saying the rosary, and attended Mass only until I moved out on my own. By the time I married, I had become so disenchanted with the religion of my childhood that for a while, though I missed the relics and ceremonies, I proclaimed myself an atheist, much to my mother's disappointment. Although she and I sometimes debated our polarized viewpoints, we grudgingly agreed to live and let live without interference.

Until after my daughter was born.

A quick trip to St. Anne's before lunch and shopping. That's all. I suspected nothing when my mother requested that we swing by the shrine in Sturbridge one afternoon during my annual summer visit from Florida, where I'd moved with my husband. My mother's best friend, a woman who had babysat me when I'd first started school, accompanied us. Della Mallon, a widow and staunch Catholic like my mother, had never gotten her driver's license, so Ma's explanation that Della wanted to come along to light a candle for someone in her family made sense to me. Once a month or so, the two of them would visit the shrine; it was pretty much their routine when they went out to lunch.

"I know you don't believe," Ma always said to me on the phone, "but I lit a candle for you anyway."

I usually rolled my eyes, something I would never do in her presence, and just let her talk. One time, I did smart-mouth her on the phone. When she said she went to St. Anne's, I beat her to the punch:

"Did you light a candle and make a wish?" I think if my mother had been the type of person to hang up on people, my sarcasm would have been answered with a dial tone. I don't remember her response, but I never said anything like that to her again.

When we arrived at St. Anne's, I picked up my infant daughter from her car seat and walked toward the shrine with Della and my mother. About ten feet or so from the door, I stopped and announced that I would wait right there in the shade while they went in. I'm not sure why I didn't want to go inside. The summer heat was brutal. I didn't know if the building was air conditioned or not, but I don't think that was my issue. I knew the layout; I'd been to the shrine many times as a child, had even, in my devout Catholic days, gone up the Holy Stairs on my knees, saying a prayer at each step. You can't get more ceremonious than that. However, something about the shrine struck me as fraudulent. Inside the Votive Shrine area, where my mother and Della were headed, in the corner, stood a statue of St. Anne herself. All around her were canes, crutches, and various types of eye glasses and eye patches, supposedly left by people who were healed through prayer. After my third eye surgery the year I turned eleven, my mother had taken me into that room and had removed an old pair of my coke-bottle glasses from her purse.

"I want to leave these under the statue," she said.

"Wait a minute," I objected, "Those are only my old glasses. My eyes haven't gotten any better. I just got new glasses."

"Before you went into the hospital, I lit a candle for you," she said. "And while you were in surgery, I prayed to St. Anne. You came out of the surgery."

"That makes no difference," I insisted. "People leave these things not because they got new ones but because they're cured." Didn't they? "My new glasses are just as thick as my old ones. My eyes are just straighter." If this whole display was a farce, I would certainly not be part of it.

We continued to argue in stage whispers until I finally turned and walked out. She followed. She hadn't left the glasses, but her mouth made a thin unhappy line.

That thin unhappy line faced me again as I stepped back into deeper shade under the drooping tree branches. "Go ahead, take your time," I told Ma. "Chloe's asleep anyway. I don't mind waiting." My mother hesitated, then followed Della into the votive shrine. I watched them enter, two elderly women in shapeless polyester slacks, hanging onto each other for balance.

Only a few minutes passed before the two emerged separately, a funny expression on my mother's face. Uncertainty? Nervousness? Is it only in retrospect that I see her pace as quicker and more determined, or did she really approach me that way? Perhaps I imagine that only now because what she did next took me completely by surprise.

"Here," she said, thrusting her suitcase-sized faux leather pocket-book at me, "take my bag."

And before I could even react, she snatched, for there is no other word more accurate, my baby from my arms and hurried with her back into the shrine. For a moment, I simply stood there, mouth open, stupidly looking at the pocketbook in my arms where only a moment before my daughter had slept. Still speechless, I turned to Della, but saw only the back of her permed head. She looked off at the skies, deliberately, I thought, avoiding my eyes.

"What is she doing?" I could barely get the words out. My shock felt like a hard, hot ball in my stomach, and something started to pound in my temples.

"I think she's baptizing Chloe." Della's voice was soft, perhaps apologetic, and she giggled as she always did in an uncomfortable situation.

My child? Without any discussion, debate, *permission*? I realized then that the afternoon had been planned by my mother, and that I had only briefly foiled her plan when I'd decided to stay outside, forcing her to improvise. In that moment, I hated her for openly overruling my position as the mother and, therefore, decision-maker of my child; further-more, she had reduced me, in that instant, from an adult to a child, strip-ping me of my dignity along with my authority. Uncertain as to what to do despite the anger forming a bitter taste in my mouth, I could only stand there, my indecision making me even angrier.

When Ma came back out of the shrine, her face flushed, I waited in the same spot, and when she reached me, I wordlessly took my daugh-ter from her arms and handed her pocketbook back to her. Then I turned and walked toward the car.

The three of us ate lunch at Friendly's in silence. I spent the entire meal planning my verbal attack. We dropped Della off, and when we got into Ma's kitchen, I turned on her.

"I cannot believe that you did that!"

"Donna, what's the harm? I know you don't believe, but she's just an innocent little baby." Clearly, my mother had decided on playing the sympathy card.

"You didn't even ask me!"

"You would have said no."

Yes, I probably would have. I'd graduated from college whereas my mother had not even finished high school, and I'd long given up on the Catholic Church and God. At twenty six, I considered myself intellectually superior to my mother. In my self-righteousness, I was sure that I knew more about the world than someone who'd never lived outside of North Brookfield and that of course my wisdom extended to child rearing. I was uncompromising and intolerant and proud of it. So even though I knew, that as an Irish Catholic who had been taught by the nuns of St. Joseph's, my mother truly feared for her granddaughter's immortal soul and that her plot had not been to disgrace me but to let the sprinkling of the holy water save Chloe from eternal damnation (and, really, what harm could it do since Chloe would never remember it anyway), I could not look past what I saw as a blatant contest of wills between me and the woman who still just assumed she could have things her way.

"That's not the point. She's my daughter. You can't just do what you want."

"You embarrassed me in front of Della. Didn't you see how uncomfortable she was at lunch?"

"*I* embarrassed *you*?"

"I will never forget this day." My mother finished, unrelenting and unapologetic, believing herself to be the victim.

But I was determined to have the last word. I met her glare with one of my own.

"Neither will I."

Usually, each time I planned a vacation back to North Brookfield, I figured on about three weeks, because right about then, Ma and I would start getting on each other's nerves. During the summer of 1994, however, I found myself drawing out my visit and putting off the return to my adult home in South Florida. This time during my stay, I'd been consumed by a feeling of nostalgia and sentimentality bordering on the melancholy. I felt as if time was slipping away from me, and I fought to hang onto each moment as long as I could.

My mother felt it too, I'm sure, though neither of us directly addressed it. We truly enjoyed each other's company that summer, shopping, going out to eat, and talking, talking, talking. A more mature thirty five, I now realized that I did not know as much as I thought I had when in my twenties and that wisdom and education are vastly different. I had mellowed and was able to accept and appreciate my mother, and she, in turn, could now relate to me as one adult to another. We were more than mother and daughter; we had become close friends.

I had driven to Massachusetts with my daughter, nine years old, and my dog, Daisy. While my mother napped in the afternoons, Chloe and I played "graces," a game of catch with sticks and a small hoop, or badminton in the back yard. One day I took her to Riverside Park, one day to Old Sturbridge Village. Ma did not go with us on these day trips because they would have been too tiring for her, but she did go with us to see the Fourth of July Parade in East Brookfield and the fireworks that night on Connie Mack Field.

I walked Daisy all over town that summer, past my old elementary school on Grove Street, converted to subsidized housing; past the Common and its run-down playground where I had spent thousands of hours as a child; and even all the way up Bell Street to St. Joseph's Cemetery where my father, my maternal grandparents, and most of my Kelley ancestors are buried.

One early evening, after yet another feast of fried haddock at Howard's Drive In, while Ma changed into her house coat and Chloe hunted up playmates on the Common, I slowly walked Daisy up Forest Street, retracing the steps I'd taken so many years earlier with Vincie Kizzle. When I reached the Fat Tree, I turned back and just stood there, looking down the street at my childhood home. I felt, in that moment, such a sadness as I contemplated the fleeting nature of life. In a way unlike ever before, I recognized the fragility of everything precious to me and I fought back tears as I reflected on all I had already lost and what I knew I would soon lose. My own childhood, long gone. My father, too, a man I never really got the chance to know, gone. My daughter, growing up so fast, fiercely independent and with a confidence I never had at her age. How many more years would she want to play games with her mother? How many more years before her adoring eyes would turn critical and reproachful to me, as mine had when I'd become focused on my own mother's flaws?

And my mother. She'd somehow shrunk this past year. I'd tried to hide my shock at how she'd aged since my previous visit. I remembered how she and I would open the Auburn Mall, stay through lunch and dinner, and shop until its closing. Now I pushed her in a wheel chair when we shopped because the angina and other health problems had made her so weak. Ever since the night my father had been killed at work just after my sixteenth birthday, I'd worried about my mother's heart condition, knowing that she, too, could be taken from me at any time, but for the first time, as I stood there under the Fat Tree during that July sunset in 1994, I felt the imminence of her death and the enormity of how her absence would affect my life.

I was right about the summer of '94 being the turning point visit with my mother. The following year, her health had deteriorated so that she didn't feel much like going out. I made five trips from Florida to Massachusetts during 1995, but none could be considered vacations. In December of that year, I took a leave of absence from teaching and moved back into the house to be close to Ma during the final months of her life. She died the following April, having left me the house on the condition that I move back to North Brookfield with my daughter.

Now, nearly nine years later, I mentally prepare myself for the ritual I want to perform on the periphery of the DiCesares' yard, conscious of the likelihood of being seen, even in the middle of the night, and feeling my heart beat a little faster as I finish delivering the newspapers at the top of Willow Street and drive back toward the Fat Tree.

As difficult as it was for my mother to accept my declarations of atheism made while in my twenties, I cannot imagine her reaction to my much later realization that the practices that most align with what I feel and believe are Wiccan. Certainly, long before I understood why, I'd been captivated by ritual, by candle-lighting, by the spirituality of Nature. When Chloe was small, I'd wake her up and drive with her to Lake Worth Beach on the Solstice, to sit in the sand and watch the sunrise. I acknowledged May Day as the rebirth of nature with roast duck and May baskets and by tying red bows on tree branches, and I lit Bayberry candles on the Yule. Despite enjoying the fun of Halloween, I still considered that night a sacred occasion to honor my deceased family members.

I don't think of myself as having "become" Wiccan; instead, I discovered Wicca to be the name for what I always was. Even during my so-called atheism, I'd never stopped searching, never stopped reading and researching because, in many ways, I had not changed from the child who had memorized the Mass and held her own pretend version, officiating over dolls and stuffed animals. Catholicism, the religion I'd been taught as a child, just hadn't been the right fit for me, but I'd never lost my spirituality.

A pamphlet I picked up at U Mass, where I briefly considered attending post-graduate school after I moved back to Massachusetts, introduced me to the term "Wicca" and led me to further research. As a registered Libertarian, I found common ground with the Wiccan philosophy "Do as ye will but harm none." I'd always believed in reincarnation, which made more sense to me than the existence of Heaven and Hell, and since I'd been raised to practice the Golden Rule, the Wiccan belief that what one puts out comes back threefold did not seem much of a stretch. I delighted in "celebrating" Nature and the passing of the seasons rather than prostrating before a capricious "God." And, in the bargain, I got back a version of the candle-lighting rituals I'd so enjoyed as a Catholic. All in all, a good fit for me.

After scanning the neighborhood and seeing no lights, I park the Tracker right at the corner of Willow and Forest, get out, and walk up to the Fat Tree. Given the past we'd shared and the feeling of safety I'd always gotten from its stalwart and reassuring presence, I have no doubt in the rightness of my choice. I take a deep breath, trying to focus on the ritual rather than on the possibility of being seen. First I remove my gloves and stuff them into my jacket pockets. Then I raise my hands to the tree, palms out, and hold them about an inch or so away from the trunk, trying to visualize the life force inside the old maple until I can imagine the warmth emanating from its core to meet my palms. After a few minutes, I cast the sacred circle around the tree, visualizing a white light surrounding the two of us that will discourage any negative forces from interfering with my ritual.

Then I speak to my old friend, the Fat Tree, explaining why I have come. My daughter, Chloe, has just this week announced that, having turned eighteen and graduated the previous May, she plans to move out on her own. Much as I long ago touched the craggy bark for luck when walking Andrea Searah home, I lay my palms over the maple's rough surface, feeling the bumps and ridges dig into my skin, and ask the Fat Tree to use whatever magic lives inside it to watch over my child.

"Please keep her safe," I whisper to the Fat Tree. "She's all I have left."

The fall leaves rustle over my head as the wind picks up. I thank the old maple and open the circle to end the ritual. Tomorrow, I will tell Mark DiCesare that if his tree ever needs anything and he doesn't want the expense or responsibility to please contact me.

When I get back into my car, having seen neither indoor lights nor headlights, I breathe a little easier. I look over my shoulder at my back seat, then glance at the dash clock as I start the engine. Time to go. I still have papers to deliver.

THE CROW FLIES OUT OF THE BELL TOWER OF THE TOWN HOUSE AND ACROSS THE STREET INTO ONE OF THE TREES NEXT TO THE CONGREGATIONAL CHURCH ON THE CORNER OF SCHOOL STREET. NEXT DOOR, QUABOUG RUBBER, THE ONLY MAJOR INDUSTRY STILL FUNCTIONING IN THE TOWN, IS JUST BEGINNING ITS FIRST – AND ONLY – SHIFT OF THE DAY. FROM THE TREE BRANCH, THE CROW WATCHES THE MEN GETTING OUT OF THEIR CARS AND GOING INSIDE THE FACTORY. SHIFTS AND MANPOWER HAVE BEEN CUT BACK BECAUSE OF THE POOR ECONOMY, BUT THERE WAS A TIME WHEN BUSINESS BOOMED. IN THE MID 1800S, NORTH BROOKFIELD WAS THE LARGEST SHOE MANUFACTURER IN THE COUNTRY, AND THE MAJOR SUPPLIER OF SHOES FOR SLAVES IN THE SOUTH, PRIMARILY DUE TO THE BATCHELOR SHOE COMPANY, WHICH IN 1916 BECAME THE QUABOUG RUBBER COMPANY. H. H. BROWNE SHOE COMPANY ALSO THRIVED JUST ONE BLOCK UP ON SCHOOL STREET.

SHOE MANUFACTURING WAS THE MAIN BUT CERTAINLY NOT THE ONLY INDUSTRY IN THIS GROWING TOWN WHOSE 1900 CENSUS LISTED 4587 RESIDENTS. THE NORTH BROOKFIELD RAILROAD CONNECTED TO THE BOSTON-ALBANY LINE, PROVIDING EASY SHIPPING AND RECEIVING ACCESS. CORSETS, LEATHER GOODS, AND OTHER PRODUCTS WENT OUT TO SUPPLIERS. THERE WERE 175 ORCHARDS AND WORKING FARMS IN TOWN. BY 1907, THE POPULATION EXCEEDED 4700. THE FIRST PAVED ROADS APPEARED IN 1910. T. C. BATES OWNED AND OPERATED THE QUABOUG SPRING WATER COMPANY, AND IN 1918 THE AZTEC ASBESTOS COMPANY BEGAN MANUFACTURING PIPE INSULATION AND BRAKE PADS FOR THE GROWING AUTOMOBILE INDUSTRY. PRODUCTION OF ASBESTOS PRODUCTS WAS BRISK, AND ON A BREEZY DAY THE ASBESTOS FIBERS FLOATED OVER THE NEIGHBORHOOD LIKE SNOWFLAKES.

5

Doppelgangers

"Come on, Mom!" My daughter runs toward the bumper cars without looking back. Still early in the day and I already feel worn out. I wonder how my mother kept up with me when I was Chloe's age. Younger by about ten years, in much better health and used to regular workouts, I should have at least as much energy as she'd had, but chasing after a nine year old is killing me. Maybe Ma had been right after all when she used to insist that rushing around in the restaurant where she worked was exercise enough to keep her in shape.

"I'm coming," I yell back, but Chloe has already gotten in line, secure in knowing that I will keep her in sight. Just as fearless as I'd been as a child, she doesn't mind riding some of the attractions alone. Bumper cars right now don't interest me. I need to find a bench where I can let my elephant ear digest.

After only a couple of days into our annual Massachusetts vacation to visit my mother, Chloe had started hounding me about Riverside Park. "You two go ahead," Ma assured me, "I'll be fine here. It's too hot for me."

I noticed a big difference in my mother this summer. The health conditions she'd struggled with since my early teens had taken their toll. She'd lost weight and seemed even more tired than last year. When we go shopping now, even only to Ames, she needs a wheel chair. She'd always looked younger than her years, but now, at seventy two, her face sags, making her appear haggard all the time. Now she takes naps every afternoon and goes to bed long before Chloe and I do. A day-long trip to an amusement park would be out of the question for her.

My thoughts focus only on sitting for a few minutes, so when I see them, the three of them, leisurely walking toward me, I stop short, stunned, caught totally off guard. Well, actually, I see HIM first. My father. Except of course, it can't be. My father was killed at fifty-one while at work at CPC Engineering in 1975, almost twenty years ago. Yet here in front of me is his younger self, like an apparition from my childhood - the large frame, the nearly bald head, the cleft in the chin of his handsome face. Then my gaze shifts to the woman and girl with him, and the breath catches in my throat. My mother and me - looking just as we had in the mid 1960s: her black hair brushed back off her forehead, her slim figure in knee-length shorts; my hair in pig tails, glasses resting on the bridge of my nose.

No. What? My mind can make no sense of what I see. Am I imagining it? I blink. Still there, solid as I am, all three oblivious to me and intent on their trek to the next ride – not the bumper cars, I realize, because they do not look in that direction. I glance over to where I last saw Chloe, thinking perhaps to take her out of line, but she's just chosen a car and the ride is about to start, so I'm stuck here.

I look back at the trio as they approach, not dead-on, but sort of on the diagonal, so I can observe without being observed. The resemblance is eerie, like one of my family's early vacation shots come to life. I'd many times heard that everyone has a double, a "doppelganger," but three at once? Like a slice out of time. Like in my favorite movie when Marty McFly goes back to the future a couple of minutes early and sees himself in the parking lot. Except this is no movie.

Once I get over the shock, I find myself feeling sentimental as I watch this little family and nostalgic for the family from my childhood, whole, before fate stepped in and ripped away one of its key elements.

Father, mother, and child, together on an excursion, a day at the amusement park, where the father and daughter will ride the scariest rides, the father laughing, the daughter clutching him and screaming in mock terror. The mother not riding any but the tamest rides, the ones with the least amount of motion, like the Ferris wheel, ever since that time she was talked into the Tilt 'o Whirl and afterwards threw up behind the Ring-Toss tent. If the carnival is on the Common, the three walking home when the rides shut down but not until the father has won the daughter a big stuffed animal, a green dinosaur or an orange shark, spending far too many quarters to shoot the moving duck targets. If the amusement park is at Canobie Lake, the roller coaster so high and so fast because this is a permanent park unlike the fly-by-night carnivals that pitch their tents on town commons, and the three afterwards riding home in the car, the father shamelessly passing gas from the beans eaten earlier and the daughter laughing when he says "pull my finger" while the mother rolls her eyes and cranks open the window.

Father, mother, and daughter shopping for school clothes the

week before the very first day of school among the racks of dresses in size 6x in solids of navy and maroon, plaids of brown / beige and deep red / green, from which the mother selects this one ("Do you like this?") and that one ("How about this?") and each being draped over the arm of the father who seems to take genuine interest. This little family eating ice cream cones from Silveo's on their front porch on muggy summer evenings, opening presents under the silver tree on Christmas mornings, going to LeBlanc's for sundaes – pineapple for the mother and hot fudge for the father and daughter – and the father putting quarters into the mini-juke box hanging from the wall at their booth. The car rides back home at night from Memere and Pepere's, Le Blanc's, or wher-ever, crickets singing somewhere beyond the open win-dows, the Rambler's wheels humming along the country roads, the father driving, the mother next to him, the

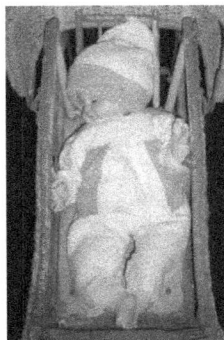

daughter dozing in the back seat, clutching Thumbelina, the rag doll, its head floppy from being re-sewn so many times, and the daughter feeling loved and secure in her perfect world.

At least, I'd once thought our life as a family was perfect, or near-ly so, but, no, I'd later realized, there'd been only perfect moments, eventually outnumbered by the stretches of hostility, disappointment, and apathy that had always been there to some degree but which a child chooses not to see. And these three? The doppelgangers? I look more closely into their faces as they come nearer. They do not speak to each other, nor do they smile. Well, they certainly have that part right because, truthfully, by the time I'd become this little girl's age – she'd have to be eight or nine – most of our family excursions had stopped being fun. I couldn't remember what had happened, if there had been a particular incident or turning point. Things just more or less deteriorated, to the extent that the three of us could no longer spend any length of time alone together without bickering and tears - to the extent that in a last ditch effort at some semblance of a family vacation before everything fell apart, my parents decided to invite their closest friends, Chill and Aurore, to accompany us one summer.

The heat blew in, a constant assault on my sunburned face. I had long ago given up on the stray strands of hair that refused to be confined in the hasty ponytail I'd put in this morning at the motel in Lake George. My neck and body itched with sweat in places I couldn't reach without squirming. I tried not to squirm because I feared reprimand. Next to me, my mother lit up another Benson & Hedges and tossed the crumpled green package on the floor, clearly irritable. Everyone was irritable, even St. Christopher on the dashboard.

I rode the hump in the Rambler, squashed between my mother and Aurore, my mother's best friend. My father drove and switched off every now and then with Chill, his best friend and Aurore's husband, who rode shotgun when not driving. Too fearful of driving, Aurore hadn't yet gotten her license (and wouldn't until well into her 60s) but my mother could have helped with the driving though I knew why she didn't offer: Dad would criticize and another argument would begin. My parents clenched their jaws in the vain effort to avoid any more arguments on this trip. For now, we all rode in silence.

I just knew Vermont had to be the biggest state in the country, despite last year's fifth grade geography lesson. Endless trees on endless roads that supposedly, eventually, would take us to Bar Harbor, Maine. No signs of habitation since the tiny restaurant where, hours (or was it days?) ago, we'd had a second breakfast. "Real maple syrup," Dad had stated to no one in particular. My mother had looked tired and unimpressed.

Nothing to look at, nothing to do, and no one willing to make conversation. Not even the car's AM radio could break the uncomfortable silence, since the road on which the Rambler's tires droned threaded through the middle of nowhere. Reading made me carsick, especially when I had to breathe in the menthol every time Mom exhaled. I licked my parched lips and wished we'd packed a cooler of drinks, but Dad and Chill hated to stop when Mom or Aurore had to pee. Certainly this week had to be the hottest week in the hottest August ever recorded.

We'd left Massachusetts only the day before yesterday. Adding Chill and Aurore on our annual vacation had seemed like a good idea if only to provide the distraction from each other that my parents needed. Evidently they hadn't realized that the Gaudettes' marriage had deteriorated even more than their own had. The arguing had begun almost immediately, before the car had backed out of our driveway.

At first, I found it amusing watching other people bicker for a change as my mother and father exchanged wary looks in the rearview mirror. After a while, though, the overall atmosphere turned tense. Chill and Aurore fought over everything, minute things, stupid things, the way people who once loved each other but no longer feel any love will fight, the way my parents would eventually fight after they lost all their love for each other and no longer tried to hide that fact from me.

That first night of our vacation, in the motel room at Lake

George, New York, my parents argued about how Chill and Aurore constantly argued and that no one was having any fun. I ignored the sharp words they flung at each other, as I always did, always had from as far back as I could remember. I slipped out of the room, quietly closing the door, and walked past all the identical doors, the identical metal chairs, past another room from which I could hear Chill and Aurore still arguing, and headed down a short dirt path to the lake's edge. I looked out over the moonlit water and wondered what it must be like to be an adult in a loveless relationship. I wondered if Chill and Aurore had ever really been in love, if my mother and father had ever really been in love.

My mother once showed me pictures labeled only "1956" and taken at some lake somewhere of the two couples, sitting in a boat, double dating, Chill and Dad leaning back with their arms around Aurore and Mom, everyone smiling. I had never actually seen my parents as happy together as they looked in those pictures. What happens to a relationship that turns love into mere tolerance, happiness into misery? I wondered, as I often had and often would, what two people as different

as my mother and father had ever seen in each other.

I listened to the gentle lapping of the water against the pier and wondered why we had to leave Lake George right after breakfast, why we couldn't just stay here and have a real vacation instead of having to drive through first Vermont, then New Hampshire, then up the coast of Maine to Boothbay and ultimately to Bar Harbor before turning around and heading back home to Massachusetts. When I returned to our room, the arguing had stopped, replaced by the customary stony silence.

In the morning, however, in the diner across the street from the motel, spirits briefly lifted. A new day, new possibilities. Dad had risen early and taken a dip in the water. He looked calm and refreshed. Coffee arrived and Chill took a sip, smiled, opened wide his eyes that matched the bottom of the motel pool, and brightly exclaimed "Good morning, world" as he looked around the room. I didn't know whether to laugh or look away in embarrassment. "He says that every morning," Aurora informed me and shrugged. After breakfast, we packed ourselves back into the car and set out for Maine.

"I hate Vermont," my mother said now as she lit still another cigarette and wiped the sweat from her forehead. "It goes on forever."

My father glared at her in the rearview mirror. "We'll spend the night in the White Mountains," he said, "and get to Maine sometime tomorrow."

"I don't see why we couldn't just stay in Lake George," she said, echoing my thoughts. She did not look at my father but instead gazed out the window, flicking the ashes into the stifling breeze as she smoked. No one answered.

My mother and Aurore wanted to relax in deck chairs, browse through gift shops, linger over restaurant dinners. Dad and Chill had an agenda: miles to cover, destinations to check off the list; however, when it became clear that we would never make it all the way to Bar Harbor without immediately having to turn around for the return trip home, the men angrily gave in and agreed to spend an entire day in Boothbay. Blaming Aurore and my mother for time lost because of bathroom stops, they sulked by a motel pool while we "girls" happily shopped for souvenirs.

Aurore spotted a ceramic vase of brilliant blue in the window of a small shop but had not brought enough money with her. We returned to the motel pool where Dad and Chill sat dripping and drinking beer.

"Look at that kid," Chill said to my father, gesturing with his beer can toward an overweight boy about my age whose bare chest looked almost like mine, which had started to develop. "He ought to have an operation and finish it," Chill said.

Dad chuckled, but my mother looked disgusted. I stared at the boy as he jumped into the pool and wondered what kind of operation Chill meant. Then I stared down at Chill's big bare feet, which caught my eye because of their size and deformity. His toes were crooked, like a hag's fingers, and some of them crossed over others. I looked down at my dad's feet for contrast; even though I already knew what they looked like because I'd so often seen him slice off his plantar warts from their undersides with a razor blade. Dad's toes lined up straight and all fit perfectly together. "I have beautiful feet," I'd heard him jokingly remark many times, "not like so many other men whose feet are ugly." Men like Chill, I figured.

When Aurore asked Chill for money, he insisted he had to see what the item was that she just had to have. He and my dad got dressed for dinner, and the five of us walked to the gift shop on the way to the restaurant. When Chill saw the vase, he reminded Aurore that she owned many vases and surely didn't need another one. Aurore became angry: who was he to tell her what she did and didn't need?

"You're not the one who works!" Chill said.

"You think taking care of a house isn't work?"

My mother fumed in silence as the two argued in the street. She hated disputes over money almost as much as she hated making a scene in public. She handled the finances in our house, so despite sticking to a budget of sorts she never had to run her purchases by my father, her philosophy being that what he didn't know wouldn't hurt him. Her mother, my grandmother Annie, had taught her well, she said. Women are more logical and organized when it comes to money. Mom had let Dad handle the bills when they first got married but had taken over when she realized the bills weren't being paid. She had already begun teaching me her methods of budgeting and saving so that I would know how to handle the money in my own household someday. She'd also taught me, by example, that if the wife is earning money, she never has to feel dependent on her husband.

Aurore never got the blue vase, and as a result, any remaining shred of civility between her and Chill vanished. I would not have thought it possible, but the car ride from Maine back to Massachusetts proved more tortuously hostile than all those seemingly endless hours of the preceding days. No one spoke the entire time except when Aurore or my mother needed to ask for a restroom.

As soon as we reached the house, Chill and Aurore, still not speaking to each other, jumped in their car. My parents barely entered our house before the yelling began. My mother accused my father of planning with Chill a vacation that was doomed to fail and then stubbornly trying to stick to the miserable plan. My father countered that my mother had had a bad attitude from the beginning and always had been incapable of making the best of a situation. Lesson learned by all of us: group vacation = failed experiment. I headed for my room before the confrontation got any uglier.

Before I'd even opened my suitcase though, my mother appeared in my doorway. "Don't unpack," she said. "We're going on a real vacation. Just you and I."

Without even saying goodbye to my father, Mom and I got back into the Rambler and headed for Hampton Beach, where we spent three days lounging on the beach and by the pool, shopping and eating in restaurants. One day the two of us rented bicycles to explore all the side streets. As far as I know, she never once called home.

Dad went on a "real" vacation too, evidently. "The beach," he vaguely answered when I asked him what he'd done while we were gone. He never said which beach or whether he'd gone alone, but he looked tan and happy. Separate vacations had thus been born in my family long before I'd even reached my teens.

Although any extended time as a family had been ruled out, we

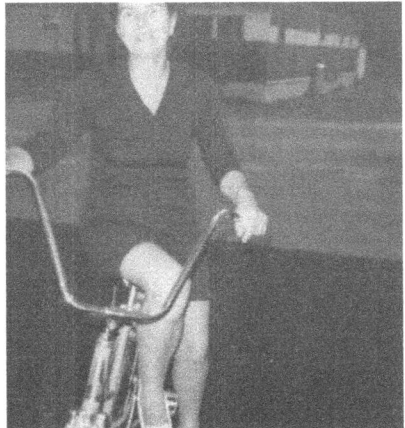

could still enjoy the occasional day-trip as long as the drive there and back didn't last too long. Always one to fall asleep quickly, my father had begun dozing off at the wheel on occasion, ironic considering his former job had been as a chauffeur because he could go without sleep for extended periods of time – twenty four hours straight if needed – and therefore could be "on call" for Mr. Krock. Sure, there was that one time - and didn't he love to tell the story? – when he'd fallen asleep while driving the limousine to the airport, the intercom waking him when Mr. Krock asked from behind the tinted divider, "Ralph, wasn't that a toll we just passed?" My father had thought fast and answered that the toll collector had waved them along. "Jesus must have been riding with him in the front seat," my mother said every time she heard him tell it, and of course he would laugh. Just an aberration. Not a problem.

Dad's increasingly more frequent fits of dozing off seemed to have little to do with how tired he was or how much sleep he'd had and became more troublesome as he neared his fifties. More accurately, they became more troublesome for my mother (since he seemed unconcerned) and added another item on the list of topics about which they argued. Cigarette burns multiplied on his recliner and on the quilt of the rollaway bed where he now slept in the spare room we called the Other Side. She feared his narcolepsy (assumed though undiagnosed) would lead to his burning down the house while we slept.

One night, on the way home from work at the steel plant, his truck went off the road, the passenger door damaged by low-hanging branches. Another night, he side-swiped a parked car.

Yet whenever the three of us went somewhere, Dad usually drove, maintaining that he was the better driver and insisting that he felt fine. Not tired at all. Wiiiiide awake. See? And he repeatedly mocked my mother's concern by pretending to yawn, loudly and exaggeratedly. Of course, she resented his playacting and spent each trip staring more at him than at the scenery, clearly unable to relax, let alone enjoy herself. When he put on his sunglasses, she could no longer see whether or not his eyelids drooped, and she worried even more, especially after one incident when she thought the car was drifting too close to the shoulder and she jerked the wheel. Then the yelling began. She accused him of deliberately endangering our lives; he accused her of overreacting, that he had been completely in control.

"I wasn't sleeping. I'm fine."

"You wouldn't admit it anyway. You're never wrong."

After he traded in his truck for an Ambassador wagon, I made a point of sitting way in the back, playing songs I'd recorded from the radio onto my cassette recorder. That way, I could pretend not to notice whatever happened between them in the front seat.

Our car rides together became less frequent and of shorter distance, ninety minutes or so being about the maximum my parents could last without any major arguments. At least we had our occasional day trips, like spending my thirteenth birthday browsing the exhibits and tourist traps of Salem, the "witch" city. Meanwhile I kept hoping that something would unite us, that we could find some joy in being together, the three of us. I knew we'd never be the Cleavers, but how about the Bunkers? They had their differences just as we did, but they still loved and stuck by each other. Had it been I who pointed out that Archie looked like an older version of Dad? And he had played along for a while, calling me "little goyle" and warning me not to marry a "meathead" someday. But even that went too far because he started calling my mother a "dingbat" and telling her to "stifle," not only privately but in front of company.

Finally, even the day trips disappeared. During my mid-teens, I rarely saw my father; whatever free time he had was not spent at home, and my mother had given up fighting about it. Then, in late July of 1975, Ma arranged for us to spend a Sunday at Hampton Beach, picking up Aunt Ruth along the way, and surprisingly, Dad decided to join us.

Despite the oppressive heat, the ocean's chill was enough to numb feet, but Dad still went in, riding the icy waves face down, stiffly stretched out, letting the current carry him towards the shore, then rising up from the foam and wading out to do it again and again while we watched. Becoming bored and wanting to shop, Ma, Aunt Ruth and I finally left him there, though, and during our absence he shopped too, secretly, for a birthday present for me – one just from him rather than from both of them: a white gauze hippie top with long, puffed sleeves gathered at the wrists and fuchsia embroidery edging the square neck. I had just that week turned sixteen.

When we later returned, carrying our shopping bags stuffed with souvenirs, my father sat alone looking out over the water, his bare sunburned back to us, his still muscular tattooed arms stretched across the green wooden bench's back. Despite the crowds on the beach, I spotted him right away, and a feeling of euphoria washed over me that there had been no arguments on this trip. I wanted to freeze time, to savor that moment of rightness as the sun beat down and the sea gulls screamed overhead, and the hope that maybe there could be a happy ending for the three of us swelled in my chest.

Though I could not possibly have known, I somehow sensed the significance of that moment, and now as I sit on the bench at Riverside Park, waiting for my daughter to step off the bumper car ride, I can still see its snapshot in my head. What were Dad's thoughts that day as he gazed at the crashing waves? Work? Bills? Us? Her – the woman who we later found out had taken my mother's place in his heart? A week later, my father was dead.

The doppelganger family has passed me, unaware of my interest, and now only their retreating backs remain visible to me. Meanwhile, Chloe is headed in my direction. Should I grab her, run after them, and say – what? Please love each other and be happy? Don't let what happened to my family happen to yours? Reason intervenes: these people are not my family. They have their own unique story. Our time has passed. There are no do-overs.

Following my head yet knowing in my heart that I will always regret my inaction, I let them go, simply watching as they fade into the crowd.

6

In Winter, Quite the Other Way

(Summer)

I'm supposed to be asleep, but I'm not tired. Besides, it's still day time. Everything is blurred without my glasses, but I can see the orange glow from the setting summer sun. The lace sheers hanging from my three open windows gently blow, creating interesting patterns of dappled light on the flowered wallpaper. It seems like hours since my mother put me to bed. While we were saying prayers, I could hear the loud cheering and occasional crack as bat met ball on the Common at the end of my street. I found it hard to concentrate on the words, especially the Our Father, which is so long, because my mind kept wandering to the Common. Not that I like baseball. Baseball is boring. Daddy will sometimes listen to a Red Sox game on the transistor radio as he putters in the garage, and I can always tell when baseball is on because it's the same guy every time who talks.

The game on the Common is over now, but I hear other sounds drifting up the street. Wump, wumpwump the big boys bouncing a basketball, then a sort of clanging sound as the ball hits the hoop. I could be playing tag, hopscotch, or kickball right now if I were down there in the playground section. There's always someone willing to start a game. I bet there are lots of kids still there, kids who can stay up late because their mothers don't have to get up for work the next morning.

My mother thinks that because I have to get up early to be babysat at Mrs. Mallon's house down the street I need to go to bed early so I won't be too tired and get sick. She doesn't understand that I'm awake for hours after she goes back downstairs, watching the light change and gradually fade, listening to the Common sounds and pretending. I pretend every night. I'm not allowed to get out of bed, but Mommy never said I couldn't sit up, and a lot of times I need to sit up to act out my parts. Some nights I'm Batgirl. I help Batman save the world from the Penguin and the Joker because he can't do it without me. We swing from buildings on the Batrope and shoot darts from our sleeves, then, after yet another successful mission, speed off in the sleek, shiny Batmobile that I love even more than the Caddy my father drives for Mr. Krock. Other nights I sail the seas with McHale's Navy. I am the only girl on the ship, but all of McHale's men love and admire me because I'm so courageous. Daddy was in the Navy and he tells me stories about all the sharks in the ocean. Unafraid though, I stand right up by the wheel, even in the storms, and sometimes Captain McHale lets me steer.

Tonight though, I'm not needed by either Batman or Captain McHale. I pick at the scabs on my knees even though I'm not supposed to and wish I had some of my dolls or stuffed animals to play with. Toys are not allowed in my bedroom though; they have to stay in the playroom downstairs. Only when I'm sick and have to stay in bed all day am I allowed to play in here and I can choose only one stuffed animal. Mommy is very strict about that - even when I had scarlet fever and I saw all the dancing pretty colors that no one else could see.

Sometimes Mommy lets me line up the plastic Madonnas that watch over me while I sleep – one from the bureau and two from the top of the built-in cabinet – but I'm not supposed to touch them without asking first. Mommy has to get them and hand them to me so I don't drop one or knock something over. They stand among the other things I'm not supposed to touch: the bottles of Holy Water and Holy Oil and the framed pictures of my brother Jay and me as babies. Directly across from my bed hangs the framed picture of Jesus pointing to his heart, which looks like it's on fire. I'm not allowed to touch that either because Jesus watches over me just like the Madonnas.

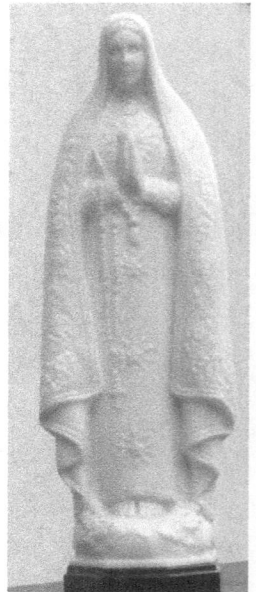

Mommy calls the statues "Blessed Virgins" and always keeps them in their exact same spots. "Mary is the Mother of God. I named you Donna Marie, after her," she has told me many times. I hate my name. Her second daughter, if she had had another, would have been named Annie after my grandmother, who died long before I was born. I have often wished that I could have been the second daughter instead of the only daughter. Maybe then bedtime wouldn't be so lonely. I look around the room, unable to make out anything but fuzzy shapes. Even though they're not toys and they all look alike, the Madonnas would be better to play with than nothing. I consider hollering down to ask Mommy to get the statues, but I know she'll say no because I'm supposed to be asleep.

Click, click, click, click…one of the ladies from up the hill passes by our house on the sidewalk, her high heels getting louder as she nears, then fading as she continues down the street. The *whole world* is still up, and I'm missing it. "Just lie there, and you'll fall asleep," Mommy always says when I complain that I'm wide awake. But how can I just lie here when I can hear grownups walking by and other kids outside playing? It's worse when we have company and they're still here after I've been put to bed. I hear the shuffle of playing cards, the clinking of glasses as Daddy makes highballs, and the laughter from jokes I will never hear. I sulk on those nights, resentment swelling in my chest, and I take an extra-long voyage with Captain McHale that often doesn't end until way after dark.

I'm allowed to bring a book, one book, to bed with me each night during the summer. If I hold the book very close to my face, I can read the words without my glasses even though the sun is setting. I've already read tonight's choice, but since it's one of my favorites, I reach for it again. I don't remember who gave me *A Child's Garden of Verses,* but I must have read it a thousand times. It's the only book of poems I have, and I know most of them by heart.

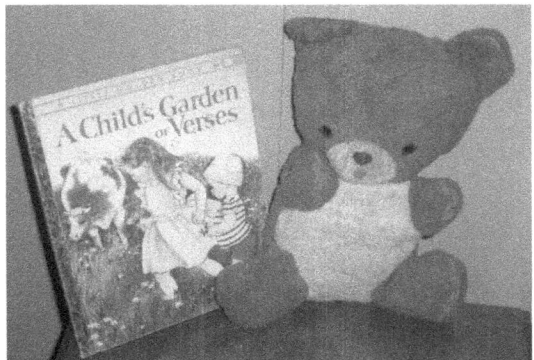

Even so, I like to reread them and stare at the old fashioned looking pictures. I turn to "Bed in Summer" and look at the little boy wearing what Mommy said is a "night-shirt."

There are no lamps in my bedroom because there are no holes in the walls to plug things into, but there is a ceiling light with a square pink glass shade that hides the light bulb underneath. A chain hangs from the light to make it go on and off, but I can't grab it from the bed even if I hold onto the footboard and reach out as far as I can reach. I wonder what it would be like to have only candles for light like the boy in the picture has by his bed. Mommy says that when she was little there were gaslights in the house because there was no electricity but that even she is not old enough to remember living by candlelight alone.

"In winter I get up at night / And dress by yellow candlelight. / In summer quite the other way, / I have to go to bed by day." I say the words aloud but softly so that I won't get caught still being awake. The little boy in the poem may not have electricity, and it doesn't look like he has very many toys, but he's still a lot like me. I feel sorry for him, that he has to go to bed when it's still light out. It's not fair. I can see he hates it as much as I do.

"I have to go to bed and see / The birds still hopping on the tree, / Or hear the grown-up people's feet / Still going past me in the street." Our only tree is Grandfather Tree, the horse chestnut in the back yard, but even if there were trees right outside my windows, I couldn't see any birds in them without my glasses. I can hear just fine though, and here comes that lady in her high heels going home from wherever it was she went a little while earlier. It's not fair.

After a while of lying down to read, my arms get tired of holding the book up, so I flop over onto my stomach. I wish I could sit up with my back against the headboard, but the wooden crucifix that Mommy nailed in there when this bed belonged to my brother Jay hangs right in the middle, and it digs into my back. I lay the book on my pillow and prop myself up with my elbows. Frustrated with being in bed and reading about being in bed, I flip to "The Swing" and again softly read the words out loud even though I know them by heart: "How do you like to go up in a swing, / Up in the air so blue?" I love my swing set even more than my spring horse. I try to imagine swinging out in the back yard, but then I start thinking about the big-kid swings on the Common – I can go really high on those – and I get mad at being in bed all over again. Also, my arms are getting tired again. It's uncomfortable being on my stomach too. Why does that crucifix have to be right in the way?

It occurs to me as I stare at it that only one nail, right over Jesus' head, attaches the cross to the maple headboard. If I had something to take the nail out, I could comfortably sit up and read as long as I remember to nail Jesus back up before I go to sleep. My thumb nail doesn't work though, and I have nothing else to dig the nail out. Then I have another idea. If I move my pillow out of the way, I think I can wedge the book under the bottom half of the crucifix. I'll still have to be on my stomach, but I won't have to lean up on my elbows to hold the book up. Jesus will hold it. After moving my pillow, I turn to the next poem I want to read and try to shove the open book under the crucifix.

Almost instantly, I hear a loud snap, and the bottom half of Jesus on the cross flies by me. Another sound lets me know that the broken piece has hit the floor somewhere well beyond the bed. I stare at what's left of Jesus and feel sick to my stomach. Only His head and the very top part of the cross are still attached to the headboard. Mommy's going to be very mad when she finds out, and I'll probably be punished. She might even think I did it on purpose because I've complained to her about its being there. I start to chew on my fingernail. Will I get a spanking? I look back over my shoulder at the picture of Jesus, which looks like a dark blob on the light wallpaper. He saw me break His body in half, but He must know it was an accident because He knows everything.

I listen very hard to see if it sounds like Mommy and Daddy are getting ready to come to bed, but I know that it's still too early for them. They have to go through my room to get to theirs, but maybe it will be so dark in here when it's time that she won't be able to see what I've done.

What's happening? The light's so bright it hurts my eyes! Why is Mommy yelling? I can't make sense of her words. *What* was her mother's? She's got something in her hand, but I can't see what it is. Then I hear the word "crucifix," and I remember. My stupid idea to use Jesus to prop up my book. I open my mouth to try to explain, but I can't seem to find the words. She'll think I'm arguing and she'll get madder. I feel small against her rage, which slices through me like knives. I drop my head and stare at my lap and say nothing. After a long time, she stops yelling and outs the light. She says we will discuss this in the morning and to go to sleep. I lie in the dark and wonder if I'll go to Hell.

(Winter)

"Okay, show's over. Time for bed." Daddy lights another cigarette and flicks the smoldering match into the ashtray that sits in a tall stand next to his chair that he calls a recliner.

Even though *The Jackie Gleason Show* is over, I still want to stay up, but I don't argue because when Daddy gets mad his voice is scary, even scarier than Mommy's. I go over to him and give him a goodnight kiss. As I leave the living room, I can hear the squeak his chair makes when he sits all the way back in it.

Now that Mommy has a job as a waitress at the snack counter in The Fair Department Store, she's not here after supper. Daddy won't put me to bed because he says I'm a big girl now that I'm in school and I should be able to put myself to bed. I haven't told him that I'm still afraid of going upstairs in the dark because, if I do, he might make fun of me. When he teases me sometimes, like when I can't see the cows or horses way over in the field he points to from the car window, he says it's just a joke, but it still hurts my feelings.

At the bottom of the stairs, I stand with my back up against the front door, feeling the cold draft leak in on my bare feet. The hall light is on, but it shines only about halfway up, so I can't see the top steps at all. The narrow stairway is like a long, dark, silent tunnel. Monsters might be up there. Or maybe evil birds like in that movie when the lady walks really slowly toward the closed door and slowly turns the knob and when the door opens birds fly out and peck her face. Mommy was right when she said I shouldn't have watched that movie because at night I can't stop thinking about it, but we were visiting Daddy's friend Benny and the television was already on. Mommy covered my eyes during the really bad parts like when the school teacher's eyes get pecked out and when the man catches on fire at the gas pump, but Benny's step-son Dale told me all about them afterwards. Dale also told me about the Booger Man, who waits in little kids' rooms at night and, if he catches them, covers them with boogers. The Booger Man could be up in my room right now waiting for me with the evil birds.

I know I have to go up the stairs anyway and soon, before Daddy realizes that I'm not in bed. I try to think good thoughts, the way you're supposed to when you're scared. I pretend that Mommy is singing to me the way she still does once in a while, if I ask her to. She sits in the rocking chair that used to be Memere's and I sit in her lap. She rocks back and forth as she sings, the way she did when I was a baby and had something called colic: "Donna Marie, as cute as can be. She's a pretty baby, and she belongs to me."

It doesn't work. Mommy's not here; she's at The Fair, serving ice cream and soda. One hand on the railing, I inch my way up, stopping after each step and waiting a long time to see if I hear any evil moving around in my room. When I get to where I can't see any farther, I have to wait until I get brave enough to run the rest of the way in the dark. Finally, I take a big gulp of air and run up the last three steps, turning left at the top because the bathroom light is closer than the one in my bedroom. Without breathing, I run past Mommy's sewing room door and reach just inside the bathroom doorway to flip on the light. Then I let the air out of my chest and wait.

Still no sound from my room. Now I can see the whole hallway and a little way into my bedroom but not far enough to see the chain that dangles from my ceiling light, so I have to get brave all over again. I stand on one foot and then the other, waiting for the right time. Then, taking another quick gulp of air and holding it in my chest, I dash down the hall and into my bedroom, frantically reaching up and waving my hand in the air where I think the pull chain might be. I'm relieved when my fingers find it and light floods my room. I can breathe, and my heart thuds a little less.

After going back down the hallway to shut off the bathroom light, I begin my search for monsters. I'm still a little scared as I open the door to Mommy and Daddy's bedroom and then to Mommy's big closet that used to be her bedroom when she was my age. Both rooms connect to mine, and I open their doors fast and look just inside without stepping over the thresholds, then close them back up after I'm satisfied that nothing is lurking in there. Next I check under the bed, lifting up the spread that I hate, pink with a giant ballerina twirling on it. I save my closet for last. The light doesn't quite reach in there, and the door sometimes sticks and is hard for me to open. It doesn't have a knob but a bolt that slides back and forth in its holder. You have to push on the door with your knee as you slide the bolt back, then grab the handle and pull hard. Even though I have trouble with this door, I make sure to check behind it because I know that monsters are strong.

My heart starts to pound again when it's time to out the ceiling light. Now that I'm bigger, I can just barely reach the chain from the foot of my bed if I lean way over, but I still have to balance myself so I don't fall off the edge. At first, the dark is always so thick that I would not be able to see any monsters that I might have missed during my search even if I strained my eyes very hard. I'm not looking, though, because after I pull the chain I'm trying too hard to get under the covers. I have to sort of wriggle into my bed because the sheet and blanket both stay tucked in all the way around so that I don't kick them off in my sleep. Mommy thinks I want them that way so that I won't be cold, but the real reason is that only when I'm covered am I safe from The Man With The Knife.

I have decided that monsters (including evil birds, The Booger Man and The Sandman, (who is not really a monster but sometimes gets

so carried away with his job that his sand might seal your eyes shut forever) cannot appear once I've searched and can't get into the house once
I'm in my room. The Man With The Knife, though, might still be hiding
(Mommy and Daddy's closet is always a possibility. I don't check there
because I'm not allowed in their room). Or, even if he's not already in
the house, he might slip in through a downstairs window or the front door
at the bottom of the stairs. The Man With The Knife has his limits
though: he can't hurt me if I'm covered up. At least I don't think he can.
Even so, I worry that he might get in the house and catch me in an off
moment, say, if an arm sticks out from the blankets while I'm sleeping.

Once my eyes get used to the darkness, I can see how the streetlight at the stop sign in front of the house shines through my windows, so
the room is not completely pitch dark. Even without my glasses, which I
always carefully set on the bureau before I out the light, I can keep an
eye on all the doors as well as the open doorway into the hall, just in case
anything tries to get in. The only good thing about putting myself to bed
is that there's no one making sure I say prayers. The one I hate the most
is the one that starts "Now I lay me down to sleep." I hate the part that
says if I die in my sleep, God will take my soul. On the nights that I have
to say that prayer with Mommy, I cross my fingers behind my back but
not so that she can see.

Alone, I lie still in my bed, keeping watch for The Man With The
Knife, blankets up to my chin, and listen to the house noises. Our house
is old. Mommy told me her parents bought it before she was born. Old
houses make a lot of noises, just like old people do. I can hear the wind
whistle through the rafters, and the creaks in the house's wood frame that
is covered up by the new yellow aluminum siding that Mommy is so
proud of. Sometimes I hear scratching over my head in the crawl space. I
know that in the winter, mice get cold outside and sneak in through the
foundation, eventually making their way over our heads to stay warm and
have their babies. I've never seen one in the house though, and by spring
they're all gone.

The blue flame in the gas stove flickers and leaps. The stove is old too and used to be in the parlor when I was a baby, before the room was made into the dining room and a new stove bought. The gas stove has a comforting smell, the same as, yet different from, the Vick's Mommy rubs on my chest when I have a cold. But each time the stove shuts off, it makes a noise that almost sounds as if someone is creeping up the stairs. Wait. *Is* someone creeping up the stairs? I'm never really sure, so I strain my ears and hold my breath, tensing my body in case I have to dive completely under the blankets, head and all.

The scariest noise I hear upstairs though doesn't happen until I am older. Now I'm in fourth grade and no longer afraid of the dark. I'm so grown up that I have my own key to the front door. My mother doesn't work in the evenings anymore; she has a day job as a waitress downtown, but even though she's home every night I go to bed by myself.

Tonight my parents and I went to visit Memere and Pepere, and on the way back in the car, Dad started to tease Mom about something stupid, and it seemed like it was just in fun. Mom laughed at first, so I figured it would be okay if I joined in too. Mostly, I just laughed or said "yeah," as if I agreed with Dad. But when Mom stopped laughing, I stopped too. Dad didn't stop though. He kept right on teasing, and it started to sound more like making fun. I could tell by Mom's silence that she was getting mad. I knew it would turn into a fight, so when we got home, I went right into my playroom in the Other Side and put on a record. After the yelling stopped, I waited a while before I opened the door to make sure the fighting was over. I saw Mom in the kitchen. I figured Dad was watching television in the living room. Now would be a good time to go upstairs to my bedroom to get into my pajamas.

I get about halfway up the stairs before I hear it: a sound I never heard before and hope never to hear again, a sound worse than any imaginary monsters could make.

My father is crying.

I stand very still on the stair, not wanting the sound to be real, and my whole body chills. Something tells me that I shouldn't be here, that I shouldn't hear this. Trying not to make any noise, I slowly back down the stairs. When I pass by the kitchen, I say nothing to my mother about what is happening in their bedroom. I walk into the Other Side and put on a record.

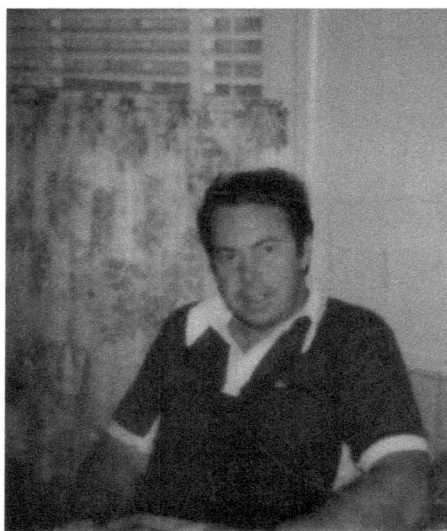

7

The Cool Factor

Sister Dorothy John had just asked a question, and I wanted to be the one to answer. "Someone give me an example of a venial sin." I had studied the catechism lesson for today, I had sat in the front row of the stuffy outdated classroom, and I was ready to prove myself. My hand flew up, and I leaned forward in my seat.

"Yes, Donna Marie?" Sister Dorothy John was my favorite of the Sisters of Saint Joseph. She wore glasses as I did, and her demeanor was gentle, almost childlike unlike many of the Sisters whose sternness sparked fear among the eight year olds in our First Holy Communion readiness class. Although her wimple covered her hair, her neck, and the edges of her face, I could tell that Sister Dorothy John was younger than most of the other nuns, and I guessed that's why she taught the younger children. Even then, she often had difficulty controlling her classes. Her soft voice and chubby chipmunk cheeks dotted with freckles and blemishes gave license to the boys to misbehave. She always looked pale and overheated in her heavy floor-length black habit. I felt sorry for her and when I tried to imagine her as a child, I saw a shy unpopular girl who probably got picked on a lot.

"A venial sin would be…" I thought fast. Of the many alternatives that came to mind, I'm not sure why I chose the one I did. Perhaps to show off. Perhaps to seem more like my classmates. Whatever I intended backfired. "…if I hit my brother."

Immediately, I heard sneering laughter behind me, and one of the Hubacz boys yelled "You don't even have a brother!" Mike and Tom, identical twins, sounded the same and sat together in the back row. Furious and humiliated, I whirled around in my seat.

"I do so have a brother!" I yelled back at both of them and at the class in general.

After I graduated from college, my mother put together two photograph albums: one for me and one for my half brother, Jay. She secretly went through all the envelopes and boxes of disorganized pictures that she'd collected over the years and selected what she considered to be the highlights from each of our backgrounds and childhoods. I never saw Jay's album, but mine begins with a couple of pictures of both sets of grandparents and of my mother and father when they were first dating and ends with my diploma from Westfield State College. The first picture after my newborn head-shot is of the infant me being held up for the camera by the grinning twenty three year old son from my mother's first marriage, outfitted entirely in khaki and wearing a crew cut. Jay, just home from the Marines, is holding his new baby sister slightly away from his body, as if I had just been placed there solely for the purpose of archiving the experience.

My album actually displays more pictures with Jay in them than with my father: Jay holding his Pekinese, Suzy, on Christmas morning as my mother leads me towards the presents; Jay as my new godfather after my First Holy Communion, standing next to me, his head tilted to one side and away from me, his hands in his pants pockets; Jay again standing next to me after my Confirmation, his expression serious, his hands behind his back. The number of pictures of the two of us in my album would seem to indicate that Jay was an integral part of my childhood. Certainly that is the fantasy that my mother always dreamed of and the impression that Jay would try to perpetuate, especially as we both got older. Appearances meant a great deal to Jay.

Several times during my early years, I would whine to my mother that I might as well not have a brother at all since Jay and I never really spent time together. "That's only because he's so much older than you," she always assured me, "but he loves you very much, and he's still your brother. Don't ever forget that." My mother told me what she wanted me to believe and what she herself wanted to believe, as if by voicing the words, the fantasy would become reality.

"He used to play with you a lot when you were a baby," she sometimes added.

I think it was my father, Jay's step-father, who told me how Jay used to laugh as he tossed me up in the air and caught me, over and over, a little higher each time, until I began to quiver and cry from the fear of falling. Still laughing but shaking his head in disgust at my timidity, Jay would put me down, releasing me to run from him to our mother's arms. Those stories sounded true. I could believe a mildly sadistic streak in Jay. I'd seen it one evening when he dropped by the house.

"I'm going to show you how to shoot dice," Jay informed me as he pulled out the kitchen chairs and moved them off to the side. Surprised and delighted at his sudden and unexpected interest in me, I eagerly crawled with him under the Formica table, one side of which abutted the wainscoting.

"Don't you think she's a little young for that?" my mother asked from the sink where she was finishing up the dishes from supper. I scowled up at her, afraid she'd ruin this rare chance for sibling bonding. Even though the last game he'd played with me, if you could call it playing, had been far from entertaining, this one already held more promise than "52 Pickup."

"Nah," Jay replied, sprawled on the floor, the dice already in his hand; whereupon, he began a brief explanation of "Craps," the name immediately sucking me in because my father had so often entertained me with stories of how he'd played it as a child with the older boys in the alleys of his Spencer neighborhood.

"Seven or eleven automatically wins if rolled first," Jay explained, "but snake eyes always lose." I tried to keep up as he rattled off the intricacies of the game. Even though I had questions, I held them back because I knew Jay's time was precious. Our mother had repeatedly told me how busy he was to explain why he always seemed to be in a hurry. Only about five or six years old at the time, I also didn't want to seem dense and risk losing his attention.

"Now we need something to bet with," Jay announced. "Ma, can you hand me some toothpicks?" I had only recently become aware that my brother did not refer to or address our mother the same way I did. Eventually, I would decide that "Ma" worked much better than "Mommy" and that saying it made me feel more grown up.

A few rolls of the dice later and before I even really fully understood the game, Jay decided we should play for real. He appointed himself as the bank and me as the shooter.

"Go get your piggy bank," he instructed, and I scurried into the playroom hearing my brother's laughter when I returned, blue plastic pig in hand. It didn't occur to me then that Jay played for keeps.

Again and again, the dice clicked in my loose fist then bounced up against the kitchen baseboard as my pile of change grew smaller. I don't remember how much money I lost that evening, but it was enough for me to decide then and there that gambling is not fun. Perhaps, without intending to, Jay did me a favor because I would never become the compulsive gambler my father would soon become. When Jay breezed out the door a while later, headed for his home in West Brookfield, he had cleaned me out of several weeks' allowance.

Somewhere around the time I was eight years old, Jay divorced his wife, Kathy. There were no children involved, and the split was amicable. Kathy moved out of their home in West Brookfield, the front portion of which had been converted to "Jay's Barber Shop" a few years earlier. After the divorce, Jay dropped by more often, especially around mealtime, which pleased my mother. My father worked as a chauffeur for Mr. Krock, the local self-made millionaire, and much to my mother's irritation had to be on-call twenty four seven, so he missed many evening suppers and Sunday dinners. It was most likely after one of these meals, while the three of us were still sitting around the table, that Jay noticed my fingers in my mouth.

"What are you doing? Let me see your fingers," he demanded.

My mother got up to clear the table as I reluctantly held out my hands, palms down, revealing my bitten fingernails, many chewed to the quick.

"That's disgusting," Jay said and thought for a minute. "I will make you a bet. You have to go ten days without chewing your nails. If you can do that, I'll give you ten dollars."

I looked at him, stunned, afraid to ask the obvious question. There had to be a catch. When I didn't respond, he continued.

"If you bite your nails, even one, during the next ten days, I will take one of your dolls and keep it."

What? I looked towards the kitchen for my mother's reaction but she had not heard what seemed to me more of an ultimatum than a bet. When told, her only response would be "Well, then, I guess you better not bite your nails." Minutes later, her son was out the back door.

For the next ten days, I obsessed over my predicament. More aware of my fingers than I ever had been or ever would be, I frequently caught myself about to tear at one of my nails through stress, daydreaming, or just plain force of habit and quickly jerked my hand away from my face each time. I worried that I would forget. What if a nail broke; would Jay be able to tell the difference? At least twice that I remember, I lined up all my dolls and tried to guess which one he would take from me if I succumbed to my nail-biting. Chatty Cathy or Suzy Smart, both of which "talked?" Danny O'Day, my ventriloquist's dummy, which came with a record for the aspiring performer? Thumbelina, my absolute favorite doll that I'd had since I was three and whose head had been twice sewed back on? Little Miss No Name, the pitiful "orphan" doll given to me one Christmas by Vincie, a neighborhood man I'd befriended? I considered hiding the very special ones but realized the dishonesty, so instead I lost sleep worrying.

Finally, the tenth day arrived, falling on a Sunday, so I knew Jay would show up for dinner. I practically danced with anticipation that the ordeal that had been forced upon me would soon end and I would emerge triumphant. Jay walked in, barely acknowledging my presence, directing most of his attention toward our mother as always. Apparently he had forgotten the day's significance. After what seemed to me enough time for pleasantries, I sidled up to my mother and nudged her with my elbow.

"Oh, yes. Donna has something to show you," she said to Jay.

I held my hands out for him once again, proudly this time, my nails healed and intact. My mother had even let me put on some clear polish.

"Oh, yeah. Well. Good." Emotionless, Jay reached into his pocket and handed me a ten from his roll of bills, then began a new topic for discussion with our mother. I almost immediately resumed my nail biting, just never in front of Jay.

The winter Jay bought his Ski-Doo, he'd already remarried. The ceremony had been a quiet, simple one with only a handful of adults gathered in the office of a Justice of the Peace, so I had not been invited. If Kathy had been Connie Francis, petite and perky with dark hair and freckles, Jay's new wife was Marilyn Monroe: tall, blonde and polished. Nancy styled hair for a living, wore sophisticated clothes and used a lot of make-up. She had two beautiful children, a girl and a boy, from a previous marriage - both younger than I.

Sherry and David had both been out with Jay on his new winter toy through the woods and on the frozen lake near his house. Crazy with jealousy but too shy to ask him myself, I hounded my mother to get Jay to take me out too. In my memory, the only time he and I had gone anywhere alone together was when he'd bought his sleek black Sting Ray convertible right after his divorce from Kathy. He'd sped down some back roads and thrown Fourth of July cherry bombs as the trees zinged by and I screeched and

114

laughed at his delicious recklessness.

Ma had to remind Jay more than once about the Ski-Doo ride before he finally appeared one day, dressed in corduroy slacks, a crewneck sweater and a suede jacket.

"Are you ready?" were his only words to me.

He drove us to West Brookfield in his Jeep, bought for plowing and towing and for driving in poor weather when the Jaguar he'd just traded for his 'Vette stayed in its heated storage unit. When we arrived, I saw a man dressed in a one-piece snowsuit unloading a Ski-Doo from a trailer backed up to the lake. It had begun to snow, so my glasses were spattered with flakes as my brother and I approached the man whom I probably would not have recognized even if he had not been wearing goggles. I had met only a couple of Jay's friends. Jay handed the man something I didn't see but assumed to be money and told him to take me "around the lake a few times." I said nothing, either to Jay as he got back in his Jeep or to his friend who attempted a cheerful tone as he told me how to sit on the Ski-Doo and hold on. At ten years old, I had already begun to be shy and awkward around males in general but especially those I didn't know. I told myself that the ride was what I wanted after all and tried not to be disappointed as the Ski-Doo swished circles and figure eights until the Jeep reappeared, ready to take me home. On the way back to North Brookfield, Jay asked if I'd had fun. I blinked back tears and assured him I had.

Although Jay and Nancy dated for over a year before they married, discord over many issues became clear, even to me, soon after she and the kids moved into Jay's house. Nancy, all too aware of her beauty, liked to flirt, even with my father (which led to arguments in *our* house on more than one occasion). Jay, the hot-tempered Italian son of my mother's first husband, Johnny Faugno, resented the attention his new wife sought from other men. Private arguments between the two often escalated to public displays that more than once involved the police. One night at Ye Olde Tavern, Nancy became so furious at Jay's jealous tirade that she decided she would not ride home with him and headed down the street on foot. Jay took off after her in the XK-E and ended up getting arrested. Supposedly, he tried to run her over. At least that's what Nancy later told the police when she got home and made the phone call.

Meanwhile, though Kathy had also remarried and moved about an hour away, both Jay and my mother maintained a close relationship with her parents, the Kretchmars. Frank Kretchmar had what Jay considered a sweet deal as the area bookie. Jay respected Frank, Frank's money, and most of all, Frank's image. Before long, Jay became well known in the Brookfields not only as a barber but as Frank's right hand. Among other "duties," my brother had been given the football pool.

Jay took to the thrill of subterfuge like the proverbial duck takes to water. He told my mother stories of buried phone lines connected to an empty apartment, of "collecting" from betters who couldn't pay off their losses, of local cops who looked the other way, and of meeting the "bosses" from Springfield. Ma listened without comment, clearly less enthusiastic about the stories than her son. Everyone now seemed to know Jay, and the money rolled in. Initially, each Sunday after he made the rounds picking up tickets and money from his growing clientele, he returned to his own house to sort and tally the winnings, but as his marriage fell apart and the arguments got more frequent and more violent, he varied his location, usually using one of Frank's "safe rooms" just in case Nancy decided to get spiteful by making more phone calls.

My mother heard about the scratch before she saw it. Jay hadn't appeared for a few days, and Ma had already started to feel uncomfortable about dropping in on him and his new family because of all the arguing. When angry, Nancy had been known to make derogatory comments about the closeness between her husband and her mother-in-law. She had figured out that reputation and a macho image were everything to Jay and didn't hesitate to use that knowledge to taunt him by accusing him of being "a spoiled Mama's boy." Somehow or other, in Nancy's eyes, my mother became the scapegoat for Jay's faults. Conversely, my father's relationship with the couple remained unaffected. He and Jay maintained the camaraderie of two mildly competitive adult males that had begun almost immediately after my parents started dating, and Nancy continued to welcome him without reservation into her home. Although my mother resented my father's closeness to a situation from which she was beginning to feel excluded, that proximity allowed her to keep up on all the news, so Ma heard about the physical violence before she saw the results.

When Jay finally did appear, days after the incident, my mother took one look at his face and started to cry. During an argument, Nancy had attacked Jay and managed to scratch his face from one cheekbone to his chin with one of her long, carefully manicured fingernails. That is the story my mother believed. To her, Nancy had now become pure evil and could never be forgiven. First she had defiled Jay's reputation by falsely claiming attempted assault with a motor vehicle; then she had marred his appearance for life. Although the wound did not require stitches, the scar it left behind never disappeared.

"Your face...your face," Ma sobbed.

A few weeks later, Jay's first wife paid my mother a visit. Bertha Kretchmar had already confided to Ma that her daughter's second marriage seemed headed for trouble. During a holiday gathering, we had met Kathy's new husband, Gus, who struck me in many ways to be Jay's polar opposite: soft-spoken and dry. At one point during the visit, as I wandered in and out of the room unobserved, I heard Kathy, clearly still feeling close to her former mother-in-law, confide her difficulty dealing with the lack of emotion from Gus. Evidently, she now felt that after fleeing from a marriage loaded with drama, she had too hastily chosen one devoid of any passion at all.

"With Gus, there's nothing there, especially when we argue. He's almost cold," I heard her say. "At least when Jay knocked me down, he'd pick me back up."

I stopped short and looked at my mother who flinched but did not respond. Kathy had no reason to lie at this point. Although I had come to dislike Nancy, partly because her beauty and sophistication intimidated me during my awkward pre-teen years and partly out of loyalty to my mother, Kathy's almost off-hand comment made me wonder about the other side of the scratch story. Perhaps Kathy had simply never fought back.

Nancy's frequent and bitter harangues regarding my mother (as reported by my father) led Jay to reduce his visits to the house until, before long, he made contact only by brief phone calls. Despite her hurt feelings, Ma tried to rationalize her son's rejection. "A son is a son 'til he takes a wife; though a daughter's a daughter all of her life," she told me. As the weeks went by and even the phone calls stopped, my mother stoically bore her pain. My father acted as go-between to some degree, bringing news from West Brookfield and relaying any messages from my mother to Jay. Ma made it clear, through my father, that she would not interfere in Jay's failing marriage, that she would always love her son, and that if and when he wanted her back in his life she would be waiting with open arms.

Around this time, Ma started feeling exceptionally tired and began experiencing frequent, pounding headaches and blurred vision. Phil's Restaurant, where she had waitressed for years, had closed, and she applied to some of the area nursing homes as kitchen staff. When Lincoln Hill Manor hired her, the manager required a complete physical. The doctor diagnosed diabetes, high blood pressure, advanced arterial sclerosis, and angina. Stress was indicated as a significant contributing factor to my mother's medical condition. The doctor prescribed medications and a new diet and advised that she reduce the stress in her life. The next day, Ma sat me and my father down and calmly explained her condition. What struck me most was the dubious expression on my father's face.

As Christmas approached that year, I witnessed a few very scary cardiac episodes my mother referred to as "angina attacks," usually occurring in the middle of or immediately following an argument with my father. Their relationship had been rocky as far back as I could remember, but of late, the bickering centered on my mother's suspicions over his frequent and sometimes unexplained absences. He no longer worked for Mr. Krock but had taken a second shift position in a steal manufacturing plant. On weekends, however, he disappeared for hours, supposedly playing cards at Duke's, a bar in nearby Spencer where he'd grown up. Ma resented the many hours he spent away from home and the household projects he ignored or left unfinished. She attacked; he counter-attacked.

As soon as she felt the tightness and stirrings of pain in her chest, Ma would reach into her enormous black pocketbook for the little vial of nitroglycerin and put one of the tiny pills under her tongue, then sit holding her head in her hands, waiting for the medicine to take effect. Unimpressed, my father would stalk off, knowing the argument had ended, while I watched, dry-mouthed and helpless.

On Christmas Eve, my parents and I were just beginning to open gifts when the phone rang. Ma got up to answer. It was Nancy. A few days earlier, Ma had sent Dad to Jay's with presents for him, Nancy and the kids. She had gotten no response. Now Nancy's shrill voice was so loud that Ma had to hold the phone away from her ear.

"I hope you have a merry Christmas because you and your son have ruined mine!" Nancy began.

My mother stood speechless, tears in her eyes, as her daughter-in-law continued to scream insults and accusations pertaining to Jay's behavior and upbringing until, after several minutes, the line went dead. The receiver still in her hand, Ma started to cough, and her hand went to her chest. That time, my father got the vial of nitroglycerin for her.

Jay's second marriage ended amid accusations of abuse and adultery. The divorce was nasty and expensive this time, but Jay paid what he had to in order to keep his house, which he'd recently remodeled. For a while, Nancy stayed in West Brookfield, the owner of her own beauty salon practically next door to Jay's barber shop. Eventually, she relocated to Florida. All that mattered to my mother, however, was that she had her son back in her life.

    Despite setbacks in his personal life, Jay's business life prospered. His barber shop probably made money, but not to the extent that the football pool and whatever else he did for Frank Kretchmar generated. By this time, Jay had "runners" who were working for him, yet he still spent so many hours occupied by his illegal business that he often had to close the barber shop. As the recession years of the early 1970s loomed, Jay upgraded his car, his clothes, and his status. He finally got to taste the good life he'd observed through Frank, and he liked it. When my mother commented on how he worked on his car in "good" clothes, he just shrugged and laughed. When he totaled his Lincoln Continental Mark III by driving too fast on an icy road and slamming into a telephone pole, he simply bought a Mark IV. The Jaguar still came out on special occasions. He didn't even try to hide his growing wealth, which anyone could clearly see did not result from a one-man barber shop that closed its doors almost as often as it opened them. Then he got arrested again – this time in a sting operation for illegal gambling.

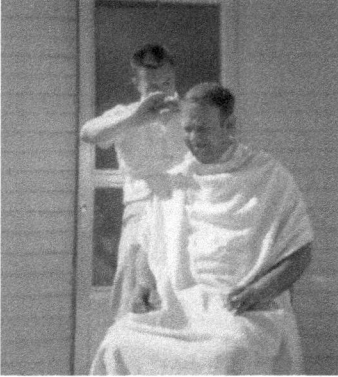

    My mother heard the news on W.A.R.E. radio one morning as I got ready for school. She knew better than to try to contact Jay, so she waited it out. As if word would not spread fast enough in the Brookfields, disc jockeys Gary James and J.P. Ellery reported the story each hour, making sure to repeat each name of those arrested, while my mother fumed at what she saw as their audacity and worried over her son. "Don't they have any other news they can talk about?" she angrily remarked. "They just want to tear him down!"

    The next day, when the article about the sting appeared in the Telegram, my mother did not cut it out to add to the collection I discovered years later while going through her things as the executrix of her estate. I found an early advertisement for the barber shop, a human interest clipping of Jay's St. Bernard sitting in the front seat of his Jeep, and an announcement Jay had put into the Wickaboug when he became dog officer:

To all West Brookfield dog owners:

The party's over!

From now on, all dogs must be registered and leashed

Or be prepared to pay the price

Love,

Jay

Nowhere did I see a clipping pertaining to Jay's arrest. It was as if it never happened.

As I recall, the charges against Jay were dropped for lack of evidence, or perhaps he was just considered a little fish by the law. Not as lucky, Frank ended up back in court with stiff fines to pay. Jay's resolve to be more careful with his football pool led to his decision to relocate his Sunday operation to a safer location. Our house. After all, who would ever suspect that a man would conduct an illegal business in his mother's house on Sundays while she was home?

Every Sunday, as had been his habit for several years (excluding the months he had been forced to choose his second wife over his mother), Jay would show up for roast beef or roast pork, but now, after dinner ended, he stationed himself in the Other Side, a combination laundry room / storage area / playroom, to sort the betting slips he and his runners had collected that morning, since his original spot, the living room, afforded him no privacy should company drop in. Jay's set-up consisted of a TV table and a folding chair. I helped stack the bills into like piles. Ma paced from the kitchen to the dining room and back, moving from window to window, often saying her rosary as she kept an eye out for strange or unusually slow moving cars.

Bertha Kretchmar had told me and my mother about the night the "Feds" broke down their door and arrested Frank. Plainclothes policemen did not give the Kretchmars a chance to open the door but kicked it in while the couple were watching television. A thorough search for betting slips and other evidence of an illegal gambling operation was conducted. As Bertha watched in tears, tables were overturned, sofa and chair cushions slashed, dresser drawers dumped out. When Ma and I got home from the Kretchmars' house that afternoon, Ma slowly walked through each room, touching things here and there and shaking her head.

Jay's business location may have changed after the sting but not his attitude. Even though she was always careful not to nag or criticize him, Ma had to comment each time her son would dash in from his car with betting slips hanging out of his pockets or clear plastic bags full of cash in his hand. She feared surveillance and subsequent destruction of her home. I feared for her health because of the additional stress I saw creasing her face and tightening her lips, beginning each Saturday evening and continuing until Jay left the house on Sunday afternoon, having wrapped his profits in foil and putting the "roast" in the freezer. The money-roast became his permanent stash, into which he would dip when he wanted a new toy, another suede jacket, a new pair of leather boots.

One of my favorite television shows in the mid 1970s was *Happy Days*, a pilot that spun off of a skit from *Love American Style*, another of my favorite shows. I even found a poster of Henry Winkler as "The Fonz" to hang on the inside of my closet door. I did not consider Arthur Fonzerelli to be sexy, but his coolness defied debate. However, I was less than impressed the first time I heard Jay growl a long, drawn out "Heeeeey," as he stuck out his thumb Fonzie-style. Please. I said nothing to Jay but eyeballed my mother, who apparently did not get the reference. Later in the evening, I showed her the poster. At fifteen, I could recognize cool, and a man in his mid thirties imitating a television character fell sadly short.

"He's just having fun," Ma dismissed my criticism. "It's so good to see him happy for a change. He had such a hard time growing up."

Here we go. Now I was in for the whole story. Again.

Born at home in 1938, with only a doctor attending the birth, Jay, at over nine pounds, should have been delivered by Caesarian. Instead, forceps clamped onto his large soft skull, altering its shape, such that our then seventeen year old mother burst into tears when she first saw him. As a baby, Jay's disproportionately large head remained slightly mis-shapen, noticeable even in photographs like the one Ma insisted I keep on the built-in cupboard in my bedroom. For years, Jay's baby face grinned at my slightly pouty / slightly cross-eyed toddler face opposite from him in the gold metal folding frame, two pictures in black and white taken twenty three years apart.

As a child, Jay still had not grown into his head. Many days re-sulted in his running home from school in tears, having been teased as "big head" or "basketball head." Ma consoled him as best she could, but her first husband Johnny had definite ideas about how to raise his son to be tough. Johnny could not tolerate the crying and advised fighting back. He also decided that if a boy could play sports, he would develop self-confidence, so he began a routine of taking Jay outside each afternoon to "play ball." Unfortunately, Jay's coordination did not measure up to Johnny's expectations, so as his mother nervously watched from the kitchen window, his father would begin to instruct, then criticize, then yell, until Jay ran into the house, in tears once again. When Johnny fol-lowed, disgusted and angry, Ma pounced, defending her child; where-upon, the arguing would begin. As an adult with a child of my own, I once heard Jay tell his third wife what a "horrible" childhood he'd had. He would never have children of his own.

As a small-time bookie and Frank Kretchmar's trusted friend and employee, Jay made plenty of money and had acquired the respect and popularity Johnny had once hoped for in his son. Jay could afford to be generous, and word got around to count on him to give to local charities, like the policemen's fund and the volunteer ambulance squad. He permitted the display of fund-raising fliers in his barber shop. Even though he no longer had time to play golf, people remembered that he'd been president of the Bay Path League a few years back and that, as a dog lover, he'd stepped up as the town's dog officer when no one else would. Jay could walk into the very expensive, very high-class Salem Cross on a busy Sunday, and Nancy Salem herself would usher him past the line of waiting customers to a table. In the Tavern, Jay was "Norm" long before the sit-com Cheers was created: everyone knew his name and greeted him when he breezed in the door.

One brisk autumn day, the Mark IV pulled into our driveway and Jay got out wearing a brand new tan, belted trench coat. He'd also started growing a beard.

"Check it out," he said, referring to the coat.

I held back as Ma exclaimed her approval. When he looked at me, I asked, "Is it a London Fog?" Just that week, Ma had driven me all the way to Steiger's in Springfield to spend my saved-up clothes allowance on the classic trench coat I decided I had to have.

"I bought this at Penny's," Jay said as I took mine down from the coat rack to show him. He turned mine around, opened it, and after a thorough examination asked me what I'd paid for it.

"You paid twice what I paid, and other than the label there's no difference," he said.

"The London Fog is of better quality. It will last longer."

"So what? When it's time, I'll just buy a new one."

"Mine is real; yours is a fake," I said, taking back my coat and hanging it up.

"No one can tell. No one's going to know," he insisted.

"I know," I answered. I pointed to the cornicello hanging from his neck. Since becoming a bookie, Jay had been flaunting his Italian heritage. "Is your Italian horn real gold?"

"That's different," and with a wave of his hand, Jay dismissed me.

The trench coat, the Lincoln, the beard, the gold jewelry, and even the "Heeeey" may have worked, but the new hat went too far. A large fedora with a wide brim all around and covered in a brown / black animal print, the hat Jay walked in wearing one night lacked only fur and a big feather. I nearly peed myself. Even Ma had to smother a laugh. Jay looked offended by our reactions.

"What?" he asked.

Only a few days later, when he showed up minus the hat, he admitted that "some of the guys" told him he looked like a pimp and asked where his "girls" were. Not exactly the image Jay was going for.

The night my father was killed at work, Jay drove me home from the hospital. When she heard the pronouncement of dead on arrival, our mother suffered a "mild cardiac incident" and remained under observation in intensive care. I spent most of the night alone in a waiting room because Jay disappeared as soon as Ma was wheeled away. Nurses and the hospital chaplain periodically checked on me until my brother finally appeared, ready to leave. Neither of us spoke in the car on the way back to North Brookfield.

When we got to the house, Jay headed straight for the phone, all business. Relatives and friends needed to be notified; arrangements had to be made. Meanwhile, I wandered through the rooms, still in shock and wondering what would happen to me if my mother died too. I had gone into survival mode. Sixteen was too young to be on my own. I did not want to live with Jay, who probably wouldn't want me there anyway. My Aunt Ruth would take me in an instant, but I had never told her the real reason I stopped spending a week with her each summer, that her husband had tried to molest me the year I turned thirteen. My Pepere and his second wife lived in a senior community that did not allow children. My father's only sister, Eleanor, her husband, and their five children were already crammed into their tiny house in Marlborough.

As I worried over my limited options, I continued to wander, exhausted but too keyed up for sleep. In the living room closet, where my father hung his clothes, I grabbed a handful of his shirts and breathed in his scent. I could hear Jay's voice in the next room, but he seemed oblivious to my whereabouts. I sat in Dad's tattered recliner and fingered each cigarette burn in the upholstery. Finally, I went into the Other Side, where Dad had been banished from the master bedroom upstairs years earlier (supposedly because of his snoring) and turned on the overhead light from the storage area of the large room that had once been my grandmother Annie's store. Dad's make-shift bedroom looked forlorn; only the roll-away bed and a small wooden nightstand gave any evidence that the space had been partly used as a bedroom. On the nightstand, a pack of cigarettes and a book of matches had been tossed next to the wind-up alarm clock and burnt orange ceramic ashtray shaped like a maple leaf. Not sure what, if anything, I was looking for, I opened the nightstand drawer, something I never would have done before this night.

The ring immediately caught my eye. My father's gold pinkie ring, bought while on a winning streak with Jay in Las Vegas, stayed in his nightstand while he worked at the steel plant so it wouldn't get dam-

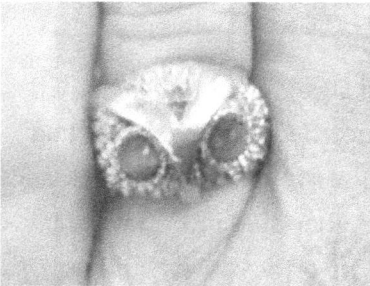

aged by the torches or be lost or stolen from his locker. As Jay often told the story, Dad had been hard at the craps table for nearly twenty hours straight, full of the single-minded determination of the compulsive gambler. Jay, who had showered, changed clothes, eaten and seen a show, found his step-father in the same spot he'd left him after the airport cab had dropped them off. Groggy, rumpled, and glassy-eyed, dice still in hand, Dad had to be physically pried away from the table just long enough to attend to necessary bodily functions and overdue hygiene, call his family, and spend some of his winnings in the lavish hotel gift shop, which was as far away from the casino as he could be persuaded to go.

I held up the heavy ring, solid gold except for the stones. Its two small emerald eyes regally gazed at me from beneath the smooth v-shaped eyebrows of a face designed to look "feathered" like an owl's. Eventually, I would have the ring re-sized to fit me, but on the night I forever lost my father, I clutched the ring in my fist, passed Jay still on the phone in the living room, and went to bed, finally able to sleep. I awoke when my Aunt Ruth came into my room, and cried while she held me.

Neither Ma nor I ever touched the foil wrapped money-roast that had become a permanent occupant of our freezer, so we had no idea how much money it contained. Jay frequently added to it or dipped into it but never made any comment about how much came and went until he bought the brand new Lincoln Mark V. His Marks III and IV had both been pre-owned, but Lincoln had just come out with its newest model, and Jay decided he wanted it.

"Ma, I'm taking the roast," he said one evening when he popped in.

The next day, the pristine, silver Mark V pulled into the drive-way. Jay called us outside and gave us the tour of what $11,000 in cash could buy.

"Was all that in the roast?" Ma asked, her eyes wide. "I'm glad I didn't know."

Jay just laughed and told us to get in.

The Lincoln glided over the roads like nothing I'd ridden in since the limousine my father once drove for Mr. Krock. Jay demonstrated one-finger steering as we cruised through town. I sat in the back and wondered what it must be like to afford such luxury.

When we returned to the house, Jay pulled alongside the curb instead of into the driveway. He turned in his seat to look at me.

"Go get your permit."

"What? Me?" My heart jumped. I had not yet driven with anyone but my mother and Mr. Boucher, my Driver's Ed teacher.

"Oh, Jay, I don't know . . . your new car." Ma looked as sick as I felt.

"Ah, you worry too much," Jay said to her, and to me he said, "Go."

Once behind the wheel, I started to shake. The Mark V responded to my slightest touch and seemed enormous compared to my mother's Rambler, which drove like a stubborn old truck. I could barely see the shoulder of Rte. 67 over the elongated hood as we made our way out of town along the mostly deserted back roads. Each time a car did approach, I held my breath and gripped the wheel tighter, hoping I could keep enough to my side of the road for the oncoming car to pass without rolling the Lincoln into the gutter. No one spoke except when Jay instructed where to turn. I couldn't wait to get back home. Peripherally, I could see my brother across from me on the couch-sized front seat, lazily stretched out and gazing out the window. I couldn't see my mother in the back, which was just as well. She was probably praying. However, during the weeks that followed, she proudly told anyone who would listen how Jay took his little sister out driving in his brand new car.

My brother never attended any of my school plays or concerts; however, he stayed informed enough (through my mother) to appear dutifully interested and knowledgeable when small talk in the barber shop turned to his family. He did not attend my high school graduation ceremony even though, as fourth in my class, I delivered a speech I wrote, nor did he attend the ceremony when I graduated from college. Both times, I received a card from him with a one hundred dollar bill in it.

After graduating from college, I moved to Florida. The year my daughter was born, Ma arrived just before the birth and stayed for another month to help me out, but almost every other year, she would fly to Florida to stay with me for at least a couple of weeks, and I spent nearly every Christmas in Massachusetts; therefore I saw my brother mainly on holidays. Between our visits, my mother and I spoke on the phone practically every day, more often than she and her son spoke, even though he lived only four miles from her.

One day, I picked up the phone and without even returning my hello, Ma asked the whereabouts of the photo album she'd made for me.

"It's right here on the bookcase," I said, stretching to reach for it. "Why, what do you need?"

"Nothing. I just wanted to know if you knew where it was, but I knew you'd know. Jay can't find his."

"Oh," was all I said, but I smiled and drew an imaginary vertical line in the air with my finger. One point for me.

The sibling rivalry between my brother and me that had been present from my birth had not become an issue for me until somewhere in my teens. I heard the sharp tone Jay often used with Ma who, instead of tearing him a new one (as she would with me when I had "a tone") would complain to me about it but never to him. I felt that she had higher expectations of me than of him. Jay never had to write thank you notes or even remember birthdays. Ma never criticized him or interfered in his decision making. Furthermore, anytime I complained about something Jay had said or done, Ma made excuses for him: "That's just the way he is."

Ma insisted that she favored neither of us over the other but treated us equally, even down to what she spent on us at Christmas. If there was any discrepancy in the cost of the gifts, one of us would get the difference in cash in an envelope. Nevertheless, Jay accused me of being spoiled. He felt Ma was more protective of me and resented the confidences that she and I shared.

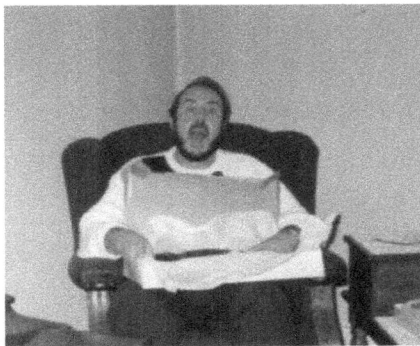

Even during Ma's final days in the hospital, when I went in every day but Sunday (Jay's day) and spent hours sitting with her, Jay could not understand how we passed the time. I had taken a leave of absence from my teaching position in Florida to be close to her. The previous summer, Ma and I had closed up the house and moved her into the studio apartment attached to Jay's house in West Brookfield. The house in North had been on the market but had not sold. During the spring of 1996 as Ma lay dying in the hospital, I lived in the house with my ten year old daughter while I waited for my divorce to become final.

"What do you talk about?" Jay asked me one night. I'd been at the hospital all that day and the next day was a Sunday.

"Nothing. Everything. Just . . . stuff." That afternoon Ma had complained that when Jay visited he spent most of the time looking out the window. "She's your mother," I reminded him, "How do you not find things to talk about?"

"I don't know. I have nothing to say."

I realized then that though I knew my brother's history, I really didn't know the man at all. He and I had never had a real conversation. Despite our mother's hope that we would bond, he and I never had a close sibling relationship.

A month or so before Ma died, she asked me to retrieve some papers from her strong box. I grabbed everything from the box without sorting through it, put it all in a white kitchen trash bag, and delivered it to her in the hospital. Blaise Berthiume, the family attorney, privately met with her while I waited outside her room. When I was called in, Ma told me, in front of Blaise and my daughter, Chloe, that she would be leaving me the family home, as she had always promised, but also that I would be the executrix of her estate.

"Jay would do what *he* wants; I know you will do what *I* want," she explained her change of heart.

I objected to being put in the awkward position of knowing her change of plans ahead of time, while Jay remained unaware. She insisted that she did not want to risk a confrontation that might alienate her son. She did not want to be cut out of his life again. Against my better judgment, I agreed to the secrecy.

Whether Jay suspected something or whether he was simply trying to protect his interests, I will never know, but the final confrontation that my mother hoped to avoid happened on what turned out to be the last day he would ever see our mother.

"I'm leaving the house to Donna," Ma reluctantly answered Jay's inquiry from her semi-prone position, then weakly turned from him to face me, standing on her left and across the hospital bed from my brother. I began to sweat.

"I thought the house would be sold, and we'd split the money." Jay's face reddened, and I could hear the anger in his voice. I looked down at the generic beige blanket that covered my mother's now barely one hundred pound frame.

"You already have a house. She doesn't. Would you sell your house and live in it?"

"No, of course not!"

"Donna is now making plans to move back home. She will live in the house."

There. Settled. No…not yet.

"What do *I* get? What's *my* share?" Jay persisted.

Shocked by his audacity and tactlessness, I looked up at him, then at her. Her eyes were wide in surprise. "You get the contents – the antiques – and the car. And she will get a small mortgage to pay you twenty thousand dollars."

Jay exploded. "Twenty thousand dollars?! That's all I get?" He leaned over Ma, his eyes bulging. "What about the money in the envelope? Where is that?"

I could see she was as surprised by this question as I was. Evidently he had been into her strongbox. Ma looked about to cry and turned toward me again. I answered for her. "I have that put aside. You'll get half."

Jay took a deep breath, struggling to regain control of his temper. Perhaps he realized the inappropriateness of his behavior or, more likely, that our family drama had become the main event for my mother's hospital roommate. "What about the arrangements? Am I still in charge of those?" he asked in a lower voice.

Wow, I thought, but instead of being furious at my brother's insensitivity, I felt an aching sorrow when I saw the pain that flashed in my mother's eyes.

"I made Donna the executrix because I know she will do things the way I want them done." Ma's voice was soft and quiet, emotionless despite the raw emotion she must have been feeling.

I tensed for the explosion, knowing Jay would interpret this reassignment of her final arrangements as an insult to his status as first-born. My own father's prophesy, voiced with a smirk anytime he was trying to get a rise out of his stepson, was that, in the end, I'd be the favorite. Did those goading words I suddenly remembered just pop into Jay's head too? I kept my head down until Jay's shaking finger appeared just inches from my face.

"*You* did this. You stay away from me. Don't you ever come near me again." My mouth dropped open. Admittedly, I had been in on the secrecy, but how was this my fault?

Jay's face turned nearly purple as he faced our mother, shaking his finger now at her, and spoke his parting words: "And you. If this is what you really want, then I will have nothing more to do with you either."

That night I called him to try to explain Ma's reasoning, figuring that once he'd calmed down, he would understand that he was not being cheated. Instead he accused me of taking advantage of Ma who, he claimed, was clearly not in her right mind.

"What did you do, put the pen in her hand and make her sign the papers?"

"Jay, be reasonable. Did you even listen to everything she said?" I asked.

"You hurt me bad. What did I ever do to you?" were his last words before he hung up on me.

The next morning, as I prepared to leave for Florida to finalize my divorce, I decided to stop by the hospital to check on my mother. I felt guilty that Jay's feelings were so hurt and worried that perhaps his suspicions regarding Ma's sanity had grounds.

"I knew you'd be by," she said when I walked in.

"I had to say goodbye again before I left," I said. "Ma, do you remember what happened yesterday?"

"Of course I do," she said, and her eyes filled with tears.

"I'm so sorry." Starting to cry, I went to her and took her hand.

"Donna, I made my decision. It's what I always said I would do except for making you the executrix, and I explained to both of you why I changed that. I know you will do things the way I want them done."

Clearly, she was well aware of what she was doing. To make doubly sure, I later approached her doctor, who assured me that he had no qualms about her grip on reality.

"Jay will get over it eventually," Ma continued. "He was always a picker for money, just like his father."

I called my mother at least once every day the week I was gone. On the drive back in the U-Haul, somewhere in Virginia, I had a bad feeling. Although (prior to my trip) her cardiologist had told her, in front of me, that the dialysis treatments needed to keep her alive could be too much strain on her weak heart, Ma changed her mind about the recently implanted defibrillator, insisting against doctors' advice and my protests that it be deactivated. She also signed a DNR. I had spoken to her this morning before hitting the road and planned on seeing her tomorrow since I would be getting back to Massachusetts very late tonight. I checked my watch; she should be in dialysis, but I found a pay phone and called the hospital anyway. I was transferred to "Mary," a nurse in the dialysis unit.

"Your Mom just passed," she told me. "We tried to call your brother, but there was no answer. He hasn't been back in to see her."

I felt sick, empty, guilty that I hadn't been with her. What kind of daughter leaves her mother alone to die? I should have been there for her, holding her hand, the way she'd been there for my grandmother Annie. I forced myself to speak, "Was she in pain?"

"No," Mary told me, "She was talking about you and how much she looked forward to seeing you tomorrow. She was smiling. Then she

133

just closed her eyes."

Bob Pillsbury, of Pillsbury Funeral Home in North Brookfield, led the way downstairs into the embalming room where he had brought my mother the night before. The call to Bob had been the second call I made from the pay phone in Virginia. The first had been to my Aunt Ruth.

I called Bob right away because I wanted my mother out of St. Vincent's as soon as possible. She'd been there over ten weeks and, despite the staff's devoted care, had hated it. She belonged back in the town where she'd been born.

Today was Sunday, the day I had planned to visit Ma after moving back to Massachusetts from Florida. The loaded U-Haul still in the driveway, I arranged to meet Bob and my brother at the funeral home to discuss the arrangements. Jay had been after Ma for several months to pre-arrange and pre-pay for everything, but she had resisted his requests because (she'd complained to me) apart from seeming morbid, discussing pre-arrangements with Jay had led to disagreements. Jay kept trying to talk her into things she didn't want, like calling hours. Years earlier, he had taken control of my father's funeral with my mother's blessing because she knew that Dad's tastes ran similar to Jay's. However, when it was her turn, Ma wanted it kept simple: cremation and a memorial service.

As I followed Bob Pillsbury down the winding stairway, I still felt shaky and in shock over losing my mother, but, in addition, I fumed over the encounter I'd just had with Jay in front of Bob. As the three of us sat around a conference table, Bob asking about the service, the burial, the cremation, the obituary and other details, he looked surprised then dismayed as, nearly every time, Jay jumped to answer before I could. Fully aware of my appointment as executrix, Bob would then look at me, whereupon I answered with, "Actually, what Ma wanted..." and continued with the instructions I had been told or had written out in front of me in Ma's hand. Jay quickly became frustrated and angry at being overruled.

"People will want to pay their respects," he argued. "Ma deserves a wake."

"She didn't want that," I insisted, unwilling to budge. "People can pay their respects at the memorial service."

Each time, Bob deferred to me, but looked progressively more uncomfortable over the bickering. Then he brought up flowers. I agreed only to a small arrangement for each side of the altar. The room just down the hall from where we were sitting had looked like a florist's shop when my father had been waked twenty one years earlier. Dad would have loved it. Ma thought it a waste of people's money.

"Donations in lieu of flowers?" Bob asked. "What charity do you want listed in the announcement?"

"Tri-Valley," Jay immediately answered, referring to the service that had brought Ma her "meals on wheels" while she lived in Jay's studio apartment.

"Actually," I said, without looking at Jay, "the West Brookfield Volunteer Ambulance Squad twice saved her life, and I'm sure they could use the donations."

"Christ," I heard Jay mutter.

"Let's put them both in, okay?" Bob said to me. "Then people can choose the one they want."

That settled the arrangements. Jay abruptly rose.

"Now would you both like to see your mother?" Bob closed his folder. "She's downstairs."

"No." Jay spat out the word and strode towards the door.

I looked at him, my mouth open. Ma would be cremated later that day.

"But . . ." Bob looked aghast as, without another word, Jay left the funeral home.

I remember only my mother's face as she lay on the table in the embalming room. Every other detail, even what she was wearing, is missing from the picture in my head. When I approached her, I stared down into her still open eyes, unable to believe she couldn't see me.

"She died peacefully," Bob said from a discreet distance behind me. "You can tell by how relaxed her expression is."

"Ma." I whispered. It was not a question; I knew there would be no answer. I bent to put my arms around her and laid my head on her chest, and as I did, a burst of air came out of her slightly open mouth, lightly caressing my face, as if she had just exhaled. I imagined that her spirit had lain there inside her, waiting for me, and now it would live inside me, and I cried, knowing how much I would miss her in my life.

Jay and I arrived at the packed church in separate cars. Seated in the pew directly behind me, he never spoke a word to me, either before or after the service. When the priest asked the parishioners to extend their hands in peace to their fellow parishioners, I turned around and offered my hand to my brother, but he simply stared straight ahead at the altar, his lips pursed in anger, his hands clasped in front of him.

In the long receiving line outside the church, only a couple of Jay's close friends approached me to express their condolences; the others just walked right by as if I weren't even there. "Shorty," who had once seen Jay fly out of the barber shop to yell at me over where I had parked when directed to do so by a policeman, tightly hugged me just as he had on that day when I had burst into tears at Jay's unexpected tongue-lashing.

"He'll come around," Shorty now whispered. "You're his sister."

Though exhausted from crying and lack of sleep, I had to smile at him. Shorty meant well. That day on the sidewalk, after Jay had abruptly turned to go back into the barber shop, Shorty had said, "He doesn't mean to be cruel. He just erupts before he thinks." I remembered all the times when my mother, too, had excused Jay's temper with "That's just the way he is."

"No, he won't," I said now to Shorty, "but thank you for caring."

One afternoon, ten years after my mother's death, the phone rang. "Donna, this is Gail Foley."

I hardly knew Gail and hadn't seen her in years. She and Jay had been friends since high school. According to my mother, Gail had always had a "thing" for Jay, but nothing had come of it but a close friendship. Gail had married a cop and lived in West Brookfield.

"I called to tell you that Jay died this morning."

"Of what?" I asked, stunned.

"Lung cancer. He's had it for over a year." Gail's voice was clipped and unfriendly.

I didn't know what to say. I'd had no contact with Jay since right after Ma's estate had gone through probate, and even my daughter had managed only limited contact, always at her initiative. Though only four miles away, we hadn't even heard he'd been sick.

"I'm only calling so that Chloe will know," Gail said. "Jay always had heart for Chloe."

Really? I thought. Then why hadn't he contacted her or gone to even one of her plays or concerts? The last time Chloe had seen her uncle was over three years earlier when she asked me to drop her off for a visit, and Jay couldn't even spare her an hour of his time. She'd given up after that. I said none of this to Gail, however. Let her believe the illusion Jay had perpetuated.

"What are the arrangements?" I asked instead.

"They'll be in tomorrow's paper. *Chloe* is welcome to attend." I got the message, loudly and clearly.

"Gail, whatever has happened, he's still my brother," I said.

"Oh, he didn't care about that." And she hung up.

I read Jay Faugno's obituary in the Telegram & Gazette. My name was not included among the list of his survivors. Anyone reading the article would think he never even had a sister.

OF ALL THE TOWN'S SHOE MANUFACTURERS, ONLY THE RUBBER SHOP HAS STAYED IN BUSINESS. ALTHOUGH THE DEPOT STILL STANDS IT IS USED ONLY FOR STORAGE; THE NORTH BROOKFIELD RAILROAD IS LONG GONE ALONG WITH ITS TRACKS THAT WERE FINALLY PULLED UP A COUPLE OF DECADES AGO. WHEN THE CROW PASSES BY QUABOUG RUBBER, SHE VEERS UP GROVE STREET AND MOMENTARILY LANDS ON THE CHAIN LINK THAT SURROUNDS THE FIVE ACRE PARCEL WHERE THE BRICK BUILDINGS OF AZTEC ASBESTOS ONCE STOOD. THE PROPERTY IS POSTED AS CONTAMINATED, AND THE TOWN IS WONDERING WHAT TO DO WITH IT, IF AND HOW IT CAN BE UTILIZED AT MINIMAL COST.

ONCE, MANY YEARS AGO, THERE WAS A LITTLE NONDESCRIPT CHURCH THAT STOOD NEXT TO THE FACTORY. WHEN NO LONGER NEEDED AS A CHURCH, IT SERVED AS A PRIVATELY OWNED HALL FOR DANCES FOR A FEW YEARS. THE CROW WAS NOT YET ALIVE FOR THAT, BUT SHE WAS PRESENT THE DAY OF THE RAZING OF THE LONG ABANDONED LITTLE BUILDING. THE DILAPIDATED CHURCH'S BELL RANG ONE LAST TIME, OVERHEARD BY THE RUBBER SHOP WORKERS WHO STOPPED FOR A FEW MOMENTS AND LINED UP AT THE FACTORY WINDOWS TO WATCH IT CAREFULLY BEING LOWERED FROM THE TOWER TO THE GROUND BEFORE DEMOLITION OF THE BUILDING. SOME PEOPLE CLAPPED; OTHERS CRIED.

8

Vincie

The late day sun beat down on my head as I played in the side yard with Pepper, my new Fox Terrier puppy. Or maybe I colored in one of my many coloring books, curled up on the cool cement of the back stoop. Perhaps my mother had carried out my spring horse for me to ride. My play options seemed endless the summer I turned five.

I remember how still the summer air could be, and other than the constant droning of the bees in the privets, silent, so that when a noise occurred, it echoed off the houses. I could hear the footsteps along the sidewalk even before he came into view from around the corner of my house, but I waited to make sure.

As soon as he appeared, wearing the matching dark green shirt and pants from his shift at the Rubber Shop, I left the dog, the coloring book, the spring horse, the tricycle or whatever and ran to him. He smiled as I approached.

"Hi, Donna."

"Hi, Vincie."

I slipped my tiny hand into his worn, calloused hand, clean but slightly stained from trimming the excess off the black rubber heels on the assembly line at the factory. As I talked about whatever came into my head, we leisurely walked up the sidewalk, past the driveway and the back yard, to the far edge of the privets. When older, I walked with Vincie all the way up the street to the Fat Tree, but at five years old, not yet in school, my boundary was at the end of our yard. When I was younger than five, I could walk with him only to the far edge of the driveway, where the privets began, but I don't remember that, just as I don't remember the day I first met Vincie.

Vincie Kizzle grew up in a middle-class two-parent household, the youngest of five children. When he was old enough, he got a job as a

141

cutter for H. H. Browne, a shoe manufacturer located within walking distance of his home, and became a valued employee: dependable, quiet, and skilled at his job. After his siblings moved out and his parents died, Vincie remained in the family home on Willow Street. A respected and well-liked member of the community, young Vincie slicked back his curly hair and donned a dark suit and tie to attend the seven o'clock Mass at St. Joseph's Church every Sunday morning. Often he could be seen tending his fruit trees or doing yard work on a typical Saturday afternoon. He lived simply, by choice rather than economic necessity, owning no car, telephone or fancy clothes. Despite being pleasant and good-natured, Vincie rarely socialized and never dated.

When H. H. Browne moved its factory to Worcester, a city forty five miles away, Vincie did not follow as many other employees did. Comfortable and satisfied with his simple, predictable life, he instead appeared at Quaboug Rubber Company, a rubber sole and heel manufacturer and the only other major industry in town and applied for a job. His reputation in the small town of North Brookfield as a conscientious employee got him hired on the spot to trim heels.

Each day after his shift, no matter what the weather, Vincie left the Rubber Shop, walked east up School Street, turned north at the railroad depot onto Forest Street, then headed east onto Willow toward his tiny yellow clapboard Cape with the sagging front porch. The walk was a short one that led him past three of North Brookfield's public drinking establishments.

About half way up Forest Street, The Knights of Columbus Hall sprawled across its double lot, a haven for the drinker who liked to play cards – except on Sunday nights when it converted to a Bingo Hall and an occasional Saturday when, for a fee, it served as a reception hall. On the other side of the street, only a few yards north next to an overgrown empty lot, squatted The American Legion Hall, a favorite with the older crowd and out-of-towners as the closest thing North had to a pool hall. Its former storefront window may have been boarded up, but its door was always open, literally in the summertime, being its only source of ventilation. One block before the end of Forest Street, wedged between two tenements and nestled farther back from the road, hid Hart's Café, the almost exclusively male local hangout whose clientele consisted primarily of married, middle-aged factory workers and married retired factory workers.

Hart's had been around since the days when Bob Kelley drove Mr. Bush's taxi-team of horses from the depot, up Forest Street and all the way out of town to deliver tourists and vacationers to the Barre Hotel. Of the three drinking establishments, Hart's was the favorite stopping off place for the Rubber Shop crowd immediately after the first shift, probably because it was the only one that served food. Vincie, who was passing right by anyway, soon fell into the habit of shooting the breeze over a few beers with the guys each weekday afternoon.

According to my mother, I was not quite four – too young to be playing outside unsupervised – when Vincie first caught my attention as he passed by our house on his way home from work and Harte's. My mother always spoke: "Hi, Vincie" – nothing more. He would then answer in his gentle voice, "Hi, Polly" and continue on his way. Evidently, after solemnly observing this interaction a few times, I began to imitate my mother's greeting, separately though, so that I would receive my own response. Ordinarily, I could be counted on to hide behind her when she spoke to strangers, and even to some of the neighbors, because I was so bashful. However, one day, after Vincie appeared and greetings were exchanged, I surprised my mother by suddenly turning to her and asking for permission to walk with Vincie on the sidewalk to the edge of the privet hedge that bordered the backyard. Permission granted, I trotted to catch up with Vincie and slipped my hand into his. He smiled indulgently at my non-stop prattle as the two of us walked to the edge of the backyard, my amazed mother watching from the porch.

I have no idea what it was about Vincie that drew me to him because I don't remember a time before our almost daily walks. I do know that once he and I connected, only the stormiest weather kept me inside before supper on weekdays. As the sun began its descent and the mouth-watering aroma of stews and roasts pervaded the air of Little Canada, I would resume my post at the edge of the side yard closest to the street so that, by peeking around my house, I could spot Vincie almost from the moment he emerged from Hart's. I then waited, silent though practically dancing with impatience, pig tails bobbing, until he crossed the intersection and stepped onto the curb, whereupon I took his hand, and we proceeded along the sidewalk while I yakked about whatever events had transpired in my life since our last meeting. Occasionally I waited to no avail; supper would be ready and my mother calling before Vincie had passed.

One Friday afternoon, supper was late, and as I watched from my post, Vincie suddenly appeared from Hart's, not with his familiar relaxed gait, but with a jerky, irregular shuffle, his head lowered. For every few steps forward, he faltered, swayed unsteadily, staggered backwards a step or two, then lurched forward again. As he neared the spot where I stood watching, Vincie, without once raising his eyes, crossed over to the other side of the street to continue his precarious trek homeward. Disappointed and confused, I remember glancing over my shoulder at my mother who had just emerged from the house, then turning back. No greetings were exchanged, no questions asked, no explanations offered. Once Vincie passed out of sight, I followed my mother into the house.

Vincie's strange behavior continued to bother me over the weekend. I knew what having too much to drink looked like because just recently I had witnessed an evening when my parents had been talked into "a couple of high balls" at the Balchunas' house across the street and had returned home slightly drunk and very sick, my father in the downstairs bathroom, my mother in the one upstairs. I also knew what Hart's was and why people went there. What I couldn't understand was why Vincie had crossed to the other side of the street and not spoken or even looked at me. My mother's explanation, when I finally asked, was that Vincie probably felt too sick and perhaps a little embarrassed for me to see him that way. She said he had acted like a gentleman and that my feelings should not be hurt. Monday afternoon I returned to my post.

As the weeks went by, I grew accustomed to gauging Vincie's gait as soon as he came into sight in order to determine whether or not he would feel up to my company on any particular day. If he staggered, his eyes on the road, I knew that he would cross the street before he reached me and that our visit would be postponed until tomorrow or the next day. If he walked normally, his head up, I would be ready to greet him and accompany him up the street. As a child, I accepted our new non-verbal arrangement matter-of-factly and non-judgmentally. I never mentioned his "bad" days, and neither did he.

When Christmas approached that year, I took stock of the growing number of presents under the silver tree set up in our living room. In addition to the multicolored ribboned and bowed packages for family members and close friends, a separate pile of small identically wrapped "token gifts" waited to be distributed to acquaintances and providers of specific services to the household such as the mailman, paperboy, babysitter and parish priest. Dismayed at not finding anything there for Vincie, I complained to my mother that he should get a gift too. A box of men's white handkerchiefs (socks and gloves would alternate with hankies over the years to follow) was hastily purchased, wrapped and tagged for me to present to Vincie during one of our walks, much to the consternation of my father who wondered aloud on more than one social occasion why, among all of the people in North Brookfield, his daughter had chosen the "town drunk" to befriend.

Vincie was an alcoholic. Of course, no one called him that; in those days, people who habitually staggered down small town streets in a half stupor, wearing slept-in clothes and reeking of booze, were simply referred to as "drunks." "Alcoholics" were the proper, well-to-do ladies or gentlemen who nipped a bit too often at the imported wine or brandy in their drawing rooms or at "the club." If there were any of those living in The Brookfields during the 1960s, they belonged to an exclusive minority. Miriam Krock, wife of multimillionaire financier and future convicted tax evader Edward Krock, was rumored to be one. It was said the reclusive Mrs. Krock languished inside their walled-off 500 acre country estate on the Brookfield Road, or at their beach house in Hyannis, rarely visible to the locals and their scrutiny, yet her reputation (as reported by live-in servants) somehow set the standard for a whole class of people. Alcoholics did not carry their vice home barely concealed in brown paper; it was delivered. They did not pass out in public places, vomit on street corners, or prompt concerned calls to the local police to be bodily removed. Alcoholics lived complicated, troubled lives and periodically required "retreats" to fancy private spas to relax and recuperate from the stresses caused by their charity appearances, philandering spouses or demanding social calendars; whereas drunks, burned out from factory or other blue-collar jobs like those in the Rubber Shop, dried out in jail cells or alone in their rented rooms or rundown homes. Alcoholics did not frequent local bars like Harte's because they did not associate with their inferiors. Drunks had no inferiors.

When I reached school age and earned the privileges that went with it, I played outside without supervision, and my boundary extended all the way to the Fat Tree that marked the north end of Forest Street where it intersected with Willow, though crossing the road by myself remained forbidden. I no longer waited for Vincie at the edge of the side yard; instead I kept an eye peeled for his passing as I played on the swing or in the back yard. On those days when he staggered by on the opposite side of the road, I continued with whatever it was I happened to be doing, watching his unsteady progress while trying hard to look as if I wasn't. When he stayed on my side of the street, I would run over to join him, leaving toys and even friends behind without a moment's hesitation. Occasionally, one of my deserted playmates would question me upon my return, puzzled as to why I seemed so eager just to accompany this odd man to the end of the street. "It's Vincie," I responded with a shrug, as if that in itself were sufficient reason.

Vincie showed genuine interest in everything I said and listened unlike most other adults I knew, remembering the names of all my friends, pets and teachers and faithfully keeping track of all the self-important details of a child's life that so obviously bore most adults. He said little beyond the friendly questions that would start me off and running at the mouth, like "Have you taught Pepper any new tricks?" or "Which dolls did you play with today?" He never revealed any personal information, and I was too focused on bringing him up to date on my life during our limited time together to ask any probing questions. I realized, years later, that our conversations were woefully one-sided, though he never seemed to mind, and that, despite our friendship, I didn't know him nearly as well as he knew me.

One Christmas when I was perhaps eight, as I was examining the displayed presents under our silver tree and reading their tags by the light of the color wheel, I discovered a tag that read "To: Donna From: Vincie." Well aware of my fondness for dolls, he had impulsively decided to add to my collection. Because of his lack of transportation, Vincie had discreetly approached my father with a ten dollar bill and instructions regarding the kind of gift to be purchased for me. The doll my father subsequently chose was called "Little Miss No Name." Barefoot and clothed in patched burlap, her long, limp blond hair hanging raggedly around her pathetic face, she came with a plastic "tear" attached to the inside corner of one of her enormous brown eyes. The gimmick (explained on the side of the box) was that the doll "cried" because she was homeless and unloved. Supposedly, as soon as she felt happy and secure, the tear would drop off. I refuse to speculate on the point my father was trying to make by selecting this particular doll, or even if there was a point; I wasn't even aware of the subterfuge until years later. All I knew when I opened the gift was that Vincie had wanted to please me. Even though the weeks stretched into months and still the tear stubbornly refused to yield to my "accidental" poking and nudging until, in sheer frustration, I pried it off with a butter knife, I treasured the doll and still have it.

After I finished elementary school and started junior high, my interests and obligations broadened, and I found myself out in the yard less often. Those activities that brought me there usually involved a lawn mower or grass clippers, so I no longer automatically dropped everything to join Vincie for a stroll to the Fat Tree, although I still greeted him when it was feasible. When I did accompany him, he never referred to my lapses, just as I'd never referred to his; our mutual acceptance remained unconditional.

As I matured and become less self-absorbed, I realized that Vincie's bouts of drinking were becoming more frequent and more debilitating. He had begun stumbling past my house at odd hours of the day, during the evening, and on weekends. There were rumors that he missed work for days at a time. While on a binge, he wouldn't shave, and his clothes looked slept in. Often, it was said, he'd be so intoxicated that he would trip himself, then lie helpless until someone came to assist him. On more than one occasion, that someone was my father who would half carry-half drag Vincie into our car and drive him home. Fortunately for me, I never saw it.

Occasionally, as I roamed past Vincie's house with one of the Searahs, who lived at the top of Willow Street, I would gaze at the peeling paint, the broken windows, and the weedy overgrown yard. I had never entered his home nor he mine. Clearly, Vincie was a man in decline but, right or wrong, our friendship went only as far as the fat tree, and I didn't know how to change it now.

One of Vincie's falls during a binge resulted in a broken nose. The swelling and blackened eyes that lasted for weeks sickened and horrified me so that I could no longer watch when he staggered up the road. I felt shame for him and averted my eyes. Neither he nor I ever referred to the incident during our brief exchanges afterward, but it was the talk of the town for weeks. A subtle shift in attitude toward Vincie Kizzle was taking place among his former friends and neighbors. He had truly become, as I'd once heard my father say, "the town drunk."

Actually, Vincie was not the only man to stagger drunk through the streets of North Brookfield, but he was, by far, the favorite target. The other one, Dave Stivick, was amiable enough when sober, but a few too many transformed him into a bitter, argumentative sort to be avoided. "Stivie" holed up inside the American Legion Hall for hours on end, despairing over the suspicious car accident that had taken his teenage son, the pneumonia that had more recently claimed his wife, and the factory accident that had left a gnarled stump where his right hand used to be. Simply put, Stivie was no fun. He was also not "safe" to pick on because of his temper and because he still had family at home who cared about his welfare.

In contrast, the mild tempered, well-mannered Vincie was an easy target. Also, by showing his obvious dependency on alcohol, Vincie had unwittingly committed the one unpardonable sin that, over the years, had gradually turned North Brookfield against him: weakness. He had allowed the liquor to control him, to reduce him to something less than a man. Because he would not (or could not) hide his problem drinking, he no longer lived up to the town's expectations of him. He ceased to be a person deserving of respect and affection, instead becoming a thing of scorn and ridicule, the town joke that provoked barely stifled laughter as it lurched by and an easy if not willing victim for any abuse directed its way.

One Sunday, my brother showed up all snickers over an incident that had occurred earlier that day in Hart's involving "Wimpy." Before Jay could even begin to relate his tale, I needed clarification as to who this person was. "Oh, you know….Vincie," Jay explained. This in itself was news. I'd had no idea that Vincie had lately acquired a nickname. Anyway, apparently Vincie had been back and forth to Hart's several times over the course of the morning (his appearance at the 7:00 Mass was a rarity by this time), so liquored up he could barely stand, when he realized he'd run out of money. Although Mr. Hart, the bar's owner, steadfastly refused to extend him credit for additional drinks, Vincie stubbornly persisted in his appeal, attracting the attention of the other customers, most of whom had just stopped by for a beer or two while their wives were preparing dinner. Having gotten nowhere with Hart, Vincie finally turned to them, his friends, for the money to satisfy his desperate craving and was met with jeers and laughter. A couple of guys who had stopped by after an early morning fishing trip had an inspiration: would Vincie eat worms in exchange for a beer? I listened, appalled, as Jay described how the dead and dying worms were lined up on the table and bets laid down as to how many Vincie could be goaded to eat until he either vomited or passed out from the beer. Jay had arrived at Hart's after the show, while Vincie was "sleeping it off" in the bar's storeroom, but had been treated to an animated account of "Wimpy's" performance.

Over the days that followed, the story spread through the town. What disgusted me most was not that a few half-drunk morons had exploited Vincie's addiction for their amusement but that no one but me seemed the least bit upset by it. Not once did I hear the word "alcoholic" or catch a note of sympathy in the incident's retelling. The attitude expressed was that he had brought it on himself. He had become, finally, after years of blatant public drunkenness, fair game. The implication repulsed but did not surprise me. What were a few worms? Just harmless fun, after all. I can only imagine what hell public life must have been for Vincie after that. I'm familiar enough with North Brookfield to know its people never forget.

I rarely saw Vincie to speak to during my high school years and when I did, it was only in passing. By then, he staggered around town almost constantly. One gray winter afternoon during a deep freeze, it occurred to me that several days had elapsed since I'd seen him pass our house. As in my childhood days, I stood watch, but from inside where it was warm and dry. As the heavy sky darkened, and Vincie still did not appear, my brother agreed to check Hart's to see how recently he had been there. A beer later, Jay returned with no news. Meanwhile, my father had come home from work. At my insistence, the two agreed to put their uneaten dinners aside and venture back out into the sub-zero weather to head for the dilapidated once-yellow Cape the inside of which probably no one but Vincie had seen for years.

Dinner was late that night. Dad phoned from the home of one of Vincie's neighbors. When he and Jay reached the shack, Jay wrenching his foot as one of the rickety porch steps gave way under his weight, they found the sagging front door not only unlocked but ajar. The house was in darkness, and yelling for Vincie brought no response. Dad got a flashlight from the car, and the men went in. The light's beam reflected off a thick sheet of ice that stretched over the bare wooden floor from the front door, through the living room, to the kitchen. Rats skittered out of its glare. The furniture consisted mostly of crates and boxes. Vincie lay curled up in a corner, barely conscious, "dead soldiers" littering the floor around him. Now Jay was trying to get hot coffee down Vincie's throat as Dad called for an ambulance and updated my mother and me.

The hospital diagnosis was pneumonia and severe malnutrition. Apparently, Vincie's gas and electricity had been shut off due to non-payment, and the water pipes had burst. A brother was contacted and the house restored to its former barely livable condition during Vincie's absence.

Vincie returned home but, from what I heard, never fully recovered. Having received no treatment for alcoholism, he fell into old habits almost immediately. Before long, his brother received another call from the hospital. This time, Vincie did not come out alive. I heard nothing regarding calling hours, and the funeral was a private affair that was over before many people were even aware of his death. Away at college, I was informed after the fact…long distance.

The next time I came home, I retraced the route on Forest Street I had walked with Vincie so many years before, continued up Willow Street, and stopped in front of the Cape that listed slightly to one side as it sat neglected in its weedy lot. A porch step, the one my brother had nearly fallen through, was missing. Holes gaped through the intricate lattice work, and roof shingles, disturbed by the harsh New England winds, were scattered around the barely visible walkway. Someone had nailed boards across all the windows and posted a "No Trespassing" sign by the front door. I knew the house would probably come down.

I can't help thinking that North Brookfield failed Vincie Kizzle because, even though it didn't cause his drinking problem, it certainly used and encouraged it for its own amusement. Perhaps if Vincie had followed H.H Browne to Worcester, he would have lived a different, more fulfilled life. Perhaps not. I know only that Forest Street seems a little emptier now that he's gone.

THE FORMER GROVE STREET SCHOOL IS THE NEXT BUILDING ON GROVE STREET. CONVERTED TO SUBSIDIZED HOUSING IN 1988, THE SCHOOL WAS BUILT IN 1857 TO ACCOMMODATE THE YOUNG TOWN'S GROWING POPULATION. WHEN THE NEW, MORE MODERN JUNIOR/SENIOR HIGH SCHOOL WAS BUILT ON THE NORTH EDGE OF THE TOWN IN 1956, THE WOODEN ELEMENTARY SCHOOL ON SCHOOL STREET WAS TORN DOWN, AND THE STURDY MULTISTORIED BRICK GROVE STREET SCHOOL SERVED GRADES K – 6 UNTIL IT CLOSED IN 1970. FOR THE NEXT EIGHTEEN YEARS, THE BUILDING SAT EMPTY, ITS SURROUNDING STONE WALL THE LOITERING SPOT FOR MANY OF THE TOWN'S TEENAGERS WHEN POLICEMEN WEREN'T WATCHING.

9

All Part of Growing Up

You wore your mini-skirt on the last day of school, the dark green one with the brown paisley sash-belt, because it was your favorite and because, on this special day, you wanted to look as grown up as you felt. You knew that, with your long hair and legs and your B cups, adults often assumed that you were at least sixteen and looked so surprised when you admitted to only eleven that it made you smile and stand a little taller.

In a couple of months, you would go from being one of the oldest in the Grove Street School to one of the youngest in the North Brookfield Junior-Senior High School, but you wouldn't think about that right now. Today, you wanted to revel in the moment of being part of the last sixth grade class to leave this crumbling multistoried brick building before it closed its doors as a school forever.

It seemed impractical, but, for the next couple of years, until completion of the new elementary school on the outskirts of town, all the lower grades would be taught in the former St. Joseph's School next to the rectory, a facility of wood and asbestos even more outdated and run-down than this one that you'd been attending since kindergarten. There the oak desks and chairs were attached to each other and bolted to the pocked floors, and the desks still had holes for inkwells. You'd nearly gone to St. Jo's, after kindergarten, because your mother and Aunt Ruth had been students there, but, thank God, there was no hot lunch program at St. Jo's, and now that your mother had just started working full time at Phil's Restaurant you couldn't go home for lunch even though you lived only a few blocks away from the Catholic school. You often thought about how lucky you were to have escaped the daily influence of the nuns (bad enough every week in Sunday School) and, besides, everybody at Grove Street knew how wild those St. Jo's kids were, how they broke into the patrol lines and tried to beat up the public school kids after having been cooped up all day and tormented by the sisters.

Although you'd often hung back after the last bell rang at Grove Street, to clap erasers or wash the blackboard for Mrs. Baker, today you stayed behind for a different reason. You slowly gathered up your things as the other kids stormed out of Mr. Leach's second floor homeroom and, once the room emptied out, you stood up and looked around, trying to memorize every detail.

All the rooms looked pretty much the same: the high narrow windows that opened with the aid of a long-handled stick with a metal hook on its end, the polished wide-board wood floors, the metal pipes that companionably sputtered and hissed their steam heat in the winter, the rows of chairs and wooden desks whose tops lifted for easy access, the single chalkboard wall, the old upright piano in the back corner where Mr. Sacco taught music, the American flag by the door. Nevertheless, you had already made up your mind to walk through the building, from top to bottom, to take it all in one last time because even at eleven you had difficulty letting go of the past.

This year, sixth grade, you'd felt the most in control, the most comfortable with yourself and better able to stand up for yourself too. Hadn't you taught Dana Gurstel a lesson? A year older because he'd stayed back, Dana had been taunting you for weeks about your thick glasses.

"Four eyes!" he'd scream right in your face during recess, "Googly eyes!"

You tried not to cry - never let them see you cry! – and you'd tell your mother when you got home. Only then did you cry as you asked what you could do to make it stop.

"Just ignore it," your mother advised. "Everybody gets teased." And she told you how she'd been teased at your age for being flat-chested. Then she reminded you that kids always looked for something, sometimes even in adults if they were different.

Like Eva.

Eva Gentile had attended St. Joseph's School with your Aunt

Ruth and had still been there ten years later when your mother was a student. Eva was a "cripple," born with one leg significantly shorter than the other, and she had a large hump on her upper back so that she limped hunched over. She lived alone in her little house right next to the Common and, because she couldn't drive, walked everywhere she needed to go, regardless of the weather. You'd so often seen the short, bent figure in her long black coat, ragged strands of her chopped, graying hair sticking out of her blue knit beret, and when you did, you always greeted her, but then hurried past in case she tried to talk to you. No one ever said whether or not Eva was retarded, but her speech impediment made her nearly impossible to understand, and you knew you'd be no good at faking it the way your mother could.

Occasionally you tried to imagine what being Eva was like, especially the girl-Eva who had gone to St. Jo's. When you told your mother how, sometimes, you heard boys yell mean things to her as she hobbled up the sidewalk – usually to the church, which she visited daily – your mother told you that Eva had probably gotten used to it by now. Not only had she been a crippled child, but a poor one. By the time your mother reached school age, Eva, in her early teens, had become a favorite of the sisters, who sent her on their errands. One day, and your mother could still see it quite clearly though she'd been only six or seven, Eva fell, having tripped over her own feet, and as she struggled to right herself, the slip of paper from one of the nuns to another still clutched in her fist, her skirt raised enough to reveal her petticoat to the whole class.

"We all laughed because there were patches of a different material sewn onto her bloomers," your mother said. "That's how poor they were."

Sister chastised the class for laughing, and your mother "got the dickens" from your grandmother when she repeated the story at home, so she'd never forgotten it.

One day, you saw, from a distance, some boy throw a rock at Eva. It missed, and when she turned around and yelled incomprehensible words through her nearly toothless mouth, the boy ran away. You felt sorry for Eva, but also, at that moment, just a little bit afraid. Obviously, for Eva at least, the teasing had continued, even now that she was nearing old age. You imagined that she must have tried everything over the years to make it stop, yet it had not, so when your mother said, referring to Dana Gurstel:

"If you ignore it, he'll get sick of it and move on to somebody else," you had your doubts.

And, of course, Dana didn't stop. He'd corner you by the backboard at the edge of the ball field and lean in close with his breath in your face "Look at her eyes!" and laugh. You fought back tears and did nothing.

One day, when it rained and recess was held inside, he started in right in front of everyone as soon as Mr. Leach left the room, "Coke bottles!" and you'd had enough of the ignoring that didn't work. With a wordless shove, your heart pounding through the fire in your chest, you sent him flying backwards over a desk, and all the kids laughed at him, and you learned that day that bullies need to be stood up to because only then will they back down.

The next time you and JoAnne Foster rode your bikes down Elm Street, you both yelled "Dana Girdle! Dana *Girdle*!" at the tops of your lungs as you passed the Gurstel farm, but only that once.

You'd taught Stephen Derrick a lesson this year too. One day while riding bikes, again on Elm Street, Stephen had come out of his little yellow house right near where the old railroad tracks cross over the road and thrown mud at your gold Huffy Stingray with the sparkly banana seat and streamers. Stephen didn't really mean any harm; you knew, in fact, that he liked you, and throwing mud was actually just his way of flirting. Still, the challenge could not be ignored.

The next day, you smuggled into school a bottle of your mother's strong-smelling Avon cologne, "Moonwind," and since Stephen sat directly in front of you, you simply waited for the right moment to give him a good squirt, right in the back of the head. He got teased for the rest of the day by the other kids who kept calling him "Stephanie." You felt kind of bad, though, because he couldn't help that he liked you and that he couldn't understand why your interest focused on Mr. Leach instead of on him.

Mr. Leach, tall and broad shouldered with dark curly hair and a cleft in his chin, was the first male teacher you'd had, except for Mr. Sacco and Mr. O'Shea, the music and art teachers whose classes were held only once a week. You saw Mr. Leach in the classroom every day for social studies (and every night in your fantasies), beginning last year, and, at the end of that year, you'd begged Mrs. Baker to make sure to assign you to his homeroom for sixth grade. Mr. Leach had a wife and kids, but you didn't care. His parents lived right across the street from your house, and on Sundays after Mass, you played records in your bedroom and kept an eye out for his car. Your brother Jay was lately keeping his distance from your mother because she and Nancy, his new wife, had argued, and your mother, too, would see "Billy" Leach's car pull up every Sunday for dinner across the street from her post at the living room window. "He's such a good son," your mother would sigh and look sad as you headed for the front door - just to yell "Hi, Mr. Leach" across the street, just to hear his voice in response.

Why did all the teachers have to seat their students alphabetically? Why did your last name have to begin with "G," landing you in the back of the class? You fumed every time the lovely Dani Ballard, first row / first seat, took Mr. Leach's messages to Miss O'Coin, the principal. Popular Dani had perfect hair and dimples and did not wear glasses. You secretly wished her dead. Some instinct told you to befriend her, and though the two of you were never close, by inviting her to your parties, you kept an eye on her all through sixth grade.

In this room, you'd played "Polly" in the class production of Tom Sawyer, and, in your talcum-powdered hair, perfectly recited your lines, even when Mark Huard, as "Tom," forgot his and yours then made no sense. You'd joined the band here, committing to the alto saxophone ("Leave it to Donna to pick the most expensive instrument," your father had complained to your mother after the parent meeting). Mr. Sacco held lessons in the school's basement, and your chest swelled with pride and accomplishment when the whole band was able to play a song together. You'd thought that Mr. Sacco's instruction would continue because he taught high school music as well as elementary and also directed the Chorus you planned to join next year, but just a couple of weeks earlier, he announced he would not be returning to teach in the fall. That night, you cried as you told your mother, and she tried to reassure you: "Oh, it's just a little crush. You'll get over it." A crush? You knew then that you loved Mr. Sacco, who had been part of your life since first grade, but definitely not in the same way you felt about Mr. Leach. Clearly, your mother couldn't understand.

On this final day of elementary school, as you left your home-room and headed towards the back stairway to the third floor, Miss O'Coin's sharp voice drifted out from the closet-sized principal's office. Probably dealing with one of the detention students. Everyone feared Miss O'Coin and her ruler, except the bigger boys who were sent to Mr. Leach for their punishment (he didn't bother with a ruler; he slammed the boys into the wall when they misbehaved). Only once had you been sent to Miss O'Coin's office: in second grade when you left the patrol line without permission because you saw your mother walking home early from the restaurant. The next morning, you stood in front of Miss O'Coin, who looked very much like the Wicked Witch in The Wizard of Oz except Miss O'Coin's hair was dark red and she wore little glasses on the end of her nose, and you trembled because you thought that at any minute she would grab her ruler and tell you to hold your hands out palms down. Instead she looked you in the eye, peering over her glasses to do so, and said "Everyone gets a *second* chance," and you got the message.

Now on the back stairwell on the way to the top floor, you paused, picturing Stephen Derrick standing right here one day just about a year ago when he'd cornered you before school.

"Do you love me like Kim loves Richard?" he'd asked, his freckled face earnest.

You'd stared at him. Did Kim Beckwith love Richard Goytt? Rumor had it that she let him put his hands down her pants. Was that love? In any case, you did not love Stephen, a mere boy, or Marty Hayden either who signed his notes to you "Forever, Marty" and made the tail of the "y" into a little heart. You had already begun fantasizing about Mr. Leach, and though you didn't admit to that, you told Stephen "no" straight out and walked away from the hurt look in his eyes. How could you have known then that in just a few years, when fifteen year old "Steve" let his dark, curly hair grow out a little and his scrawny body became more muscular that you would look into those suddenly amazing azure eyes and wish that you could take it all back?

Once on the third floor, you headed into Mrs. Baker's room to say goodbye. She didn't drive, so her husband picked her up every day at 4:00 after he got out of work. Even after starting sixth grade, you often helped Mrs. Baker with the boards and erasers until it was almost time for *Dark Shadows*. Mrs. Baker was old and fat and wore flowered dresses. Some of the kids called her "Shake and Bake" because if anyone talked in class she'd grab him by the shoulders and shake until everyone could hear his teeth rattle. You liked her, though, and you were glad when she got promoted to teach fifth grade math instead of second grade so you could have her again.

The boards already looked clean, so you didn't have to feel guilty about taking a last tour instead of helping. Mrs. Baker seemed to know that you didn't really feel like small talk today as you absently wandered around this room where Doug Fedler once pointed out the long hairs on your calves and told you that you needed to shave. He said he knew about that because his older sister shaved. In that moment, you resented your older half-sister Karen for living an hour away and for not taking more of an interest. That night you told your mother who said that you were too young to shave because "once you start, the hair grows in dark and coarse," but she finally agreed to let you use her razor when you showed her how your hairs were already dark and coarse.

Over there by the bulletin board, Michael Buzzell once watched as you hung up a poster and, as soon as your arms were raised, he stuck his finger in your bare armpit. You'd jerked back and stared at him, neither of you speaking, then turned your body away from him to resume the hanging. Maybe you should have told on him because sometime after that you saw him on the stairway cupping his hand under Debbie Searah's boob through her thin cotton dress and gleefully announcing, "I caught a ball!" Debbie just turned red and squirmed away as the boys laughed and the other girls looked disgusted.

The panic attacks had begun here in your fifth grade homeroom too, except you didn't know that's what they were. Just sometimes, for a few seconds, your head would feel a little heavy and then the room began to swim and darken as your heart beat harder, like a scared, trapped thing trying to burst out of your chest. After a few of those, your mother took you to the doctor for tests. For three days in the hospital, doctors took x-rays and took blood because they thought you might have fits or some other serious disease, but at the end, they said it was just nerves and gave your mother some tiny yellow pills for you to try. She broke them in half because, otherwise, they made you sleepy.

After you said goodbye to Mrs. Baker, you walked fast past the wing where Mrs. Clark's homeroom and her auction drawer were. Mrs. Clark taught science and liked to wear bright red lipstick and polka dots. Usually her hair was bright red too, like Lucille Ball's. Mrs. Clark and her husband, "The Captain," went to Mt. Vesuvius one summer, and every year she showed the slides to her science classes and talked about how she bravely "descended into an active volcano." Nobody knew what Mrs. Clark's husband was captain of and nobody dared to ask because Mrs. Clark might consider the question discourteous. Anybody who was discourteous had to spell out "courtesy" three times in front of the class while Mrs. Clark counted on her fingers, holding each of them up in the air, her bright red fingernails flashing like stop lights. Everyone else always stopped whatever they were working on to watch the offender spell out his penance. Mrs. Clark hated disruptions and noises of any kind, which was why she invented the auction drawer.

On the very first day of fifth grade and your first time with different teachers teaching different subjects, your pencil rolled off your desk and onto the floor while Mrs. Clark was speaking.

"Who dropped something?" she asked, and her face looked angry.

You said nothing, only raised your hand.

"Bring it up," she barked at you and glared like you'd dropped it on purpose.

"This will be the first item in this year's auction drawer," she said and explained that anything – no matter what it was - that hit the floor during her class ended up a special drawer in her homeroom across the hall. Every Friday afternoon, just before school let out, she conducted her "auction," during which she called by name those students of hers who had excelled that week to pick any item from the drawer to keep.

"So from now on, hold onto your things," she ordered your science class, "or others will have them."

The next period, in English, you had to raise your hand and tell Miss Triffilo that you needed a pencil.

"Do you always come to class unprepared?" she asked, frowning.

"No, Miss Trifilo. I brought a pencil, but Mrs. Clark took it."

Miss Trifilo turned to reach for one of her own pencils for you to use but not before you saw her roll her eyes. "From now on, bring two," she said, "and be more careful."

Mrs. Clark had probably already gone home, but even so, you didn't want to run into her on this last day of school, so you rushed toward the library, tucked into one of the eaves on the far end of the third floor. Mrs. Bennett, the librarian, must have already gone home too because the library was empty. You only glanced in as you passed. You didn't use this library much; preferring to walk to the town library on Main Street even though Mrs. Miller still gave you mean looks over her glasses when you checked books out.

"You can't check out these books," she'd said the day you approached her desk with a stack from the main part of the library instead of from the children's section. "You're not old enough."

"But I've read everything in there," you gestured toward the alcove where the storybooks were kept.

Mrs. Frizzell, who was the head librarian and whose husband was on the school committee, overheard and walked over to the main desk. Both librarians could be crabby, but you always thought Mrs. Frizzell was the nicer of the two. She looked at the books, one by one, then looked up and down at you.

"How old are you?"

"Nine. But I'll be ten soon."

"I'll have to have a note from your mother if you want to borrow books from the adult section. Bring it with you next time. I'll hold these for you," said Mrs. Frizzell.

Mrs. Miller frowned and adjusted her little glasses. You ran back home and since it was Saturday morning your mother was home. In less than an hour, you once again stood before the main desk, and you handed your note to Mrs. Miller who had to call over Mrs. Frizzell to read it even though Mrs. Frizzell had already said it would be okay.

So the only time you really went into the school library was when Mrs. Dobeck, in her starched white uniform and little hat with its red cross on the front, called the classes in there for their eye tests. Every fall, just after the start of school, each class paraded into the library, even though Mrs. Dobeck's office was in the school's basement where the "special" kids were, and took turns showing with their hands which direction the Es on the eye chart went. You dreaded that day, but after first grade, you made sure to be prepared for it with a note from your mother excusing you from the test since you had your own eye doctor. You knew that even with your thick glasses you would probably not pass because when you got nervous the letters jittered. The doctor said the letters didn't move; your eyes did. He called them "dancing eyes," but at least, since the last surgery, the lazy one no longer turned in. Unfortunately, your eyes only *looked* better; they couldn't see any better.

Back on the second floor, you saw that Miss O'Coin's door had now closed, so you slipped by it into your fourth grade classroom. Miss

Dowgielewitz, who still wore her hair in a frosted beehive (and had for as long as you could remember), had some sort of speech impediment, so it took each year's fourth graders a while to get used to her, and even then, she occasionally would have to write a word she'd said on the board for it to be understood. She hated seeing misspellings of her name and made all her students spell it out loud several times over the first few days of school until it was burned into your brains forever.

Here, in this room, you'd recited as "Marcia from Russia" in your class play Children from around the World, and when Miss Dowgielewitz found out you'd started taking guitar lessons from Mary Coffee, she insisted that you play for the class. You knew only a few chords, so you played "Rock-a My Soul," an easy song. Everybody clapped, but you still felt a little embarrassed being the center of attention like that.

At least Miss Dowgielewitz let you play from your seat, so it wasn't like being alone onstage. At home, when you had to play for company, your mother pulled out one of the kitchen chairs and set up your music stand in front of it right at the threshold. You had to sit in the doorway, playing and singing as you faced the whole kitchen. When you complained about being forced to perform, especially for Jay who always looked like he had something better to do, your mother once again told you how your grandmother Annie used to roll up the living room rug so that your mother, as a girl, wouldn't trip on it when she danced the jig to the Victrola for company.

When you played the guitar and sang, you tried to tell yourself that it was no different from singing in Mr. Sacco's music class. You loved singing for him, even though the selections in the school songbook were mostly about people dying, like "My Grandfather's Clock" and "Oh My Darling, Clementine," which actually struck you as funny, being Huckleberry Hound's theme song and all.

Once you got better on the guitar, you started playing popular folk music and the grownups listening in your kitchen seemed to like it. Everyone praised you, especially when after hours of practice, you performed "Mon Vrai Destin" from your Peter, Paul and Mary guitar songbook.

Except that when your mother insisted you perform it for Jay, instead of clapping he said, "What language is that?"

"It's French," your mother said, smiling at you and looking proud.

"Doesn't sound like French to me," said Jay who couldn't speak anything but English anyway.

"Oh, yes," your mother said. "She has the book and the record to go with it."

Jay only looked at his watch.

Now you glanced at your watch and headed for the second floor stairwell of the Grove Street School, hoping you wouldn't run into Mr. Bouchard, the janitor, on the first floor.

Mr. Bouchard lived with his wife, Leah, in the house behind yours, so he walked to work. Wrinkled and stick-like, he had a loud, raspy voice and a cackle that ricocheted when he thought he was being funny. Your dog Pepper hated him and went crazy at the sound of his voice. Then Mr. Bouchard, whose real name was Ulric but who went by Henry, always yelled, "Another country heard from!" and then cackled louder at his own joke, making Pepper bark even more.

A few months ago and for no reason, Mr. Bouchard had started calling you "Stinky Donna" when he saw you on the sidewalk on his way home. The first time, you were shocked and immediately went inside to ask your mother if you smelled.

"Of course not," she said, and when you told her what happened, she added, "He's an ignorant Canuck, a thick-headed Frenchman. Just ignore him."

Ignoring didn't work with Mr. Bouchard, any more than it had with Dana Gurstel, and even avoiding him didn't work because you never knew what corner he'd be lurking around. After the day he yelled, or so it seemed, "Stinky Donna, Stinky Donna!" in the school hallway and ricocheted his cackle, and all the kids turned to stare, you decided to retaliate. So what if he was a grownup? He was ignorant. Your mother had said so. So instead of avoiding him, you watched for him, and then before he saw you, you yelled, "Stinky Mr. Bouchard!" hoping none of the teachers would hear. Your friends howled. Mr. Bouchard turned red and silently looked away. It took only that once to make it stop, but you still preferred not running into him.

Now as you opened the stairway door to the first floor lobby, you could hear the janitor's cart, so you scurried over to Mrs. Derrick's third grade classroom before you could be seen. By now, it was highly likely that only you, Mrs. Baker and Mr. Bouchard were left in the building.

You liked Mrs. Derrick even though she had a reputation for being very strict. She didn't tolerate any misbehaving, but at least she didn't grab kids' chin skin and twist the way you'd heard Mrs. Turner, the other third grade teacher, did. Mrs. Derrick had white hair and an interesting face behind her large black framed glasses – not wrinkled so much as covered by a network of deep interconnecting lines, like when mud has dried from the sun. She not only lived in town but went to your church and knew your mother, so she kept an extra eye on you.

You memorized times tables in Mrs. Derrick's class, alternating between writing them and reciting them, and you learned to square dance. Every Friday, after the noon whistle had sounded from the fire station and lunch had ended, the desks were moved aside, Mrs. Derrick took out her records, and dance partners were chosen. Because both Ray Dwelly and Marty Hayden wanted to dance with you and pouted every time you chose the other, you couldn't help but stall, just a little bit, over making the weekly choice. That year, the whole class learned to bow or curtsy and how to extend or accept an invitation to dance. Mrs. Derrick's eyes snapped when she stressed that good manners never go out of style.

Third grade was the last year you could wear undershirts instead of brassieres, and unlike the hair on your legs, nobody in your class had to tell you. One day, your mother just walked into your room, removed all your undershirts from their dresser drawer and announced that the two of you were going shopping.

Third grade was also the year that you first saw someone you knew in a cast, when Helen Corbeil broke her leg and came to school on crutches. Everyone signed or drew on the white plaster, and you felt a little jealous of the attention she got. When Martha Salem, whose mother had gone to school with yours, announced one morning that she had a new baby sister, laughing and rolling her eyes at the unusual name "Heather," she got lots of attention too as all the kids offered their theories of where babies come from until Mrs. Derrick rapped on her desk for silence.

On Parents Night that year, both your mother and father came to see you perform as "the second stewardess" in the class play and to look at your carefully laid out schoolwork, and, afterwards, you watched as they walked over to Bradley Earle's desk and looked at his because no one else had come to see it. When you sulked because you wanted all their attention, your mother explained to you that Bradley's mother had just recently "run away" from her family and that his father must be working and that you should be extra nice to Bradley from now on since he had no mother.

A few weeks later, during one of your parents' arguments, you overheard your mother tell your father that maybe someday she would just leave, and wouldn't he be happy then? You felt fear stab at your chest, and you ran crying into the playroom. Later, when your mother found you sitting in a chair facing the wall as if you were being punished, she hugged you and assured you that she would never leave you.

After Mrs. Derrick's room, you decided to skip your second grade classroom on this final tour because janitor-sounds seemed still to be coming from that direction, so you crossed the big foyer, passing the wide wooden stairway to the building's main entrance, and proceeded to the classroom that used to be Mrs. Lyons'. Here, first graders had to get used to being in school all day long, since kindergarten sessions ran only half-days. Full days of school meant getting used to more structure like not talking out of turn, staying seated at the desks, eating and drinking only at recess and lunch, and holding back pee. Mrs. Lyons had taught for years; she had even been your brother Jay's teacher, long before your birth. She believed in strict discipline, and even if someone raised a hand to ask to use the bathroom, she usually said no. She thought that children needed to learn to do the things they had to do during the time allowed, even if the lines to the bathroom were so long that not everybody got in before the bell sounded. Sometimes, someone couldn't hold it anymore and had an accident.

One day, Deborah Hague raised her hand and said she really had to go, that she hadn't gotten a turn at recess, and Mrs. Lyons told her that she could wait until lunch. Except that Deborah couldn't wait, and you noticed the puddle around her desk first because Deborah sat right next to you. Deborah stared straight ahead, not crying but just frowning, her large eyes unblinking, and you couldn't tell whether she looked angry or sad. Mrs. Lyons had to call for Mr. Bouchard to clean the floor as Deborah was made to stand and watch, her dress still wet and dripping into her white ankle socks, her eyes still dryly staring straight ahead.

Mrs. Lyons died towards the end of your first grade year, but before she did, a string of young substitutes came in to take her class. You never really knew, from one morning to the next, who would be standing at the board, copying down the day's assignment for each reading group. Even though the class had early on been divided into four groups according to reading ability, everyone used the same Dick and Jane series. Whether a student belonged to Group 1, Group 2, Group 3, or "The Three Girls" only determined from which book and where in the series they would read aloud.

Martha Salem, Claire Goddard and you, as "The Three Girls," had grown tired of breezing through readers that held no challenge, so you mutually agreed to ask one of the more-or-less regular substitutes (whose name you forgot long ago but whose black French braid and red lipstick you could still picture) if, perhaps, you could move on to something else.

Miss Whoever raised a perfectly penciled eyebrow and looked each of you in the eye before asking, "Do you girls think you're better than the other students?"

Martha, Claire and you, suddenly timid before her glare, giggled a little and looked at each other. Well, when it came to reading, you *were* better, weren't you? Oblivious to the shame she had evidently intended you to feel, one of you, or maybe all of you, said something like "Well, yes, and can't we please read something harder?"

Miss Whoever snapped her Dick and Jane shut, and said, "Your reading class is over for today. You three can go back to your seats."

The three of you hung your heads as you returned to your desks, chastised but still not quite sure why. However, the next day, when your group met in the back of the room, you all brought the same old books and meekly read aloud from them when called on.

Another glance at your watch and you realized you did not have time to visit the Grove Street School's basement on your tour, not that there was much to see there anyway. You'd attended afternoon kindergarten sessions in one of the larger rooms, where you'd learned shapes and colors, and where you'd been punished more than once for refusing to share your coloring books with kids you just knew would ruin them. Your mother had taught you to take care of your things, but you already knew that lots of mothers apparently did not teach that to their children. Despite your protests, Mrs. Pease repeatedly banished you to the corner for being "selfish," especially that time when Dean Ringgard helped himself to whatever you were playing with and you slugged him the way Lucy always threatened to slug Linus in the Peanuts cartoons.

No, you didn't need to see your kindergarten room where you'd taken tap dancing classes for months and, despite being so uncoordinated, had learned all the steps for the recital that you ultimately missed because of the scarlet fever that put you in the hospital. You didn't need to see the band rehearsal room down there either because you already missed Mr. Sacco so much that thinking about band might make you cry again. The only other rooms in the basement were the boiler room, the janitor's room, Mrs. Dobeck's room, and the windowless room where the "special" kids went for extra help.

You went out the side exit of the Grove Street School, the one facing South Common Street, and down the steep concrete steps, hearing the heavy green door thunk behind you for the last time. After you crossed the empty street, you stepped onto the playground, planning to cut through the Common to get home just in time to see who Barnabus Collins would attack in today's episode. You walked over the cracked asphalt where you'd skipped a hundred ropes, tossed thousands of flat rocks onto hopscotch squares, and played kickball or dodge ball with whoever wanted to play regardless of age or gender. Although you passed the rotting sandboxes, the peeling metal jungle gym and the merry-go-round that listed slightly to one side, you momentarily paused at the swings, wishing you had more time, but reassuring yourself that they would still be here tomorrow.

You had your own swing set at home – even now that you'd outgrown all the store-bought models. Because your dad worked in a steel manufacturing plant, he had designed and built a larger, sturdier, adult-sized set for you, using heavy pipes and welding the joints together himself. Nevertheless, at every recess, you'd been first among the group racing through the playground to grab for these canvas seats to the clouds. When you were younger, and if you lucked out, Diane Carlson might have remembered to hold one for you when she wandered over from her house on the corner.

Older, taller, and much larger than all the other kids on the playground at recess, Diane did not go to your school like her younger brother Richard, one of the "special kids" who regularly visited the room in the basement. Nor did she attend the school in Worcester like her older sister Carol, who could at least speak in whole sentences. Diane was so severely retarded that she could not form real words, let alone read or do math. She hung around the Common in her billowy house dresses and thin pink cardigan, her lank hair uncombed, her tiny eyes lost in her fleshy copper-colored face.

Little kids feared Diane because she looked and sounded so different, and so had you at first. Was she a Mongoloid? You didn't really know because you'd never actually seen one. Well, no, actually you had, but you couldn't remember it. Your mother had told you about Marguerite St. Jacques who lived across the street from your house when you were very small and how her mother Cecile would carry her over when she came to visit.

"She had to be carried because she couldn't walk," your mother said. "And even though she was, oh, around eight or nine, she still had a very small body. But her head had kept growing, so it was too big for her neck to support."

Marguerite couldn't speak, but she made sounds and she fixed her slanted eyes on you and laughed out of her toothless mouth. Your mother told you how when Cecile walked in with Marguerite, you cried, then ran to hide because you thought she was a monster. Marguerite eventually went somewhere else to live because Cecile couldn't care for her anymore. She died before her thirteenth birthday.

Diane Carlson didn't look like a baby with a grownup's head, but she didn't look exactly "normal" either. Still, she stayed around the Common so much that the kids got used to her being there. Nobody really played with her though, except that when she did remember to save you the swings as you'd asked her to, her heavy weight made her a great partner for "Spider." You and a couple of your friends would take turns on one swing while Diane sat on the other. Each rider started at diagonally opposite corners, and the trick was to run at each other clockwise, and sort of throw your body up and around each other so that the long chains holding the swings would twist together. Once the momentum ceased, the chains unwound, and the lighter child got a dizzying "ride" that spun faster and faster until the swings finally freed themselves. Because of her bulk, Diane's swing didn't move much, but she seemed to like the attention. You and your friends had even taught her to count the number of loops made during the game, and she yelled louder than anybody: "Waa, too, eee, faa . . ."

But that one day in fourth grade when you realized that the monsters were not the ones with large heads and small bodies or the ones who had humps on their backs but the ones who looked just like everyone else, you and your friends had tired of the swings and were playing on the slide at the far end of the playground, so you didn't notice anything unusual until the circle of children had already formed around Diane. As you hesitated at the top of the slide, trying to decide whether to go down head first or backwards, the commotion way over past the jungle gym, louder than ordinary playground noise, broke your concentration and caused you to turn your head.

Most of grades four through six, maybe a hundred or so children, normally scattered over the playground, seemed to be gathered in one spot. The group of bodies fanned out, then closed in, over and over, but you couldn't see what held their attention at the center. You only vaguely heard your friends on the ground calling to you to hurry up as you strained to make sense of what you couldn't quite see. Then the crowd fanned out again, revealing Diane's pink cardigan at its center.

When you reached the circle of children, most of them older and taller than you, you had to squeeze between the bodies to get a good look. In the small clearing, Diane stood tall and alone her red face even redder with rage, bellowing her wordless words as children, mostly boys, took turns poking her in the back, the general audience taunting and cheering when contact was made. Each time she felt the offense, Diane whirled on the attacker, and that part of the circle fanned out in retreat as, simultaneously, another part of the circle closed in with another attack from behind.

One boy stepped forward with a baseball bat, attempting to jab her in the side, but was too slow in his retreat. Diane grabbed the bat and began randomly swinging it at the group. Surely, now, a teacher would step in. You stood on tiptoes and looked back toward the playground entrance where you could just make out the frosted beehive next to the bright Lucille Ball curls, neither of which seemed to be moving any closer.

As Diane's meaty arm swung the bat back and forth in a protective arc around her body, the crowd of children momentarily froze as if unsure of the next move yet unwilling to let go of the moment. Then one boy stooped to pick something up, and the first stone was thrown. It bounced off of Diane's shoulder, and, as it did, the expression on her face changed from rage to surprise, then to a darker rage that was almost beast -like.

As if they had been given a silent command, dozens of children now bent, searching for rocks, sticks, anything they could throw and Diane's face got redder and redder as she screamed and roared and the rocks sailed from all directions and you kept looking to see who these boys were but the faces just blurred and where were the teachers and Diane's tiny eyes looked like bright blue stones in her scrunched up, tear -stained face as she swung the bat, trying but failing to hit the source of the stones because there were so many that she ended up just turning in circles as the children danced just out of her reach and the teachers still didn't come and even the ones who weren't throwing the stones laughed and taunted and you were jostled back and forth as the crowd ebbed and flowed and just before Diane dropped to the ground you saw her brother Richard's face among the others.

You could hear the crows scolding from the trees around the Common in the sudden silence. All the children gaped as Diane's body shook and thrashed. Miss Dowgielewitz appeared with a pink rat-tailed comb she had fished out of her pocketbook and attempted to force the end between Diane's frothing lips, "to hold down her tongue, so she wouldn't choke on it" she told us later on in class. Meanwhile, Mrs. Clark simply called for everyone to line up to reenter the building.

You never followed up on what happened to Diane after that day. For you, life went on pretty much as it had before, and you assumed that her absence from the playground during recess only meant that she was being kept home. Besides, nothing that had happened out here or in the brick school, whose shadow had begun to lengthen as the sun dropped in the sky, mattered now anyway. Tomorrow morning, your summer vacation would officially begin, with bike riding, and swimming lessons, and camping with Aunt Ruth and Uncle Chuck. And best of all, the two weeks your older half-brother Brucie would be spending at your house, giving the two of you, you hoped, the opportunity to become closer, like a real brother and sister.

Right now, though, you sprinted through the Common and up North Common Street, your house key already in your hand. *Dark Shadows* was about to start.

THE CROW PAYS NO ATTENTION TO THE FORMER SCHOOL, NOR TO THE PLAYGROUND NEXT TO IT, THE ASPHALT CRACKED AND WEEDY, THE SLIDES RUSTED, THE MERRY-GO-ROUND SAGGING TO ONE SIDE, THE STONE BUBBLER UNUSABLE. SHE HEADS FOR THE ADJOINING COMMON, ANOTHER STAGING PLACE OF HERS BECAUSE, LIKE THE CEMETERY, ITS OPEN AREA MEANS A SAFE AND FERTILE HUNTING GROUND. JUST AS SHE EXPECTED, SHE SEES MANY MEMBERS OF HER MURDER ALREADY FEEDING IN THE DENSE GRASS WHILE OTHERS LINE THE CHAIN LINK FENCING AS SENTRIES. SHE PERCHES IN THEIR MIDST AND SURVEYS THE GROUNDS.

CONNIE MACK, "THE GRAND OLD MAN OF BASEBALL," PLAYED BALL HERE IN THE 1880S, AND ON JULY 10, 1934, THE TOWN HONORED HIM WITH ITS "CONNIE MACK DAY" CELEBRATION WITH GEORGE M. COHAN THE MASTER OF CEREMONIES. MACK AND COHAN ARRIVED TOGETHER IN A SPECIAL CAR ON THE NORTH BROOKFIELD RAILROAD. OVER THE YEARS, VARIOUS CIRCUSES AND CARNIVALS HAVE SET UP ON THE COMMON, AND MANY SPORTS PRACTICES AND GAMES HAVE BEEN HELD HERE. LATELY, INHABITANTS IN THE SURROUNDING HOUSES ON GROVE, NORTH COMMON, AND FOREST STREETS HAVE NOTICED THE GRADUALLY INCREASING CROW POPULATION, ANYWHERE FROM A DOZEN TO SEVERAL DOZEN AT ONE TIME ON THE FENCE AND IN THE GRASS AND SURROUNDING TREES, ESPECIALLY IN THE MORNINGS. THE BIRDS DON'T SEEM TO BOTHER ANYONE OR CAUSE ANY DAMAGE; STILL, THE SIGHT OF SO MANY MAKES SOME PEOPLE UNEASY, PARTICULARLY THE OLD IRISH WHO WERE RAISED TO BELIEVE THAT CROWS ARE THE EARTHLY REPRESENTATIVES OF SOULS IN PURGATORY.

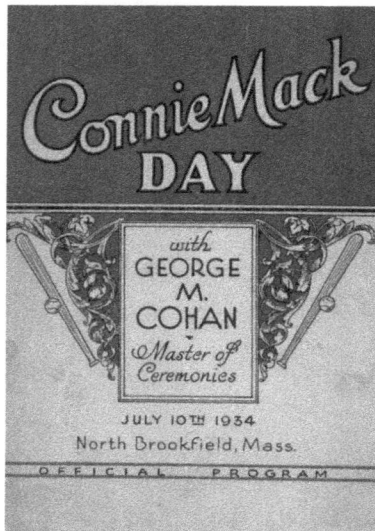

ConnieMack DAY
with
GEORGE M. COHAN
Master of Ceremonies
JULY 10TH 1934
North Brookfield, Mass.
OFFICIAL PROGRAM

10

Not Appropriate for Children

"What does it taste like?" I asked, more appalled than curious but not knowing what else to say. This morning out of the blue, after waking from a sleepover at my house, my best friend Amy revealed that her father had been sexually abusing her in various ways for the past year. We were eleven years old.

"It tastes like...skin," she replied. Later, after Amy went home, I would lick my own arm and try to imagine the unimaginable.

"Do you...isn't *stuff* supposed to come out?" I stammered as I struggled with my meager knowledge of male physiology. A year or so earlier, my mother had been unable to look me in the eyes when she handed me a slim volume on menstruation and reproduction. The passages that covered the male's role in the process lacked detail and used technical terms that I'd never heard spoken. As she turned away that day, Ma said that if I had any questions after reading the book just to ask. I had questions, all right, but I sensed her embarrassment, which, in turn, fueled my embarrassment, so I looked to other sources for clarification, to the same font of knowledge tapped by previous generations (and most likely by those to come): the streets, where I had no trouble soliciting the sage wisdom of all of my just as sexually ignorant friends. At least, I had assumed them all to be ignorant. How should I ask this? "Do you---?"

"He stops before that happens," Amy interrupted me, "and 'goes' into a hankie."

We were in bed, I in the maple twin bed that had been Jay's when he still lived at home before I was born and Amy in a folding guest bed a few feet away. I'd been complaining for a couple of years about my "little girl" bedroom, so earlier that summer, my father and mother had decided to update and redecorate. The project entailed a total gut job, my father doing most of the work himself, which included demolishing not only the wallpaper of pink and white roses but the horsehair plaster un-

derneath in favor of honey maple wood paneling, as well as rewiring to add outlets and a wall switch instead of a pull chain for the new ceiling light: a basketball-sized frosted plastic globe that hung by a gold chain from the exact center of the formerly cream colored ceiling, causing my mother to whack her head and curse every time she vacuumed. I chose purple for the paint – trim and ceiling – because purple was "cool" and the dominant color of the junior-senior high school I would be attending in the fall. Satiny purple drapes held back with gold tasseled cords replaced the lacey cream "shears" of my early childhood, and a faux fur area rug with a zebra pattern lay under the new Boston rocker. Wall space being at a premium thanks to the room's three windows and three doorways, I'd insisted on removing for good the crucifixes and pictures of the Sacred Heart and the Virgin Mary and carefully selected as their replacements posters of David Cassidy and Bobby Sherman, a psychedel-

ic "black light" poster of a mushroom, and a Harland Young print I'd purchased with my allowance of a black stallion galloping along a churning ocean shore under a leaden sky. A stereo console, the most recent birthday present from my parents, had replaced my old phonograph and stood within easy

reach right next to my bed. I was proud of my room and considered it very grown up, but as my eyes flicked back and forth at everything in the room but Amy, pride was not the emotion I was feeling, nor was I feeling very grown up.

"How- when does this happen?" I asked, still unable to believe what I heard. "I mean, with all of your brothers and sisters . . ."

"While Mom works. He sends them outside to play."

Could Amy tell that I couldn't look at her right now? I squirmed under the sheet.

"But . . . why do you do it? Can't you just say no?" I asked the ceiling.

"He won't let me leave the house unless I do what he tells me."

Realization suddenly dawned on me that Amy's almost obsessive desire to walk down North Common Street to my house for supper and sleepovers or just to hang out not only got her away from the noise and chaos of five younger siblings, it gave her father something to hang over her head. How many times had I called her house to invite her over and heard her father's curt "no" in the background only for our phone to ring a half hour or so later with the news that he'd changed his mind. Now I knew why.

"One time . . ." she hesitated, then blurted, "he made Brownie lick me. You know, 'there.'"

I had no words, no response. What could I say to that? Amy's parents, younger by far than my own, had always seemed kind of cool to me, especially her father. On the rare occasions when I went to Amy's house, he kidded around and often complimented me, telling me how grown up I looked, that even at eleven I could easily pass for sixteen. Mr. Rose's thick, dark hair, side burns, and charming smile had struck me as rather attractive, and when I teased back that he looked like Graham Kerr, The Galloping Gourmet, he laughed and galloped across their kitchen. I didn't want to picture him bringing Amy's dog, Brownie, up to her and making him – no, I couldn't even let that image form in my head.

Then another thought occurred to me. "What happened to Brownie? I haven't seen him around the neighborhood lately."

Silence.

This time I turned to Amy. Her face was turned away from me. Was she crying? I waited.

Finally she spoke, the words coming out in a rush. "He wanted to put Brownie's thing in me, but I wouldn't let him, so he took Brownie away. He told me he drove Brownie to the woods and left him there."

Now I felt like crying, imagining Amy's dog lost in the woods or walking alongside a back road about to be hit by a car. Immediately, I imagined my own dog, Pepper, facing scary, lonely nights, cold and far from home, and I felt tears sting my eyes. I was such a wimp with anything involving dogs, that movies like *Lad: A Dog* and *The Incredible Journey* reduced me to tears, and even when I watched *Lassie* on television, I had to remind myself that she would always survive whatever dangers she faced to reappear in the following week's episode.

"Why are you telling me all this?" I asked, hearing the whine in my voice and not caring. Amy had kept her secret for almost a year, after all. I didn't want to know this, any of it!

"Because he wants me to invite you over. For a sleepover."

Yikes! Dogs forgotten, I felt my stomach flip. I had never spent the night at Amy's. The thought had never even occurred to me because there simply wasn't room in their small, crowded house.

"*He* wants you to?"

"Remember that day after school when no one was home, and I showed you those magazines?"

Did I ever. Amy had pulled out a couple of magazines from under some underwear in a dresser drawer, and we sat on the floor, leafing through glossy pictures of women in high heels and stockings fastened by garters, wearing different colored fancy underwear of a type I'd never before seen ("bustiers," I would find out years later). Each page featured a different woman but all sat spread-eagle, facing out, opening themselves with their fingers, their manicured nails garishly polished to match their outfits. I had stared at each one, repulsed yet fascinated, while Amy watched my reaction. "These are gross!" I'd declared, meanwhile wondering if all women looked like that "down there." Did I? I never told anyone, not even Amy, that later on that day, in the privacy of the upstairs bathroom at home, I examined myself with a hand-held mirror while sitting on the toilet lid and wondered why anyone would find what I was looking at appealing enough to put in a magazine.

"Well, that was his idea. Showing you those. He told me to. Afterwards he asked me what you said."

I could feel my face flush in embarrassment over what I thought had been a mischievous spur of the moment idea having instead been planned by and later discussed with an adult – and a man no less!

"Now he keeps asking when you're going to sleep over. He says that the three of us could 'have some fun.' I thought I better warn you."

Wrong, wrong, wrong. The thought whirled through my head that this was all so wrong. Only years later did it occur to me that I never thanked Amy. So overwhelmed that I couldn't even comprehend how brave she was to have spared me her father's perversions, I had only one response:

"I have to tell."

"I know," she said.

After Amy went home, I lay on my bed for a long time, thinking about how to bring up the subject with my mother. I even briefly reconsidered telling her at all because I remembered how unfazed she'd seemed two years earlier when I told her about Mr. Hart, a neighborhood man who'd confronted me one day after swimming lessons.

I didn't mind the swimming lessons held at Camp Atwater; they gave me something different to do during the summer, but I hated the bus ride back home from East Brookfield. The old school busses themselves were "nifty" (a word I picked up from *Mister Rogers' Neighborhood*), although I may have thought so only because of their novelty (I lived close enough to my elementary school to walk). However, sitting in my still-wet, now-clammy bathing suit, sand from Lake Lashaway's beach between my toes, I felt grungy on the way back.

The bus always dropped me and the rest of the kids off by the playground, where a few mothers waited in their cars. Most of us walked home, scattering in different directions. I lived closer than anyone else - just a block away – so I cut through the Common, then headed up North Common Street, eager to get into dry clothes and eat the sandwich Ma had left for me. Because I was older now, having just turned nine, I no longer needed a babysitter. This summer, I did not go to Mrs. Mallon's house, four doors down from mine, after swimming lessons. I had my own house key, and I had proven myself responsible enough to be home alone during the day while my mother worked downtown at Phil's Restaurant. The other neat thing about being nine was being allowed to wear a two-piece bathing suit.

My suit was white lace over a background of hot pink, and the cut was fairly conservative for 1968 despite being a two-piece. The bottom piece reached my belly button, and the top piece actually covered more skin than the average brassiere, so that barely any cleavage could be seen. I didn't have a great deal of cleavage yet anyway, although my body had already begun to develop. For me, the idea of the two-piece mattered, not what it did or did not reveal. One-piece suits were for babies, and even though only about a two inch strip of my skin showed between the top and bottom, I felt grown up. I had no thought of trying to look sexy, since I had no concept of what "sexy" implied. When I watched Goldie Hawn dance in her bikini on television, her exposed skin "painted" in multi-colored designs, I did not see "sex." I saw only a new, more grown-up style.

If I strutted as I crossed the Common the day of my encounter with Mr. Hart, I certainly didn't mean to. In retrospect, I should have kept my beach towel wrapped around me for decorum's sake, but in my defense, what nine year old knows about decorum? The sun beat down, and the light breeze felt delicious on my skin. I remember savoring the perfect summer day as I walked (strutted?) from the bus toward my house and barely noticed the elderly man who had just turned onto North Common Street as I stepped off the Common and crossed the road to the sidewalk. I did not know Mr. Hart – only that he lived up the hill from me and was somehow related to the Mr. Hart who owned the bar near my house. I knew his name only because I had once or twice heard my mother speak to him in passing. He must have rushed to catch up to me, or perhaps, in my reverie, I dallied because two houses down from my own, he appeared by my side, startling me when he spoke.

"Hey, how's your coconuts?"

My brain made no sense of what I thought I'd just heard. Coconuts? I stopped walking and turned towards him. In my mind's eye, I see a smallish, very wrinkled man, black-rimmed glasses magnifying his owlish eyes, some sort of black derby on his head, a long tan raincoat open and loosely fitting his stooped frame. That image cannot be accurate, however, if for no other reason than the time of year this incident occurred. I do remember a moment of utter confusion, wondering if somehow this man thought that my family grew coconuts on our property. Or, perhaps I simply misheard since I'd been daydreaming.

I'm guessing that I dumbly stared at him, trying not to appear, well, dumb. The second time he spoke, he clarified his question by leering and pointing at my chest.

"I said 'how's your coconuts?'"

Shame crept over my face as if I had done something wrong. I wordlessly turned away from Mr. Hart and broke into a run, terrified he would follow me. As I cut through the yard between my house and the house next door, I heard the words again, yelled from somewhere behind me, then the laughter, an old man's cackle. I went around my house, to the back, but for some reason, I did not let myself in; instead I stood pressed against the cool aluminum siding, hiding from some perceived but not fully understood danger while my heart thudded and my stomach churned. When enough time had passed for him to have gone up the hill, I peeked around the house just to be sure and went inside.

As soon as Ma got home from work, I told her what had happened with Mr. Hart. She looked a bit cross but said only "He's a dirty old man. Stay away from him."

My internal debate over whether or not to tell my mother about Amy and her dad lasted all afternoon. Though I knew enough of the world to recognize the wrongness of Mr. Rose's behavior (despite my ignorance of the terms themselves), I hesitated partly due to my own self-consciousness but also because I had no idea what kind of fallout, if any, would result from my disclosure. It seemed pretty plain to me that Amy's treatment by her father far surpassed a crude remark made to me by a near stranger on the street, yet I still supposed I could be sticking my nose where it didn't belong. Would I simply be told to "stay away" from Mr. Rose? On the other hand, what if telling my mother made things worse for Amy? Could her father go to jail for what he was doing? I had no frame of reference as to how to handle the situation. Ultimately, I decided to dump the whole thing in my mother's lap. Let her decide what, if anything, should be done.

I don't remember the words I used that day, but Ma's reaction was only to tell me that my father would be informed as soon as he got home and that, together, they would figure out what to do. I didn't want to be in the room for that discussion because I was too embarrassed, so I sat on the hall stairs where I could still hear the voices from the kitchen. Judging from the delicate, almost vague references to the sexual acts themselves, my parents either were just as embarrassed as I was or assumed I was listening in. Both remained eerily calm, and the conversation ended after only a few minutes. Instead of notifying the police, they decided to call the Parrish priest, Father Hughes, a decision I thought odd since my dad attended Mass only on Easter and Christmas. As far as I knew, he'd never even spoken to our priest. Furthermore, the Roses were not Catholic. My mother made the phone call.

The events that followed my parents' visit to the rectory that evening happened quickly and apart from me. I was told how Father Hughes called Amy's house and asked that Mrs. Rose bring Amy in to talk to him. He spoke privately to her, while my parents stayed in the outer office with Mrs. Rose who, when she was called in and informed of her husband's abuse, broke down in tears. Mother and daughter held each other and cried.

Amy did not attend school on Monday or Tuesday, but when I did finally get the chance to talk to her, she told me that her mother had immediately reacted by telling her husband to pack his bags and get out. He ended up renting an apartment in a nearby town with his new girlfriend who was closer to Amy's age than to his. Meanwhile, Amy's home life certainly changed but whether one could say it improved is debatable. Not only was Amy, as the oldest child, now saddled with the care of her siblings while their mother worked, but as money became tighter with only one regular income, Mrs. Rose's initial compassion for her daughter's abuse gradually turned to resentment. Amy became the scapegoat not only for her mother's failed marriage and current financial problems but for the marriage having taken place at all, since Mrs. Rose had accidentally gotten pregnant at fifteen with Amy. Furthermore, the other children, too young to understand the reason their parents were divorcing, quickly picked up on the tension between their mother and sister and surmised that whatever had happened had been Amy's fault. Although she never complained about my having told on her father, Amy frequently confided to me about feeling blamed and alienated. Her grades suffered, and she started acting out in school: sassing the teachers and getting into fights with classmates.

The revelation of my best friend's abuse also inevitably affected my own household. By the time I was eleven, my parents had long been sleeping in separate rooms. I believe that my mother had already begun to question my father's fidelity and commitment to their marriage. Their arguments – about money, unfinished projects, and too much time spent God knows where - were frequent and loud. Mr. Rose's impropriety contributed another element to their stew of discord. My mother became fixated on how both my father and I dressed at home.

From as far back as I can remember, my father had been known to lounge around the house in his underwear. In cooler weather, he added a bathrobe, often unbelted and hanging open, but during warm weather, he wore only briefs and slippers. Big deal. Except, suddenly, his outfit became a big deal to my mother, who decided a man should not be walking around in his underwear in front of his eleven year old daughter. I heard the argument from my room one day when my mother came home from work to find my father in his recliner prior to getting ready for the second shift at the steel manufacturing plant. From what I could piece together, he'd been dozing with his knees up and bent, the soles of his feet on the edge of the footrest, legs slightly splayed open and, apparently, my mother had seen quite an eyeful when she walked in. I heard her yell the words "hanging out" and he yelled back that I was upstairs in my room.

"She could have come down and seen that," Ma yelled.

Actually, I had come downstairs for something earlier, and I had glanced in at my father but all that had registered with me was that he'd been asleep.

Being told of Mr. Rose's abuse had already begun to affect the way I viewed men. I'd also had "the talk" with my mother who told me that boys are after only "one thing" and that a young lady always has to be careful around them. I could feel myself pulling away from my father, partly because of his frequent absences and the constant arguing between him and my mother but also through my own self-consciousness. I did not want to have to deal with the fact that my father was also a man, so I withdrew. The daughter who once loved sitting in his lap and listening to his stories became distant and uncomfortable around him.

One night, I listened on the stairs as Dad commented that he couldn't understand why he and I weren't closer. In a rare moment of support, Ma assured him that I was just going through a phase. I wanted to cry. Deep down I knew Dad was not like Mr. Rose, but I was so uncomfortable with my own newly developed body that now I felt like the target of every man's evil intentions.

Then my mother turned her attention to *my* outfits, primarily to my pajamas, making me even more self-conscious. Since Dad worked second shift, he got up after my mother had already gone to work. On Saturdays or when there was no school, I would sometimes laze around in my baby doll pajamas. I hated robes, so I rarely wore one. My pajamas were all cotton, some like mini-dresses with matching brief-style bottoms and others more like short shorts with sleeveless tops. I saw nothing inherently wrong with any of my baby dolls until my mother pointed out the size of the arm holes one very warm night when she and I were watching television while Dad was working.

"Do you wear a robe when your father's home?" she began.

"No." Why would I?

"You're going to have to start," she said.

"Why?"

She hooked one finger onto the material under my arm and tugged. "Because you can see everything through here."

I cringed and pulled away from her.

"He's my Dad." I felt dirty and ashamed. Mr. Rose used to look at my chest sometimes; did my father? Mr. Hart's "coconuts" comment flashed through my head, and I crossed my arms.

"A young lady should not be showing herself," my mother said, ending any further debate.

When school let out for summer, Amy still had to babysit, but she sometimes managed to get away so we could hang out – usually in the evenings or on the weekends. The fact that we saw each other less often didn't really bother me since I had other friends in the neighborhood. Besides, the summer I turned twelve, I became obsessed with two things: reading Gone with the Wind, which I'd found among some old books in the garage, and redecorating the shed to make it "mine."

The original old barn behind our house had been razed two summers earlier, the plan being that a garage would be built with enough room in it for a workshop for my father. Previously, he had partitioned off the rear section of the Other Side, the huge space that had once been my grandmother's store, as his makeshift workshop (which came to be known as "the shed") for his table saw and other tools. Construction of the new garage began shortly after demoli-

tion of the barn. Dad and my brother, Jay, spent the better part of a year on the structure, doing most of the work themselves. Once the garage was finished, my father moved everything out of the shed and set up shop under the newly installed fluorescents in his new space. He had designed a built-in work bench with cabinets below and pegboards above for all of his tools. One area even had a long wooden shelf the underside of which he had screwed in the lids of baby food jars, each jar to be designated for nails or screws of various sizes. The garage had no ceiling; instead, Dad left the rafters and exposed beams accessible for storage of lumber, sheet-
rock and tools not used on a regular
basis. He spent many hours organizing
the workshop-half of the new garage
until, finally, the shed had been emptied of all of his things.

I don't know what about the shed appealed to me – probably its privacy since it had its own entrance onto the back porch, whereas my bedroom opened directly into my mother's room and my playroom shared space with my mother's storage / laundry room in what remained of the Other Side. In any case, I staked a claim on the empty shed as my three season hangout. An old Shaker hutch left behind by the first owners of the house when my grandparents moved in and my mother's first kitchen table, enamel with slide-out leaves, had both been discarded by Ma in favor of more modern pieces, so I laid claim to those as well. The hutch made a great bookcase. I found a couple of odd chairs, one a rock-er, the other a rickety captain's chair that had been in the attic since my grandfather's death in 1949. Dad supplied paint: little sample cans of different colors that I splashed on the walls and wainscoting in designs meant to look groovy. In fact, just in case any of my guests missed the point, I painted the word "Groovy" in fat multi-colored letters, along with "Flower Power" and "Far Out." Ma helped me pick out and tack down linoleum to cover the old oiled wood floor, and gave me curtains from one of the attic trunks for the shed's two windows. The shed's ample floor space allowed plenty of room for sleepovers, and the separate entrance meant my friends and I could (and did) sneak out for many a moonlight stroll to the Common while my father worked and my mother slept undisturbed in her room at the other end of the house. My old phonograph, portable unlike the stereo in my bedroom, made the trip back and forth from the playroom to my hangout, as did many of my records. The shed was where my friends and I tried to imitate the dance moves of Goldie Hawn, Jo Anne Worley, and Chelsea Brown on Laugh-In. No one objected to how loudly the music played or how hard we stomped on the floor. I could shut the double doors to the outside world and lock them from the inside.

The early summer Saturday that Amy and I spent practicing our moves to the blaring strains of The Surfaris' was still cool enough for both shed windows to be left open, as opposed to the very hot days when the windows were closed and shades drawn to keep the heat out. I wore denim cut-off short shorts, which we called "hot pants," and one of my many "poor boys," a loosely fitting, short sleeved, scoop-necked top of ribbed cotton. I preferred tops of a looser fit these days since my breasts had decided to increase another cup-size, and I was still not comfortable with my new, more adult looking figure.

Amy and I danced, flipping our long hair and shaking our hips, oblivious to anything but getting it right. During the school year, weekly dances were held in The Town House, open to kids in Junior High and older, and we wanted to be ready by fall. Over and over, one of us lifted the stylus to replay "Wipe-Out" or "Tequila," unaware of the presence lurking outside at the windows. When I heard the knock on the door, I was more annoyed at being interrupted than anything else.

My mother's older sister Ruth and her husband Chuck had arrived from New Hampshire for a visit, and now Chuck stood in the doorway of my hangout wanting to know why I hadn't come into the house to say hello.

"Sorry. I didn't hear you. We were dancing." I said.

"I know. I was watching you girls from outside." He gestured toward the window.

I could feel myself blush. How long had he been watching? My Aunt Ruth was ten years older than my mother and Chuck was even older than that. He had to be in his sixties; why would he be interested in watching us dance?

"You girls dance well. Don't let me interrupt. I just wanted to say hi." He stepped forward to greet me with a hug and a kiss, the way all my relatives greet me and each other. Wait, did he just lick his lips? The kiss happened so fast that I'm sure no one seeing would have suspected the wet open mouth that descended on my own. I quickly pulled away but said nothing.

Uncle Chuck sat down in my grandfather's captain's chair, clearly prepared to stay for a while.

"Go ahead, dance. Just pretend I'm not here."

No longer interested in dancing but not wanting to be rude, I looked at Amy and wondered what to do. Hesitating only a moment, she headed over to the record player, placed the stylus onto the 33, and began to dance. I played along but my moves were self-conscious and awkward, and I made sure that my body was turned slightly away from the captain's chair. Only once through the song, I decided I'd had enough.

"I don't want to dance anymore," I announced and turned off the record player. Chuck looked disappointed. I looked at Amy. "Let's go outside."

The next couple of times my aunt and uncle visited, I managed to avoid any physical contact by waiting until they were both already seated before walking in to say hello. The more I thought about the kiss, the more I rationalized that I was being paranoid. Chuck was my uncle, after all, and he was known to be a kidder and practical joker. At worst, he was only annoying, like the way he would come up from behind and try to surprise the unaware with a quick jab to the side while saying a sound like "brrrrt!" Or the time he put a lock on our telephone dial, undiscovered until after he and my aunt had already gone. My father had to go to a neighbor's house to call his brother-in-law and, even though the hour was late, Dad demanded his immediate return to remove the device. My parents argued that night, and I overheard my father object to more than Chuck's jokes.

"I don't like the way he pulls you down into his lap," my dad said, "Why do you let him do that?"

"He doesn't mean anything by it," Ma answered. "He's just kidding around."

It became clear to me that night that my father really didn't like Chuck, but even so, I told myself that he was harmless.

Every summer, from as far back as I can remember, I spent a couple of weeks with Aunt Ruth and Uncle Chuck. I loved their apartment in the three-decker house in Cambridge right next door to a house where two girls roughly my age lived. Sharon and Sheila and I spent many hours playing on their porch or in their yard during the day while my aunt and uncle worked and my much older cousins, Francis and Richard, alternated keeping an eye out for me. On rainy days or when the girls next door weren't home, Francis entertained me by playing records, telling me stories, or getting right down on the floor with me to play with Matchbox cars. When my aunt wasn't working, she and I would walk to the trolley station and then take the subway into Boston, where we made our annual visit to the Public Gardens and their Swan Boats, Revere Beach, or the toy department in the biggest Jordan Marsh store I had ever seen, where I could pick out my birthday present.

By the summer of 1972, however, Aunt Ruth had retired, and though Chuck still worked part time as a school bus driver, the apartment in Cambridge had been exchanged for a mobile home in a retirement community in Salem, New Hampshire. No children my age lived anywhere near the park, there was no public transportation to take us to the beach or anywhere other than restaurants and shopping malls, and my aunt had never learned to drive. The prospect of spending two weeks in a retirement village held little appeal to a twelve year old, but I could see no gracious way of getting out of the two-week summer tradition. I brought Gone with the Wind with me and decided to make the best of the situation.

Only a day or two passed before I discovered the paperback book, casually left out on the nightstand in the master bedroom. Already bored, I spent some of my time trying to win over the two Siamese cats, Kim and Torah, who were not as fearsome as they'd been in their prime and who liked to curl up on Ruth and Chuck's bed during the afternoons. The book caught my eye because only the newspaper, *Yankee* magazine, and my aunt's craft books ever lay about the house; any other reading material I'd ever seen there was stacked on bookcases in Richard's room (and had boring titles like *Flowers of New England*) or was lined up in a small bookcase that had glass doors behind which lived mostly encyclopedias. I had never seen either my aunt or uncle actually read a book.

I picked up the paperback, and immediately put it down as if I'd touched something unclean. On the cover, a naked, grinning, heavily made-up black woman appeared to be dancing, her arms raised, her hands in her hair, her breasts adorned with what looked like glittery stars – one over each nipple. Behind her, a naked blonde woman on her hands and knees looked back over her shoulder. The dark-skinned man who sat between them looked like a business man in a button-down shirt and tie. I knew that *Cajun Sex Club* could not be something my aunt had chosen to read, and I felt almost sick with disgust.

However, for some reason I couldn't understand, I also felt drawn to the book. The cats provided the perfect cover for my being in the bedroom, and I found myself leafing through the pages, skipping over the gangster parts to read and reread some of the other scenes. I didn't understand all of the words I read; I remember having to look up "ejaculate" to find out what one of the men had done after the woman he was with had "taken him in her mouth" and later vomited when he wasn't looking. *I* nearly vomited when I figured it out. I went back to that part in the book several times, until I could recite the scene in my head almost word for word.

My morbid curiosity turned me into a thief, stealing any spare moment (while my aunt baked or cleaned and Chuck tinkered around the yard) to return to the goings on at the "sex club." Each time I heard someone coming, I carefully replaced the book the same way I'd found it so as not to be detected as having snooped. I burned with shame at my duplicity, but I could not seem to leave the book alone. After the second or third day of my discovery though, the book slipped through my hands and fell down behind the heavy nightstand. I had no time to fish it out, and when I returned the next morning the book was nowhere to be seen. No one ever said anything to me about it, but I had already started making a list of things to tell Amy when I got back home.

Topping the list were the sounds I heard nearly every night from the master bedroom. Francis now lived in a house of his own, and Richard had taken a two-week vacation somewhere, so I'd been assigned Richard's room during my stay, but even though a small bathroom separated the two bedrooms, the mobile home's paper thin walls kept no secrets. I went to bed first, so perhaps they assumed I slept through it, but shortly after Ruth and Chuck got into their bed, my aunt would start giggling. The first night, I rolled my eyes at Richard's ceiling, figuring Chuck was tickling her. Then I heard her playfully scolding "Oh, Chuck!" in the tone she sometimes used when he told a slightly off-color joke, followed by his snickering that sounded just. . . wrong and threatened to disturb the contents of my stomach. Artie Johnson snickered like that when he played the dirty old man to Ruth Buzzi's scandalized prissy old lady on *Laugh-In*. Make it stop, I asked the ceiling. I wished Aunt Ruth would whack Chuck the way Buzzi's character always whacked Johnson over the head with her purse. Of course, the giggling and snickering did stop, replaced by the sound of mattress springs and heavy breathing. Oh my God, *they still did it*.

At twelve years old, I hadn't yet made up my mind whether sex was something dirty or not, but I had decided that, regardless, "doing the deed" was reserved only for young and good looking people who were

not related to me. Obviously my mere existence indicated that, once anyway, my parents had had sex, but I found even the thought of it distaste-
ful and appreciated the fact that they now slept in separate rooms, the only sign of any physical affection between them being the customary hello
or goodbye peck. Now, here were my aunt and uncle, old people who had
been married to each other over fifty years, evidently still doing things I
could only imagine after reading about them in Chuck's paperback. I
dreaded bedtime. I tried plugging my ears with my fingers, but I could
still hear the giggling and the snickering and the "Oh, Chuck!" followed
by the springs and the heavy breathing.

Yet, despite my revulsion, part of me felt as if I missed out on
something. All too aware of the frequent stirrings in my own body and
the vague PG-rated fantasies that dominated my consciousness (many of
them involving Mr. Leach, my handsome former sixth grade teacher), I
struggled to reconcile my recently acquired sexual knowledge as an ab-
stract concept with the realization that these acts existed in reality, had
existed between Amy and her father, and were being carried out right
down the hall in my aunt's bedroom. Sex was not the make-believe of
television or storybooks; real people did these things. I began to wonder
if every older person I knew was "doing it," and doubted if I could look
at anyone in the same way ever again. I felt ashamed for them and embarrassed at my revelation, yet, simultaneously, I resented being an out-
sider barred from an exclusive club to which everyone but me seemed to
belong.

I spent most of my time in Salem reading on Richard's bed, making small talk with my aunt, and avoiding being alone with my uncle.
Although, prior to my visit, I had half convinced myself that his kiss that
day in the shed had been blown out of proportion in my mind, I still kept
my distance whenever I could, accompanying my aunt even when she
just walked across the street to the grocery store, so I would not risk being caught alone with Chuck. After having discovered his paperback, I
became more determined than ever not to be alone with him. However,
one afternoon about ten days into my two week visit, my aunt announced

she would be spending an hour or so with one of the other residents in the park, and I could think of no plausible excuse to go with her. A peek through the window assured me of Chuck's whereabouts in their shed, so I went into the master bedroom to visit the two Siamese - for real now that the paperback had disappeared.

I didn't hear the footsteps, but when I looked up from where I sat, Indian-style on the middle of the bed, Chuck was standing in the doorway watching me. I looked back down at Kim and Torah and continued patting their sleeping bodies, ignoring my uncle but all too aware of his approach toward the bed.

"You know," he began, leaning toward me over the footboard, "You owe me something."

Already uncomfortable with his proximity, I faked nonchalance. "What?"

"For the last few visits, you have not kissed me hello. I've been keeping track, and you owe me quite a few." He leaned in farther.

I felt trapped, caught in my plan to avoid his kiss. I could feel my muscles tense and my stomach knot as I tried to think of a way out of what I saw coming.

"I don't know what you're talking about," I tried, knowing how lame it sounded, but unable to summon any indignation in my tone. I had been raised to respect the authority of my elders.

"Sure you do," Chuck said, his voice soft, "and now's the time to pay up."

I didn't even resist. How bad could it be? As his face came closer to mine, I simply shut my eyes pretending I was somewhere else. When his wet lips touched mine, I felt my stomach turn, but as his tongue slithered between my lips and probed around in my mouth, I truly thought I would vomit. Thinking about other things or imagining being somewhere else did not work for me. I was completely stuck in this moment that seemed to last forever. I could taste the Canada Mints that he always sucked on, and feel his toothless gums up against my lips as his tongue continued its assault. When Chuck finally pulled away, I realized I'd been holding my breath. Not wanting to ingest his saliva, I had to force myself to swallow. I looked at the light blue chenille bedspread, trying to lose myself in its pattern.

"One," he said.

I don't remember how many kisses I had to endure that afternoon because somewhere along the way my mind went numb. At least until the moment he finally pulled away and stood up to speak. His first words brought me back to reality but threw me entirely off guard because I thought conversation meant escape.

"I've wanted to ask you about something. Remember that day you and your friend were dancing in the shed?"

I only nodded and edged farther back from the footboard.

"Why did you stop?"

I shrugged, straining to hear any sound that might signal the approach of my aunt.

"You can tell me," Chuck persisted.

No, I couldn't. I felt my face flush in embarrassment. Why wouldn't he just leave me alone?

"Was it because you had your period?"

"No." I spoke quickly and shook my head, wanting the questioning to end. How could I explain that even though I'd turned my body away from him that day, I'd been ashamed of the jiggling of my breasts as I danced? I hated bras, which either rode up or dug in, but I had enough of a figure, even at twelve, that I had to wear them, so I had two sets: one style that offered more support for when I would be "seen" and another style that I wore only when I hung around the house. That particular day in the shed, I'd worn one of my more comfortable bras, so despite the loosely fitting shirt, I'd been self-conscious dancing in front of Chuck, who, it now became clear, would not be put off.

Finally, I took a deep breath and spoke in a rush.

"I was embarrassed because I was wearing an old bra." Now would it end?

"Oh." A pause. Then, "You have trouble with them?"

Oh God. "With what?" Bras? Let him mean bras.

"Them," and he gestured toward my breasts, just as Mr. Hart had, roughly three years earlier.

I had no answer. I still had not looked at his face but continued to stare down at the bedspread. Out of the corner of my eye, I saw his hand, still outstretched from his gesture, now motionless and only inches away from my body. I shrunk back, wordless.

"Can I see 'em?" he asked, his voice even softer. "It's okay, you can show me."

I shook my head and shrunk back even farther.

Chuck must have sensed the panic I felt at that moment, or maybe some inkling of common sense took over because he pulled back his hand and straightened up. I heard the different tone in his voice when he spoke again.

"Do you always tell your mother everything?"

I don't remember whether I shrugged, shook my head, or nodded, but his response was, "Well, you don't have to tell her about this."

When he turned to leave, I started to shake and gulped big mouthfuls of air. My heart pounded wildly, and I fought against dizziness as adrenaline coursed through my body.

Chuck was outside when Aunt Ruth returned from the neighbor's. As soon as she was settled, I asked if I could call home. My mother answered the phone. I made small talk, trying to keep my voice neutral, until Aunt Ruth left the room. Then my words spilled out.

"Ma, I want to come home. Can you come get me?"

"Why? What happened?" My mother sounded concerned but there was also something else, something sharper behind her words.

"I just want to come home. But I feel bad telling Aunt Ruth," I whispered into the phone.

"Put my sister on," Ma said.

I shadowed my aunt for the rest of the day, and the following morning she and Chuck drove me back to North Brookfield. Homesickness had been the excuse my mother had given for the abrupt end to the vacation that would be my last with them. Aunt Ruth never questioned it.

As soon as their car backed out of the driveway, Ma asked for an explanation. I told her everything. Well, almost everything. I left out the part about the paperback book, and I didn't see much point in clueing her in on the fact that her older sister was still having sex on a regular basis. Those stories could wait for Amy. But I left no details out of my encounter with Chuck in the bedroom, and I also filled Ma in on the afternoon in the shed while I was at it. She silently listened until I finished. I waited for a reaction, but I was unprepared for what she said

"I was wondering when something like that would happen."

I stared at her. "What do you mean?"

"I figured he'd try something like this, but I thought you'd be a little older."

"*What do you mean?*" I asked again. I felt anger and resentment building. If Ma had somehow seen this coming, how could she have let me stay there with them, with him?

Ma sighed. Then she told me about how one day not long after she had married her first husband, Johnny, Chuck had come to town alone to see her. Though he hadn't touched her, he had propositioned her in her own kitchen over coffee. "We could keep it in the family," he'd said. Newly married and in her late teens, my mother had not been shy in telling off her brother-in-law.

"I told him if he ever tried anything, I'd tell my sister," Ma said. "I never told Johnny."

I thought of all the times I'd seen Chuck pull her into his lap. I also thought of the argument between my parents the night Chuck put the lock on our phone.

"Does Dad know?"

"No." My mother's tone was sharp. "And don't you tell him about any of this."

"We're not going to tell Dad?" I looked at her, aghast. I wanted retribution.

"If your father knew about this, he'd kill Chuck. I'd never see my sister again."

I couldn't make sense out of her logic. I remembered how calm Dad had been the night Ma had told him about Amy, but then again that had been someone else's daughter.

"I know how he'd react," Ma said. "It's happened before. With Karen."

I listened in amazement as my mother told me how my half sister had been molested when she was just a child. As Ma remembered the story, the abuser had been an uncle on Karen's mother's side of the family. In any case, Flo, my father's first wife, had seen Karen either getting into or out of the bathtub, marks the size and shape of fingerprints on her not yet developed breasts. Flo had called my father into the bathroom, and, between the two of them, they got the truth out of their daughter. Apparently Dad reacted by beating up the uncle (who had been staying with them) and then literally pitching him out the front door.

"I will handle this," Ma said now, her tone firm. "You don't have to worry. I'll make sure it doesn't happen again."

The next time the Vernons came to our house, my mother discreetly handed Chuck a slip of paper. He took it into the bathroom. When he came out, his ears were red, but he never said a word. As far as Ma was concerned, the problem had been taken care of.

The next time we went to New Hampshire, I arranged for Amy to come too. I could make myself scarce in my own house, but keeping a low profile in the mobile home would be difficult. I wanted to be invisible, but the next best thing would be to have the moral support of the only person (apart from my mother) who knew what had happened between me and my uncle: Amy. While my mother acted as if everything was just as it had always been, Amy remained glued to my side during the entire visit, even accompanying me into the bathroom. In retrospect, I realize how selfish I was to draw her into my drama as my confidante and protector, considering what she had gone through, but at the time she was the only one I could talk to about my anger and humiliation. I could see that my mother expected me to behave normally, to pretend, just as she was pretending, but I felt awkward and wounded. Although I did not want my aunt to be hurt, a large part of me wanted my father to know what had happened because I knew he would fight for me. I wanted someone to fight for me.

Amy and I were in the bathroom practicing with eye liner when Chuck knocked on the door and walked in.

"What's going on with you girls?" he asked.

"What?" I said, more of a challenge than a question. Amy's presence gave me courage. In my head, I dared him to make a move.

"You girls have been avoiding me like the plague."

Was he serious? Did he expect otherwise? Did he really think that I'd just forget all about that afternoon in the bedroom? I wanted to scream at him, yell for my father, have it all out in the open here and now. I said nothing. I ignored him until he walked away.

As things turned out, I would never feel avenged because I never confronted Chuck. Even as an adult, I would be standoffish with him, but I never had my say, except in the occasional dream in which I railed at him for his abuse of my trust. In reality, however, I never demanded an apology from him, so I never got one.

I never told my father either, and though I initially felt resentment for being forced to keep quiet, when I accidentally discovered his stash of paperbacks (all with illustrations of naked women on their covers) stacked in a box on the floor of the living room closet, I lost my initiative. Maybe my mother was right after all when she said that all men are alike.

Meanwhile, despite our confidences, my friendship with Amy began to deteriorate. Once Junior High School started, we found ourselves developing separate interests and new relationships. Beyond that, though, Amy expressed an interest in me that crossed the line into something that I found unappealing and a little frightening. The Halloween night that I threw a party in our garage and invited all of my female friends (boys were as yet unchartered territory), I can't swear that it was Amy who initiated the kissing contest. I'm not even sure how we ended up as partners, whether by choice or default. I do know that we won the contest. Certainly the kiss was chaste; both our mouths were closed and dry, and at the time, I thought nothing of it since everyone present participated. Nor did I suspect anything unusual about our role playing, when Amy and I devised dating scenarios as practice for the real thing later on. Playacting, that's all. At least, on my end. By this time, my brain overflowed with fantasies so real that I could easily supplant Amy with Bobby Sherman or David Selby. I became the innocent yet smitten young girl looking for a husband in the Seattle wilderness or destined to marry the heir to the Collins' fortune. My verbal overtures and responses addressed "Jeremy Bolt" or "Quentin Collins," not Amy Rose. And since we had no one to teach us how to slow dance, we practiced with each other, and as we turned and swayed, I imagined myself in the arms of a dashing young man, perhaps "Nick Barclay" from *The Big Valley*, who hoped to win my heart.

Perhaps the innocent pretense gave Amy the wrong idea, or perhaps she was just experimenting, as I was, but in a different way, but the first real fracture in our friendship occurred one afternoon as we both sat talking at the kitchen table, our chairs just inches from each other. I leaned over to pick up something that had fallen to the floor, a pen or slip of paper, and as I did, Amy reached down to cup my breast. I jerked back up, startled, and just stared at her. She stared back.

Then she said, "That's how I am. Now you know."

When I did not respond, she said, "Do you still want to be my friend?"

"Yes," I said and meant it, "but don't ever do that again."

Amy and I never spoke of that incident, but something changed between us. The pretending and dancing stopped as if by mutual agreement. For a while, we still walked to and from school together, but we also both branched out into friendships apart from each other. Amy started running with a rougher crowd from out of town, and the incidents of her acting out in school became more frequent. She became belligerent to the teachers and administrators and once was even suspended. As time passed, we saw far less of each other. Before we finished high school, Amy and her family had moved out of North Brookfield. There were no teary goodbyes. There were no goodbyes at all. Amy was just . . . gone.

THE OLD CROW TAKES FLIGHT AND HEADS UP NORTH COMMON STREET INTO THE HEART OF LITTLE CANADA, AN AREA OF TOWN ONCE INHABITED PRIMARILY BY FRENCH-CANADIAN IMMIGRANTS AND THEIR FAMILIES. IN THIS SECTION OF TOWN LIVED THE FACTORY WORKERS AND THE MERCHANTS WHO RAN BUSINESSES OUT OF THEIR HOMES; THEREFORE, MOST OF THE HOUSES WERE CONSTRUCTED AS TWO-FAMILIES, OFTEN WITH ANOTHER POR-TION DESIGNED FOR THE MERCHANT'S USE. IN A NEIGHBORHOOD THAT ONCE BOASTED A BAK-ERY, A GROCERY, A BAR, AND A DRY GOODS STORE, ONLY THE BAR – HART'S CAFE (RENAMED "STILL HART'S CAFE") - HAS SURVIVED.

AS THE CROW PASSES OVER THE STOP SIGN AT THE INTERSECTION OF NORTH COM-MON AND FOREST STREETS, SOMETHING TO HER LEFT CATCHES HER EYE, SOMETHING OUT OF PLACE THAT WASN'T THERE THE DAY BEFORE. A LARGE YELLOW TRUCK WITH A RAMP EX-TENDING FROM ITS REAR IS PARKED DIAGONALLY ACROSS THE DRIVEWAY OF ONE OF THE COR-NER HOUSES, THE ONE WITH THE RECONSTRUCTED FARMER'S PORCH. THE YELLOW TRUCK HAS DISPLACED THE SMALL DARK GREEN SUV USUALLY PARKED THERE THAT IS NOW OFF TO THE SIDE. THE OLD CROW HAS SEEN OTHER TRUCKS SIMILAR TO THIS ONE, PARKED IN OTHER DRIVEWAYS, ESPECIALLY OVER RECENT MONTHS. SHE PERCHES ON A TELEPHONE WIRE AND GAZES DOWN AT THE HOUSE, COCKING HER HEAD. SHE IS FAMILIAR WITH THIS HOUSE BE-CAUSE A FEW YEARS BACK, THE ELDERLY WOMAN WHO LIVED THERE ALONE WOULD THROW SCRAPS OF BREAD INTO THE SIDE YARD EVERY MORNING AND TAP AN ALUMINUM PIE PLATE TO CALL THE SMALLER BIRDS: THE ROBINS, CHICKADEES, AND BLUE JAYS. OCCASIONALLY, THE PAIR OF MOURNING DOVES THAT LIKED TO COO ON THE GARAGE ROOF WOULD ALSO SWOOP DOWN FOR FOOD. THE CROW, HOWEVER, SOMEHOW KNEW THAT THE BREAD WAS NOT PUT OUT FOR HER KIND, SO SHE WOULD WAIT UNTIL THE OTHERS HAD EATEN AND GONE AND THEN TAKE WHATEVER REMAINED.

ONE DAY, THERE WAS NO BREAD. (THE HOUSE'S OWNER, DAUGHTER OF ANNIE KEL-LEY, HAD DIED.) THE HOUSE STOOD EMPTY FOR OVER A YEAR, AND AFTER A WHILE, THE SMALLER BIRDS STOPPED COMING AROUND. THEN ANOTHER FAMILY MOVED IN BUT DID NOT PUT BREAD OUT. HOWEVER THE CROW STILL STOPPED BY EVERY MORNING AS WAS HER HABIT. OVER THE NEXT FEW YEARS, SHE CONTINUED TO KEEP A KEEN EYE ON THIS PARTICU-LAR HOUSE (NOW OWNED BY ANNIE'S GRANDDAUGHTER), SO SHE NOTICED WHEN A LARGE SIGN APPEARED OUT FRONT A FEW MONTHS AGO, A SIGN SIMILAR TO THE OTHERS SHE'D RECENTLY SEEN IN FRONT OF OTHER HOUSES, SOME OF THEM LONG EMPTY.

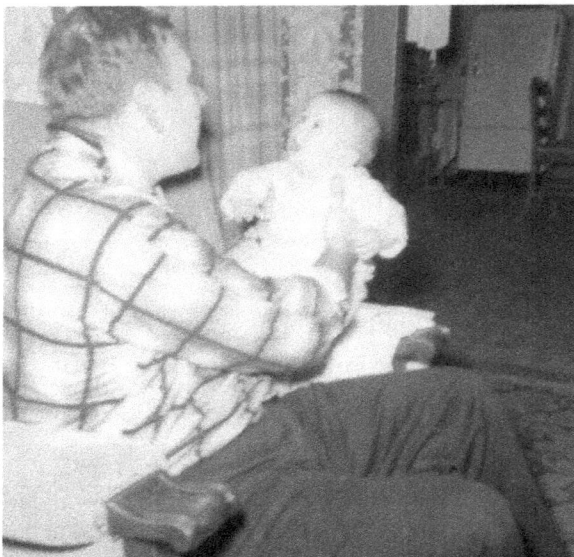

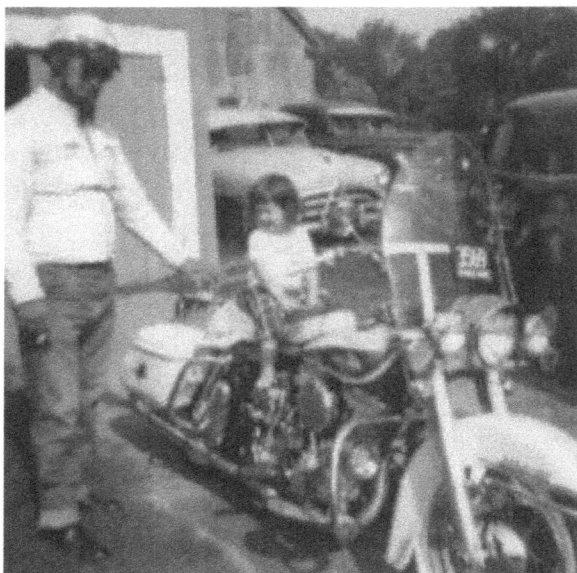

11
The Most Important Thing in the World

The baritone voice calling my name brought me scurrying from the playroom. Daddy had settled into his scarred mustard-yellow recliner, which was torn and pock-marked by ciga-rette burns. His feet were already propped up on the footrest and waiting for me. He lit a cigarette and pulled closer the glass ash-tray in its metal stand as my small fingers pulled the shoestrings of first one then the other of his black wingtips. I carefully loos-ened the laces so I could slip the heavy shoes off of his sore feet but paused, trans-

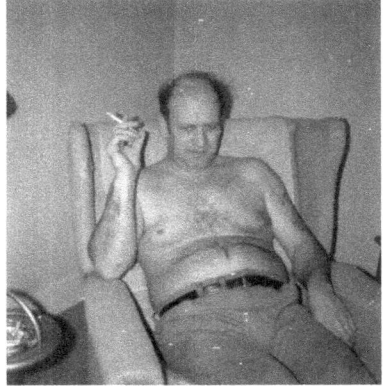

fixed, when he exhaled a perfect smoke ring toward the ceiling. "Do it again," I urged, but he smiled and motioned with his foot. I obediently slipped off his shoes, carefully lining them up next to the recliner (as I'd been taught) and climbed over the footrest into his lap. Smoke rings of all sizes soon drifted around us, and I reached out to stab at the closest ones before they got away. Somewhere between puffs, I asked him to "open wide," so I could gaze for a moment at the gold molar that never lost its fascination for me. When the cigarette became too short to hold and had joined the other discards in the littered ashtray, I nestled closer and won-dered what would come next today.

Sometimes he told me stories of skip-ping school, of shooting marbles or rolling dice in back alleys, or playing pranks on neighbors by shifting their unlocked Packards and Deso-tos into neutral to be rolled down the steep streets of Spencer, where he'd grown up. Per-haps I'd be treated to a tale of his Navy days, and I would reverently touch the tattooed dag-

ger on his forearm or the anchor on his bicep while he described the sea spray that pounded Destroyer 474 as thunderclouds rolled over the Pacif-

ic and squid and hammerhead sharks glided by. If my mother happened to overhear, she would shake her head at his exaggerations: "Buck, why do you lie to her?" but her words were usually ignored. If I was really lucky, he sang to me, Maurice Chevalier whose accent he could easily imitate: "Thank Heaven…for little girls…" Whatever tale he told or song he sang would predictably be followed by the same question to me: "What's the most important thing in the world?" I knew the answer but always played along. "Money?" I asked, giggling. "Noooo…," he always shook his head in mock severity. "Ummmm…" I stalled, not wanting the game to end, "jewelry?" "Noooo…" he growled. Then, together, we shouted the right answer: "LOVIN'"

A few years later, when I turned nine, I joined the Girl Scouts, bras replaced my white cotton undershirts, and my father moved out of the master bedroom. A rollaway bed and odd nightstand that Pepere had in his attic appeared one day in the Other Side, the storage room that ran almost the length of the house where my maternal grandmother, Annie, once operated her dry goods store. By this time, Dad had already partitioned off his shed, and the remainder of the space was being used as a combination of my playroom and a laundry/storage area for my mother. However, upon seeing the rollaway bed in there, clearly not being stored but already made up with sheets, pillow and one of Memere's patchwork quilts, I stopped short, the fate of yesterday's victim of Barnabus Collins no longer the dominant thought it had been just seconds before when I'd raced home from school and once again (despite repeated warnings) hurriedly dumped my school books on the antique dining room table. The television show abruptly forgotten, I sought out my mother for an explanation. The snoring, she claimed, had finally gotten to her and no amount of whining or complaining from me would change the result: Dad's "bedroom" would be smack in the middle of the Other Side, virtually dividing the room into thirds with my playroom on one end and the now smaller storage area on the other.

My fear of intrusion into my private playroom life proved to be unfounded – at least until a year or so later when my father quit his underpaid job as Mr. Krock's chauffeur to work second shift in a steel manufacturing plant (and even then, I suffered only during the mornings of the summer months when his right to sleep superseded my right to play). On the weekends, he still rose fairly early, so I was not inconvenienced by his proximity to my turf, and I noticed very little change in the overall behavior of my parents toward each other. They frequently and often vigorously disagreed, but they always had. The yelling, door slamming, and table pounding (as well as the long, angry silences that followed) had all been just as much a part of my childhood as their exchanged hello or goodbye kisses. Apart from the discomfort I experienced when they argued, their volatile relationship did not directly affect me since I felt relatively secure in their love and neither had yet asked me to choose sides. That would come later.

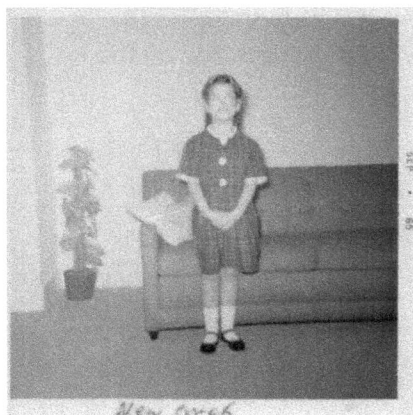

New couch

One particularly memorable argument from my early childhood, even before my father's banishment from the master bedroom, began after the delivery of the new couch. The living room walls had just that week been painted a pale tangerine, with cream trim and white swirly ceiling. Beige wall-to-wall had been installed and clear plastic mats put down on the anticipated heavy traffic pathways. As I recall, I impulsively requested permission to "camp out" on the burnt orange couch, anticipating the adventure of spending the night in a room other than my own boring bedroom. For some reason never made clear to me, my father challenged my request by staking his own claim on the couch's first night in our home. I cried foul, something to the effect that I had "called it" first and that he wasn't being fair. I don't remember the details, but I know that my mother jumped in to take my side, whereupon Dad became stubborn, insisting that since he'd paid for the couch, he should be the first to try it out. As their voices grew in volume and intensity, I melted into the woodwork. Too young to realize that the fight extended far beyond who should sleep on the new couch, my only thought - as always when they really got going- was to be unobtrusive and tune out as much as possible. I now wonder if I somehow sensed that the day would come when I'd be forced to take sides and therefore stayed out of the way simply to postpone that no-win situation for as long as possible. This particular argument however, unlike most of the thousands of others I'd witnessed, rapidly escalated beyond any point of reason. An image that remains with me to this day is of my father backing towards the door, his eyes wide in anger and surprise, his hand raised to ward off my mother who was advancing on him while wielding one of the kitchen chairs over her head and screaming at him to get out - the only time, at least to my knowledge, that either one threatened physical violence to the other. Sometime during the night, as I fitfully dozed on the hard, uncomfortable couch cushions, regretting my request but determined to stick it out, I heard my father's quiet footsteps on the porch, in the hall, and then up the stairs.

My parents' new sleeping arrangement actually established a temporary sense of peace in the household, especially after Dad's job changed to second shift. The less time he and my mother spent together, the less they fought - a fact finally realized after several family vacations had turned ugly, resulting in mutually agreed upon separate vacations. Although I was not invited to accompany my father on his trips and saw him less often, I remained the equal fan of both of my parents. Ma and I shopped, baked, and talked, and talked, and, well actually, I talked while she mostly listened. Meanwhile, Dad still found time to entertain me with tales of his younger days, although I'd become too grown up to sit in his lap, and taught me air guitar before it was called air guitar, for which I displayed considerable raw talent and natural ability. From the living room stereo would twang the songs of Al Green, Ben Colder, or (Dad's favorite) Buck Owens and the Buckaroos. I knew all the words so when Dad, as Buck, sang from his recliner, I joined in to harmonize from one of the other chairs or from the floor as his sidekick, Roy Clark. If the song had a guitar solo, Dad would say "Take it away, Roy!" and I would pick or strum the part with great finesse and enthusiasm, Dad "yee ha-ing" his approval.

Once situated in his new job at the factory, Dad would still be sleeping when I left for school; he'd be leaving for work when I got home from school; and I'd be in bed when he returned from work, so except for school vacations and weekends, our encounters occurred mainly in passing. He'd always had his "nights out" before, when he'd play cards with the guys at Duke's, the bar from his old neighborhood about fifteen miles away; now because of the new work schedule, his nights out just shifted to the weekend nights. Perhaps because I was so caught up in my own riveting and demanding childhood world or perhaps because my mother remained such a large part of my life, it took me a while to notice the gradual and subtle shift in the family dynamic taking place right in front of me.

When I had the second largest part in the third grade play, for example, Dad still worked days, so not only were both my parents there to watch my performance as "the 2nd stewardess," but the next morning my father got up early and drove me to school in the stretch limousine, the way all famous, talented actresses traveled. As Mr. Krock's sleek, dark Cadillac pulled up to the playground, swings slowed, balls and bats dropped, and jump ropes ceased to twirl. My six foot tall, broad shouldered, handsome father stepped out from behind the wheel in full uniform and walked to the very back of the limo to open my door. Enjoying this part even more than the one of the previous night, I regally offered my hand, to be helped down from my seat. I demurely nodded my thanks, he tipped his hat, and, wrapped in my new plush coat of midnight blue that exactly matched the velvety carpet in the Caddy, I sedately made my way toward the bulging eyes and open mouths of my school-mates. The following year, when I played "Marcia from Russia" in the fourth grade play, however, Dad was working at the shop, but since my mother made such a fuss over my success, even allowing me a sleepover with my best friend, Andrea, his absence that night was of no great consequence to me.

As the months passed, I became only peripherally aware that Dad spent less and less time at home. On weekends, instead of accomplishing household chores or puttering in his workshop as he had during my early childhood, he seemed to find more frequent excuses to be elsewhere, usually at Duke's or helping one of his friends – George, Benny, Don or Chill - with some task of theirs, having apparently lost interest in most of his own, especially once his summer-long project of constructing a new garage had been completed. If I had paid more attention, I might have sooner noticed that my parents' arguments had begun to cover additional ground: the unfinished and neglected maintenance and repairs that Ma now had to hire outsiders to handle, as well as her new-found suspicions about where and how he was spending so much of his time for instance, instead of just finances and his compulsive gambling. Sometimes Dad called from somewhere to say he'd run into an old friend or that he had lost at cards and wanted a chance to win back his money. Gambling had always been an issue for him, so hours-long pinochle games at Duke's seemed plausible. On occasion, I answered the phone, and I could hear the raucous bar sounds in the background - the half drunk voices, the clinking glasses, the jukebox, the laughter. Some nights, he'd be very late; I'd fall asleep hearing my mother pace in her bedroom, which adjoined mine. The mornings that followed those nights were the quietest, with a silence that could last for days. Occasionally, though, he wouldn't appear until daylight, explaining that he'd been so tired (and perhaps a little drunk) that he'd spent the night at a buddy's or on a cot in the bar's back room. I kept a low profile on those days to avoid being caught in the crossfire of their anger and sleeplessness.

Eventually, unless there was a specific family activity that required his presence; such as a birthday, holiday dinner, or trip to visit a

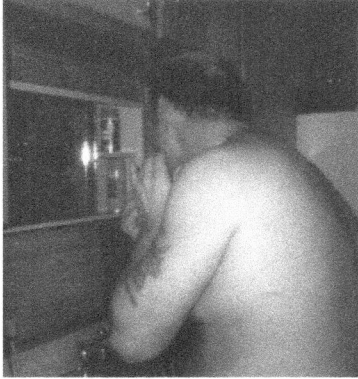

relative; Dad's "nights out" morphed into entire weekends out, and even I noticed that his preparations before leaving the house had become more extensive. After he showered, he took exceptional care in shaving and applying cologne, slicking back and combing his thinning hair, and choosing just the right outfit. I often plunked myself down to watch him get ready to leave on Saturday mornings after he'd made the two of us breakfast, deeply inhaling the scents of

Irish Spring, Old Spice and Vitalis while he happily sang or whistled. Sometimes my opinion on which shirt matched which slacks was requested, and I readily obliged, thrilled by even this crumb of attention, so seldom did I see him by this point. My mother, having just awakened, might pass through and, if so, she would question why a nearly fifty year old mar-

ried man cared so much about his appearance only to spend a weekend playing cards and hanging around with his buddies. Only kidding, I thought, because Dad kidded back that the ladies at Duke's appreciated a good smelling guy. If she then got angry, he'd say of course he was just teasing; then he would quickly kiss her and be out the door like a kid headed to the carnival, careful not to provoke an argument that might delay his departure and reminding her that he could always be found if she needed him. Certainly, his assurances appeared to be true the day Ma smelled the gas leak.

     I was playing in the back yard when I heard my name called from the house. When I was ushered into the Other Side, I agreed that there was a distinct whiff of natural gas in the air. Since it was fairly late on a Saturday afternoon, Ma doubted that the gas company could be reached and decided the situation should be handled by the man of the house. The call to Duke's was answered by Duke himself who indicated that, yes, Buck had been playing cards there all afternoon but had just stepped into the men's room. As soon as he emerged, he would be informed of the urgent need for his return home. After nearly half an hour had elapsed and Dad's car had not appeared nor had the phone rung, Ma called a neighbor from across the street to see if he might know where to find the shut-off. As Andy rooted around in the shrubbery at the house's foundation, Dad pulled into the driveway. A mixture of relief and irritation replaced the fury in my mother's eyes as Dad explained that Duke hadn't immediately seen him exit the bathroom.

As far as I was concerned, Dad had vindicated himself: he had in fact been where he said he would be and though I had already come to realize (even if it hadn't recently been implied by my mother) that he fell far short in his role of the ideal husband, I wondered if perhaps Ma's paranoia and tendency to overreact might be partially to blame for his preference to spending nearly every Saturday morning through Monday morning away from home. In time, the gas leak story would actually take on a humorous light and often be retold with a smirk by my mother since, as soon as Dad arrived home that day (and before he'd been told of Andy's assistance), he'd bolted into the Other Side and headed straight for a stack of tin pie plates, between two of which he had secretly hidden several fifty dollar bills. The punch line of the story was that Dad had rushed home to rescue not his wife and daughter but his secret stash of fifties.

As time went on, Ma seemed almost resigned to Dad's time away and began, I think, to develop a more fulfilling life of her own, free from the bitter arguing and his sometimes bullying jokes. More than once in his zeal to be the entertainment at a Saturday or Sunday occasion he'd sulked at being required by her to attend, Dad retaliated by making her the butt of his humor, persisting until her feelings were hurt and yet another argument sparked.

"I never saw anybody consistently dealt such poor cards," Dad might say, shaking his head. "The cards hate her. But of course, it would help if she could remember what cards were played…" And from there, he would animatedly relate a particular game of Canasta they had played as partners with another couple, during which Ma had apparently not followed his lead or made the right play or done whatever she was supposed to have done. Embellishments got more laughs.

For variety, he might discuss my mother's inability to circumnavigate the crater-sized potholes on Crompton Street in Worcester (where his parents had relocated): "Last time, she hit them all!" he would crow with a smirk, "I said, 'Poll, congratulations, you didn't miss a single one!'" whereupon followed details of which parts nearly fell off the car *that* time.

Later, alone in the car and continuing into the house, he would object to her pouting or tears and loudly accuse her of not being able to take a joke, and she always shrilly accused him of deliberately goading her into the argument so that he'd have an excuse to walk out, which, of course, he inevitably did - after the customary table pounding and cabinet door slamming. Having reached the age to realize the likelihood of overhearing words and accusations that I had no wish to overhear, I began to rely on the stereo upstairs in my bedroom as my escape and usually cranked up The Beatles or The Stones to drown out the drama below. In my room I could remain aloof and safe from involvement, or so I thought until the day I was called downstairs by my mother during an argument.

"Tell your daughter what you just called me!" my mother screamed after she led me to the living room doorway to face my father who sat smoking in his recliner.

I hung my head, wishing I could be anywhere else in the world. I couldn't look at either of my parents. I may have been only thirteen or fourteen at the time, but I was still old enough to know that this confrontation should not involve me.

My father refused to answer, even when my mother repeated her command, her voice slicing me in half. He shook his head and tried to wave us both away, but she would not be put off. I could feel the pain and anger rolling off of her as she stood there shaking, but somehow, at that moment, though I sensed that whatever he'd said crossed the line, my sympathy lay with him because I felt just as awkward as he looked. Finally he mumbled, "I said I was sorry," and I instantly forgave him.

"He called me an asshole!" my mother shrieked, far from being mollified. I had an insane and completely inappropriate urge to laugh. That was it? I had imagined much worse things. Worse, actually, than what he had said was the fact that I was standing there to hear it.

"Fine. Now she knows. Can she go back to her room now?" The back door slammed shut before I had even reached the top of the stairs. From that day on, when the fighting began, I quickly found things to do outside.

Christmas Eve had, for as far back as I can remember, meant gathering with all of Dad's side of the family to exchange presents, eat large quantities of food and play loud music. The festivities took place at Pepere and Memere's until Memere died Christmas Eve morning the winter Dad moved into the Other Side. That year the family gathered only for Mass and the funeral services. Over the months that followed, much discussion took place by phone as to whether and where to continue the family tradition, and it was finally agreed that, from that year on, since Memere's anniversary Mass would take place in Spencer, where she had raised her family, everyone would first meet at the French Catholic church and after Mass drive to Dad's cousin Jeanette's house, hers being the closest, to eat and open presents.

I took one last look at myself in the mirror, hating the glasses through which my severely near-sighted eyes stared back. I had already started hounding my parents for contact lenses, convinced that my popularity, not to mention my sex appeal, would soar once the gold frames disappeared for good. Other than that one flaw, I felt satisfied by my appearance: clingy red turtleneck sweater, short red plaid wool skirt and black knee length boots – very Christmas-y. Surely, my shorter, stouter cousin Monique, also fifteen, would be jealous.

Ma did not look happy when I got downstairs. "Your father still isn't here," she informed me, "but if we wait any longer, we'll be late for Mass."

At the church, Aunt Eleanor asked where Dad was and frowned her displeasure when Ma said she had no idea. "He said he had some errands to run, but that was this afternoon." My father's younger sister and my mother had developed a barely polite relationship that I could attribute only to the fact that Aunt Eleanor always said exactly what was on her mind regardless of whose feelings or sensibilities might be offended. Tonight, however, she had nothing further to say. Pepere gathered me into his customary bear hug, then patted my mother's shoulder. "He'll be here."

As we filed into the pew, I made sure to leave room on the end. My father finally arrived during the First Reading of the Liturgy, genuflected, and seated himself next to me. Immediately I smelled the alcohol and looked out of the corner of my eye to assess my mother's reaction. She remained impassive, staring up at the altar. Well, though unusual behavior for my father, consuming too much drink on Christmas Eve could be understandable and forgiven, couldn't it, especially on the anniversary of his mother's death? I hoped my mother would see it that way. I tried to concentrate on the Gospel.

"Wake your father up," Ma's voice hissed in my ear, startling me. Dad sat slumped in the pew, his eyes closed, his head drooping on his chest. I poked him in the ribs with my elbow in a way that I hoped would be discreet and unnoticeable to the other parishioners around us. Thank God Aunt Eleanor had chosen a pew closer to the front. Dad's head jerked up, but I could see that his eyes struggled to remain open. Had he had that much to drink? The night ahead loomed ominous.

During the sermon for his mother's anniversary Mass, my father not only slept but snored. Loudly. Such that I repeatedly and forcefully had to nudge him while the priest spoke, beyond caring what the nearby parishioners thought as they nudged each other, pointed and either snickered or shook their heads in disgust. On my right, Ma fumed in an embarrassment that I didn't even need to see to know existed; I could feel it matching my own. This fight promised to be a beaut.

In the parking lot, I lagged behind so I wouldn't hear whatever it was my parents had to say to each other, confident that at least their voices would remain low since Ma hated putting on a public show and was already mortified by Dad's behavior. Their encounter did not take long. Within minutes, Dad stormed to his car and careened out of the lot.

Aunt Eleanor reached my mother even before I could. "He's drunk," she spat out.

Ma, making an effort to keep her composure, did not reply.

"Where's he going?" Aunt Eleanor boomed.

Ma bit her lip and shrugged. Did I actually see a glimmer of sympathy in my large and imposing aunt's eyes before she turned away? I did not dance to rock oldies with Monique and my other cousins in Jeanette's basement that night. Ma and I went home and opened our presents alone.

The early spring Saturday afternoon our swimming pool collapsed, my father could not be located. Taking the railings into account, the massive redwood structure stood almost as high as our garage and had just begun its sixth year of use in our back yard, having seen me through one-piece summers into two-piece summers into, finally, bikini summers. The pool's purchase had been my mother's idea, paid for by several years' accumulation of tips from her full time job as a waitress. Dad had noticed some rot under the supposedly weather-treated deck, and arrangements had already been made for its repair even before its sixth annual Memorial weekend opening. Urgent enquiries into the company itself had led to our discovery of its recent bankruptcy; still, apart from the few visible suspect areas, the pool appeared to have several years of life left. Not so.

The unseasonably warm late May weather had prompted Ma to replace the back door's storm window with its screen, so as I entered the kitchen, I clearly heard the wrenching, splintering groan of tearing wood followed by the rushing gallons of water gushing out of the pool's just split corner seam. When I looked out toward the yard, I saw the crazy tilted angle at which the whole structure now leaned, and yelled for my mother as I flew out the door. Already the side yard was under water, and a river was snaking its way down the street along the sidewalk. The far corner of the pool, split from the railing to the ground, fanned out, revealing soft rotted wood at the inner seams. Right behind me, Ma began to cry, fretting not only about the pool but about our house's foundation and the fate of its dirt and bedrock cellar that had never before seen a wet day even during the heaviest rainstorm. With no way to control or divert the pool water's furious onslaught, there was nothing to do but go back into the house.

Once again faced with a household crisis without her spouse by her side, my nearly hysterical mother picked up the receiver and started dialing, first Duke's then one by one all of Dad's friends. No one had seen him. Relatives followed. Still no luck. Since Christmas, communication in our house had been strained and mostly through notes or through me. As Ma continued to search through the phonebook for more numbers to call, I could see that she'd made it her mission to track down her errant husband who had either disappeared or found new friends.

I never found out who eventually relayed the message to my father to come home. Looking sheepish and a little scared, he showed up late the next morning, long after the chlorinated water had emptied out of the pool and the fear of a flooded cellar had proved to be unwarranted. I had begun planting sweet pea seeds in the red metal planter by the back porch and ignored his subdued greeting as he passed. I tensed in anticipation of the hollering and banging I would surely hear from inside at any moment, but the house stayed oddly quiet. My heart beat faster as I repeatedly stuck my index finger into the dirt to make holes for the seeds. When Dad emerged from the house and walked over to me, I didn't look up.

"I'm sorry I scared you and your mother," he said softly. "That wasn't fair of me." He offered no explanation for his whereabouts, and I was trying too hard not to cry to ask for one, so I just nodded. Did he expect a hug? Part of me wanted to oblige, but this time, caught in his lies, he could not so easily be forgiven. After a few moments, he turned away, and I concentrated on the sweet peas.

I decided Mother's Day that year would be extra special, so instead of sneaking away from Ma during one of our many shopping trips and trying to smuggle some little thing or two into the car when she wasn't looking, I enlisted Dad's help. The two of us rarely spent any time alone together anymore, so I looked forward to the occasion. Having agonized over the perfect gift, lush yet affordable, I'd found my answer at the library. A terrarium, its plants hand chosen by me and lovingly arranged in a store-bought container, would show effort, creativity, and love without costing more than my allowance could handle. Its purchase required only one stop: the local nursery, so Dad's entire Saturday would not be eaten up by my errand. As we set out, it didn't even occur to me to wonder why my father didn't take this rare opportunity to treat me to lunch or even an ice cream along the way. Library book and shopping list in hand, my mind focused strictly on business.

For the container, I opted for large and plastic rather than small and glass. Pear-shaped and of a circumference such that, full, it could barely be carried by one person, the two-piece structure screwed apart (for planting and weeding) and funneled up to an opening with a dial-like lid, which could be adjusted to regulate air and moisture. Anticipating adequate light but only limited direct sunlight for my creation, I chose baby tears, spider plants, and ivy, with dracaena and coleus for color, and philodendron because of its hardiness and longevity. (The philodendron actually outlived all of the other plants and even years later, long after I'd graduated from college and gotten married, still thrived in the clear plastic container, having climbed its way out through the lid and latched onto a nearby window frame where it lay draped over the curtain rod.) A bag of terrarium gravel and two bags of potting soil mix completed my purchases.

At the last minute, just as we reached the cashier's counter, Dad

picked up a similar container about a third of the size of the one I'd chosen and asked if I thought I'd have enough plants left over to fill it. Scanning the nursery packs laid out in front of me, I thought I would but why?
While managing to avoid my eyes, Dad explained that he'd recently befriended a "very nice couple," the wife of which would certainly be
pleased to receive such a gift as thanks for kindness they'd extended to
him. I pressed for more details but got only vague answers, and I could
tell my father would shortly lose his patience with me if I persisted.

As I worked the rest of the afternoon, arranging and securing the
plants in their new home, I tossed over and over in my head Dad's sudden revelation about this mysterious "couple" in his life and couldn't
help but doubt its truth and innocence. The smaller container he'd
bought, already prepared with gravel and soil, sat off to the side, waiting
for its plants, but I'd already determined that it would receive only the
leftovers from my mother's arrangement, hers taking top priority.

The multi-colored coleus, being by far the most striking variety
I'd chosen, commanded center stage in Ma's terrarium: two specimens
tucked in with the other less vibrant greenery spread out around them.
One lone coleus remained unused in its cell pack. I looked over at the
smaller container and the other leftover plants, and a flush of resentment
heated my face and tightened my chest. No. There would be only green
plants in this second container.

Deliberately squeezing the third coleus in next to its planted pack-
mates, I rationalized that, after all, I'd not received any specific instructions regarding the layout of the other terrarium and, furthermore, had
paid for all the plants myself. This "wife," whoever she was, would never
know about the coleus anyway, and she should consider herself lucky to
get whatever she gets. Satisfied with my work (and my decision), I hid
Ma's terrarium upstairs until the next day and left out the smaller, much
less impressive but still nicely arranged terrarium for Dad to take with
him when he left later on.

I was in my bedroom, reading, when I heard Dad's sarcastic one-
liner called up from the bottom of the stairs a couple of hours later:

"Couldn't find it in your heart to put one of those pretty colored plants in there, could you?" I'd been waiting for it, knowing he wouldn't be able to let it go. Feeling mean but triumphant, I did not reply.

On Father's Day that year, I had a shirt I'd picked out for him boxed and wrapped in white paper with gold ribbon, card attached. Nothing had changed in the weeks since the pool's collapse except that the back yard now had only a large sand pad next to the garage instead of a sagging, broken redwood skeleton. All day Sunday, I hung around the house, waiting for Dad to show up to receive his gift and cut the cake I'd baked for him, but as the sun dropped in the sky, and I realized that, despite the holiday, he probably would not return home until Monday just in time to get ready for work, I angrily hid the box in an upstairs closet where it remained forgotten until several months later when I would accidentally find it and tearfully regret my decision. Ma and I each had a piece of cake with our dinner that night.

Monday afternoon, true to form, Dad walked in the door with barely enough time to change into his work clothes. I noticed a slight expectant smile on his face as he attempted a bit of small talk with me and felt a little of the resentment my mother had no doubt been experiencing over the last several years. Where had he been all day yesterday when he should have been home to celebrate his special day with his daughter? I spoke curtly and never mentioned the day, his gift, or the cut cake he'd no doubt noticed in the fridge, and I triumphed over the hurt expression in his eyes caused by my responses.

We were led into a small examination room, much too brightly lit for the middle of the night – Ma, Jay, and I. I entered first, and immediately looked around for my father. That's why we were here, to see him. The phone call had come not an hour before, the call that Ma had been dreading for years, one that would change both our lives. Ma had then called my half-brother, Jay, because she hadn't felt steady enough to drive. Or, perhaps she sensed she needed more emotional support than her sixteen year old daughter could give. It crossed my mind as we all stood there under the searing lights that it must be really bad if they had to prepare us first.

An "accident." But ironically not a car accident, despite the countless times Dad had fallen asleep at the wheel. Ordinarily he would be on his way home from the plant by 1:00 A.M., but this week Dad had requested more overtime to pay off some of his mounting gambling debts. I'd seen the area where he worked third shift as a steel burner and assistant foreman, but that steamy summer night when he'd shown me his station, I'd been more interested in the enormous mutant-like insects drawn in from the pitch black swamps through the lighted open doors and buzzing against the unpainted cement walls, their magnified winged shadows the size of bats as they swooped and swirled. The cranes and pulleys that hoisted the heavy pieces of steel from station to station to be cut or welded were for me mere backdrop to the insect antics, although the giant gas-fed torches had briefly held my interest as my father's as-bestos-gloved hands deftly guided their blue flames through the irregular cuts and patterns indicated on the blueprints in front of him. The torches, the heavy machinery, the massive slabs of steel - any of those could have turned against a man to send him to the emergency room.

Now as I stood with Ma and Jay, I tried to imagine the extent of my father's injuries and how much care would be required. No doubt there would be convalescence; would there be disability? I envisioned myself his care-giver, bringing extra pillows, spooning food into his mouth, seeing the love and approval I craved in his eyes. Simultaneously, however, I dreaded the prospect, remembering his recovery from a sim-ple tonsillectomy roughly two years earlier. Being out of school for sum-mer vacation, I'd fully expected to prepare his lunches while Ma worked, but I had not anticipated repeatedly being called away from my books and stereo to fetch slippers or cigarettes or to change the television chan-nel with never a thank you in return. Dad's persistent complaining had quickly exhausted whatever sympathy I may have had for his discomfort and boredom, until, in desperation, I privately whined to Ma, "...but there's nothing wrong with his *legs*," to which she'd rolled her eyes and quipped, "What can I do? I can't kill him."

The examination room door abruptly swung open, and a man in bright green scrubs breezed in.

"I'm sorry," he said, "There was nothing we could do."

I stared at his face, his eyes behind the gold rimmed glasses, the hideously green surgeon's mask hanging around his neck as a sound like rushing water filled my ears like the day our pool split itself down the side. The man's lips continued to move, but even though I could see every detail in his face, every pore in his skin under the harsh fluorescent light, all I could hear was the water, thunderous yet somehow muted, as if I were standing just inside a cave next to a waterfall.

"What?" I screamed, or maybe it was "No!" but my screams were only in my head, blocked by the waterfall, which was impenetrable until…one sound broke through: my mother started to cough, could not stop coughing, and I heard Jay's panicked voice, "She has a bad heart." The room was suddenly full of movement: nurses, doctors, hundreds of people, thousands even - and colors flashed by, buzzers went off, and gurney wheels screeched on the tile floors. The picture had thrust itself into fast forward while I stood, immobile and hollow, screaming in my head. Hours, or maybe just seconds, later, I realized I was alone in the room and wondered if I was an orphan.

The services the following week had everything my father would have planned for himself if he'd been a planner. Three nights of mourning and each of those nights, a limousine slunk up to the house to pick us up and slunk back with us three hours later. Relatives and old friends arrived from all over, even some old biker buddies who had lost touch after Ma made Dad sell his Harley when I was a toddler. Of course Karen was there with her husband and baby, and Bruce too, who had driven them all in his new canary yellow Camaro. Although I felt more comfortable around my half sister and her little family, having seen them more often, it was Bruce, virtually absent from my life since he was sixteen and I was eleven, toward whom I gravitated, partly because we were closer in age than Karen and I were but partly because his thick curly hair and star-tlingly light blue eyes unexpectedly aroused some very un-sisterly stir-rings in me. I couldn't stop imagining his leanness under his olive green corduroy leisure suit, and despite the mild guilt I felt as I fantasized, I pictured the two of us flying down the back roads in his Camaro, ulti-mately parking in a clearing and making out on the black vinyl back seat.

When I was in sixth grade, I read *The Adventures of Tom Sawyer* and as I sat during the wake I half believed that my father hid among the crowd, watching us the way Tom watches his friends and family mourn his own supposed death, because I had already nearly convinced myself that the man in the casket wasn't Dad. The face bore some resemblance, enough to be a pretty good likeness, but where was the recent Hampton Beach tan? This mask, this mannequin-face of pasty-white rubber could not be my father's face. Pancake make-up, I'd been forewarned, would be covering the cuts and bruises. I remained unconvinced. The nose was not right either; it was flat and askew, supposedly broken when he'd been knocked facedown onto the concrete floor, crushed by a five thousand pound piece of steel. Nope, still not buying it.

"He looks so natural," I heard a neighbor announce from the back of the room, "as if he might just sit up and ask 'what's going on?'"

That's about the stupidest thing I have ever heard, I yelled back in my head. I could almost hear Dad snicker at such a remark; perhaps he actually was snickering somewhere among the countless vases and sprays of cut flowers - out of sight but not out of earshot. Was I the only one who needed proof that this day was not some elaborate joke he or some-one on his behalf was playing? Did the mouth of this mannequin have his gold molar? Were Dad's tattoos there under the sleeves of the navy blue suit? I wanted to pull up the eyelids to prove that the fake head was hol-low. To whom could I express my disbelief?

Ma had been pretty out of it since her release from the hospital. I'd seen the bottle of blue and white capsules in the medicine cabinet when I went in looking for Alka Seltzer. Even now, her eyes looked glazed, and she kept repeating how much her husband would have loved this since he always loved to be the center of attention. No one contradicted her because everyone here knew that to be accurate.

Jay? Although he had been useful in making all the necessary calls and arrangements, Jay had made himself predictably scarce around me. Supposedly he had identified the body as our mother was being wheeled into intensive care, but as far as I was concerned he was not to be trusted. After all, *his* father was most likely stretched out on a couch somewhere watching a ballgame. Besides, Jay obviously believed this farce because now, as he once again stood before the casket, he exchanged the customary finger-entwined rosary beads for a brand new deck of cards. Those closest to the casket murmured their approval. I kept silent.

At St. Joseph's Church, the farce became even less believable since, now that the casket's lid was sealed, I could more easily convince myself that my father wasn't inside. Two rows of men, dressed completely in black, lined the church's walkway: coworkers from the shop, given the day off to attend the funeral. Rifles pointed at the sky and shot blanks at the clouds, military honors for a veteran of the Navy. Though only a step-son, Jay knew my father well, knew what he'd like. Through the ceremony and fanfare, I stubbornly kept one eye peeled for a glimpse of my Dad through the crowd.

Out of nowhere, a thin, pale man with brilliant red hair and thick glasses with heavy black frames approached first my mother, then me, hugging each of us in turn, crying and stammering his apologies. We'd never met, he explained, but he'd been the only one to witness the accident. A fairly recent employee at the shop, he'd been struggling with the machinery at his station and had asked for "Buck's" help. The walkway led right past a large randomly placed piece of solid steel that stood on its end.

"I saw it!" the man bawled. "He walked by, and it was like the hand of God knocked over that piece of steel." Shivering and shaking in his black trench coat, the man who had not given his name and who would shortly after quietly quit his job and leave the area, raised his own hand high in the air as he spoke, palm out and fingertips pointing up-ward, then to illustrate his point, swung his forearm down in one swift motion so that his palm was flat, parallel to the ground. Splat. How clev-er. Always include a grain of truth to make a lie more believable.

We already knew about the steel slab. Dad had told us over a rarely shared supper one night. Worried that sooner or later someone might be injured, he had registered a complaint to Omar, his boss, regard-ing its placement and was disgusted that his concerns had been dis-missed. Was I really supposed to believe that after weeks of hulking si-lent and immobile, the steel piece had spontaneously taken it upon itself to tip over at the precise moment my father passed by while working an overtime shift?

"Like the hand of God!" the man repeated, shaking his head at the tragic irony just before he stepped back and melted into the crowd. Wait, tell me why you're lying, I wanted to scream. Who put you up to this?

The package arrived a few days later. About the size of a coat box and wrapped in plain brown paper, it was addressed to Mrs. Ralph Girouard but had no return address. The postmark read Woodstock, CT, a city about forty five miles away. Neither Ma nor I knew anyone from Woodstock. Inside the box, all freshly laundered and neatly folded, were a pair of Dad's slacks, a couple of his shirts and undershirts, and several pairs of his socks and briefs. One of his leather belts lay coiled under-neath the clothes. I watched my mother pick up the items one at a time, examining each as if it had a story to tell, and wondered who could have made such a cruel effort to confirm her years of suspicions at a time when she was already in so much pain. I knew my father often showered at the shop after his shift and therefore always kept a change or two of clothes in his locker, so missing clothes had never raised any eyebrows on laundry days, but I also knew that Jay had already cleaned out the locker days ago. My stomach turned over as I waited for the tears or the yelling or whatever reaction this evidence of her husband's infidelity would bring, but, calm and dry-eyed, Ma made only one comment as she finished sorting through the box: "I wondered where these things had disappeared to." That afternoon, she and I began cleaning out Dad's closet and bureau.

My father's duplicity as evidenced by the anonymous package proved to me his capability of so much more than just the random lies that had rolled so glibly off of his tongue over the years when confronted by my mother's questions and accusations. Even when caught, seemingly trapped by his inconsistencies, his contrite, soothing voice and innocent blue eyes, his charm and ease with which he could manipulate an argument, would have deterred even the most expert inquisitor and were certainly no match for an overly emotional jealous wife who, deep down, still wanted to believe in her marriage. The Woodstock package told of another man with another life, separate from us, a life that he had apparently frequently visited and to which, perhaps for months, he may have been planning to escape. It fed my fantasy of the mannequin look-alike in the casket and fueled my hope that my father still lived and breathed somewhere out there in the world. The bills, the debts, the arguments had just reached the point of intolerance for him, had tipped the scales in favor of this "other" life, and so he had staged this elaborate scheme to convince the world of his death so that he could disappear with no fear of pursuit.

I toyed with the idea that the package was Dad's secret message of this to me because he knew I'd be the only one not fooled by the subterfuge. Perhaps, as the weeks and months passed, he would regret his decision, miss his daughter, and decide to return, tears in his eyes as he apologized for the deception. Or better yet, I fantasized, the double life itself might have weighed too heavily on him, causing so much pain that he had chosen neither life but instead had gone much farther than Woodstock, to think it through or maybe even start over but might still someday return.

For years, I kept my fantasy alive by scanning the crowds at Disney World or Miami Beach or countless other tourist spots, hoping I'd spot my father's face, older but still familiar to me. I would rush up, catch him by surprise; Dad would instantly recognize me and we would embrace. Many times through my college years and even after my first marriage and the birth of my daughter I would see a man in the crowded street of some festival or parade who, from his profile or from behind, just by the way he walked or carried himself, struck me as familiar and my heart would palpate, the breath catch in my throat until a closer look would disappoint me.

One day, after having moved back to North Brookfield from Florida, I sat alone in the Fallon Clinic in Spencer, impatiently waiting for my second husband's name to be called so I could pay for his prescription and return home before he'd had a chance to dwell too long on my absence. The last thing I wanted tonight was an argument. Over the past several weeks, the pain from an injured back together with too much idle time on his hands had turned Bob belligerent and unreasonable. I glanced at my watch and sighed.

"Leon Gaudette?" When I heard the name I immediately looked around the waiting area to see who would respond. I hadn't thought of Chill in years, hadn't seen him since his wife, Aurore, had died after skidding into a tree not five miles from home while driving through a sleet storm. Chill and my father had been long time friends as had my mother and Aurore. Chill and Aurore had dated while my parents were dating and each couple had "stood up" for the other's wedding. Aurore had been a shoulder for my mother when Dad had been killed, and her unexpected death not long after had been a harsh blow. I had just assumed that with so much time having passed - twenty? twenty five years? – that Chill had died, as had my mother.

A short, plump woman with curly white hair and glasses who, I assumed must be the "new" wife, had risen and was approaching the prescription counter. On impulse, I decided to introduce myself.

"Excuse me. Are you…Mrs. Gaudette? Chill's wife?"

"Yes, I am." She answered without looking up, distracted by the wallet or checkbook search she had begun in her tote-sized purse.

Having already put myself out there, I persisted, "I'm Donna

Girouard. Ralph's daughter."

At that, she looked up, blinking nearsightedly through her thick lenses. "Who?"

"Buck Girouard's daughter," I tried instead.

"'Buck?' Buck! Yes! Oh, I remember Buck so well." She was nodding and smiling. "Such a shame what happened. And you're his daughter?"

"Yes, I am. How is Chill?"

"Oh, Leon is hanging in there. Nothing serious." She went back to rummaging in her purse, then found her wallet and began looking through it as the pharmacist waited.

A bit self-conscious that I was holding up the process, I meant to end the encounter by just telling her to say "hi" to Chill when she returned home, but I never got the chance. Still intent on her search, she said, "He used to go with my best friend, you know."

I froze. "I'm sorry?"

"Buck. He used to go with my best friend," now she was handing a card to the pharmacist, looking at him. "Rita." She turned back to me as she spoke the name. "Didn't he ever tell you about her?"

I couldn't seem to make my brain work. In retrospect, this should have been my opportunity to get the answers to so many unanswered questions. Tell me what you know! Let's go have coffee. Or better yet, may I follow you home and talk to you and Chill together! Instead, I stood there, stupidly looking at her, trying to form words. "No," I finally managed.

"That's odd. I wonder why he never told you about her. Rita Kamuda. I haven't seen her in years." She continued, her voice picking up speed. "I wonder if she's still in Connecticut . . ."

I may have said goodbye, or even thank you, or maybe I just mumbled unintelligible sounds under my breath. Screw Bob's prescription, I had to get out of there. Right now. I ran out the automatic doors and across the parking lot. I barely had time to unlock my car and slide in behind the wheel before the tears came - huge, choking sobs – and I

pounded the steering wheel with my fists. "You bastard, you bastard."
Did I scream it? Whisper it? Or just think it? I have no idea. If there were
passersby, I didn't see them.

P.S.

All kidding aside I want you to know that I love you very
much and as the card says I think that I got the better half
of the deal. You should know by now that I wouldn't cheat
on you or do anything wrong I haven't done so yet and
have no reason to do so now. Every thing i want is right at
home and i don't have to go any further. You know if we
didn't have our little spats once in a while9 (just like every
one elese0) then we wouldn't have the fun of making up
HAPPY BIRTHDAY DARLING and I love you VERY VERY
MUCH.

2nd. P.S.

Make sure that you take the money and get something
for yourself. I'd get it my self but you said that you even
had trouble getting the right zi sizes yourself and I wanted t
to get you a skirt or a good blouse for yourself.

Your Loverboy Husband;
Ralph

AFTER OBSERVING NO VISIBLE SIGNS OF ACTIVITY AT THE CORNER HOUSE, THE OLD CROW DECIDES TO CONTINUE WITH HER DAILY ROUTINE. THE NEXT PART OF HER FLIGHT TAKES HER BEYOND MT. GUYOT STREET, OVER HILLSVILLE ROAD TOWARD THE FIVEMILE RIVER ON THE OUTSKIRTS OF TOWN, WHERE SHE ONCE STOPPED TO WATCH A GROUP OF MEN GATHERED ALONG THE SHORE. THAT DAY, A LIFE-LONG TOWN RESIDENT - ONE OF HART'S REGULARS - HAD DIED, AND, AFTER A FEW DRINKS IN THE BAR, HIS CLOSEST FRIENDS LINED UP AT THE FIVEMILE TO HONOR HIM BY SALUTING AS THEY ALL PEED IN THE RIVER.

AFTER FLYING OVER AN AREA WHERE SHE AND HER FAMILY ONCE FLOCKED TO DINE IN THE CORNFIELDS BUT THAT LAST YEAR HAD BEEN LEFT NAKED AND SCARRED BY THE BULLDOZERS SENT TO MAKE WAY FOR A DEVELOPMENT THAT NEVER HAPPENED, THE OLD CROW CIRCLES BACK OVER ONE OF THE FEW REMAINING FARMS AND ITS ORIGINAL BARN TO HEAD TOWARDS BROOKFIELD ORCHARDS, THE ONLY ONE OF IT'S KIND LEFT IN TOWN. ONCE BUSTLING WITH CARTLOADS OF MIGRANT WORKERS, SOME OF THE ORCHARD PARCELS HAVE SINCE BEEN SOLD AS HOUSE LOTS. THE CROW PASSES OVER THE LITTLE "COUNTRY STORE" AND THE EMPTY SWINGS, SANDBOXES, AND PICNIC TABLES OUT FRONT AND CONTINUES OVER ELM STREET, VEERING SLIGHTLY NORTH. SHE FLIES OVER WARD STREET WHERE MORE HOUS-ING FOR THE ELDERLY HAS REPLACED ONE OF THE ONCE THRIVING CHICKEN FARMS, THEN OVER GILBERT STREET, WHERE THE ONCE STATELY AND WELL-MAINTAINED VICTORIAN HOMES HAVE BECOME RUNDOWN, NO LONGER OWNER OCCUPIED BUT INSTEAD DIVIDED INTO APARTMENTS AND ROOMS FOR RENT OR LISTED FOR SALE.

THE OLD CROW ABRUPTLY TURNS SOUTH WEST, TOWARD THE TOWN FOREST, A PARCEL OF SEVERAL ACRES THAT ABUTS THE WEST BROOKFIELD ROAD. ORIGINALLY SET ASIDE TO SUPPLY FREE FIREWOOD TO THOSE RESIDENTS WHO COULD NOT AFFORD TO BUY IT, THE TOWN FOREST IS "PERPETUALLY PROTECTED" FROM DEVELOPMENT ACCORDING TO NORTH BROOKFIELD ZONING RESTRICTIONS. ASIDE A LARGE CIRCLE OF TRAMPLED GRASS, THE RESULT OF REPEATED ASSAULTS BY PICKUP TRUCKS ENTERING THE FOREST TO DUMP RAKED LEAVES, LIE THE WEATHERED REMAINS OF A DISCARDED MATTRESS, LEFT, NO DOUBT, IN AN ATTEMPT TO AVOID PAYING AN ADDITIONAL FEE AT THE TOWN DUMP. THE APPROXI-MATELY 3500 CURRENT RESIDENTS, MANY POST-RETIREMENT, HAVE AVIDLY OPPOSED THE INCREASING TAXES AND FEES LEVIED BY SELECTMEN, AND SOME LOOK FOR CREATIVE WAYS TO AVOID THEM. NON-WORKING APPLIANCES AND BAGS OF TRASH ARE NOT AN UNCOMMON SIGHT ALONGSIDE THE TOWN'S RURAL ROADS. THE CROW SWOOPS DOWN ON A FAMILY OF MICE LIV-ING IN THE GUMMY COTTONY DEPTHS OF THE MATTRESS, THEN HEADS OVER TO THE WET-LANDS OF NEARBY COYS BROOK TO TEASE THE BEAVERS BUSILY REPAIRING THEIR HOMES DIS-TURBED BY THE SPRING RAINS.

12
Your Father's Children

I sat in the back seat, directly behind the driver, so I had a clear view of the building. Karen sat next to me, squeezed into the middle, sobbing, a hankie clutched in her fist, and Bruce sat on the other side of her, silent and pale. My mother, the passenger in the front seat, sat up straight in her smart suit and kept her gaze under the little veil of her matching hat leveled straight ahead. She did not turn around to us, nor did she look toward the funeral home. Although the barbiturates, pre-scribed just days before, had slightly dulled her reactions, she remained cognizant enough to notice details, slights to focus on as distractions from the bigger picture. Right now, she was still angry because the lim-ousine would not accommodate four people in the back seat; therefore, her son, Jay, had to follow us in his own car, second in line after the hearse.

"Jay should be sitting in the 'family car,'" she'd said to me earli-er, her voice low and shaking with fury, "He was more of a son to your father than his own son was."

I'd said nothing.

The door to Pillsbury's Funeral Home opened, and I watched my father's casket, draped with an American flag to signify his time served in the Navy, being wheeled the few feet to the hearse whose rear door already leaned open, waiting.

"Donna, that's Dad in there!" Karen's voice was almost a scream. She grabbed my arm and I cried with her as we leaned into each other.

In the photo album my mother assembled for me after I graduated from college, there are only two pictures as acknowledgement that Karen and Bruce ever existed as even a remote part of my childhood. Both were taken on my fifth Christmas, in Memere's living room. One is a picture of all of us grandchildren; the other, unlikely to have been my mother's idea, shows my father with his three children: Karen, about fifteen years old at the time and already beautiful in high heels, long hair, and lipstick; Bruce, a slightly awkward ten year old with his father's eyes; and me, front and center, the ugly duckling with bangs and pigtails, the light glaring off the thick lenses of my cat's eye glasses. Someone posed us for this picture, but I can't remember who. My father has one arm around Karen and the other around Bruce, whose hand has been placed, somewhat awkwardly it seems, on my shoulder. My father leans slightly forward and smiles over my head, but almost shyly, as if afraid to be too proud.

That Christmas day in the home of my father's parents, I first became aware, if only vaguely, that I did not hold the only position as my father's child. I don't even remember the dynamic (although knowing my mother so well I can imagine it) because, at five, I tended to focus on those closer to my age - in this case, my cousin Monique, a month older than I and the immediate rival for my grandparents' attention. When we were small, Monique and I competed and fought during every Girouard family gathering, often to the extent that we had to be separated and threatened with "the strap" if we didn't behave. In retrospect, therefore, I most likely was too busy comparing height, clothes, and presents with Monique than to dwell on two older near-strangers with whom I posed for a couple of photographs.

Over the next couple of years, I saw Karen and Bruce only at Memere and Pepere's and only on major holidays. Occasionally I overheard my parents discussing them, in the context of money spent or extra money requested by someone named "Flo," who I later found out had been my father's first wife. Clearly my mother resented the financial intrusion, and I remember how happy both she and my father were when Flo remarried. I learned the word "alimony" that day.

Bruce was a shadowy figure back then and rarely discussed; however, whatever information I got about Karen was either vented by my mother or overheard when she and my father argued. Karen had "gone wild" and hung around with Puerto Rican boys. She was caught smoking and sneaking out at night and sure to end up "in trouble" (whatever that meant), and, on more than one occasion, my mother grimly handed the phone to my father with the words "It's Flo." Still unclear on the relationships, I picked up whatever I could by listening on the stairs; I had already learned that, though she freely talked about her own past, talking about my father's past angered my mother, and, for some reason, I couldn't bring myself to go directly to my father.

My chronology of events is sketchy, but certainly, had I not fully understood the intricacies of our sibling relationship before I turned seven, they became clear that year when my father, my mother, and I attended Karen's wedding. Now I wanted to know exactly who this person was and how she was related to me. I hammered my mother with questions she didn't want to answer. In the end, I still could not understand why Dad was in the wedding and I was not.

"But if she's Dad's daughter, then that makes me her sister – and Brucie's sister. Sisters are supposed to be in the wedding." I insisted.

"This is different," my mother said, frustrated by my persistence.

"*How* is it different?"

"She's not your sister. She's your father's daughter, so she's your half-sister. And Bruce is your half-brother because he's your father's son."

"But you call Jay my brother and he's just your son. So Jay is only my half-brother, like Brucie?" I struggled to make sense out of her explanation. I wanted everything clear-cut.

"No." Her tone was firm, nearing anger. "Jay is your brother, and don't you forget that."

"But how is it not the same?" I could not let this go.

"You and Jay have the same mother. Karen and Bruce are just your father's children."

I don't remember much about the wedding. I didn't know most of the people there. When I asked where Bruce was, I was given a vague answer. I didn't notice that Karen's mother also did not attend, although both of my parents must have been relieved. I didn't find out until years later that Flo had given Karen an ultimatum: she could choose either her or our father to be there that day.

"And I chose Dad," Karen told me.

Once Karen married and moved out of her mother's house, she and her husband came to our house on occasion, and we reciprocated. When she and her husband Franny opened a diner, Dad and I ate there. My mother and I attended Karen's baby shower. What I remember most about Karen from those days is that her hair changed color quite often. I picture her in short skirts and boots, with Johnny Cash droning in the background. Being so young, I found small talk boring, so typically, when we went to see her, I climbed her fruit trees and played with Major, her Beagle. Karen and I never spent time alone to develop any kind of sisterly bond, and even if we had tried, a ten year age difference is significant. Karen's husband drove truck and was often on the road. The diner failed; another baby came. As a busy young mother, Karen had no time for a little sister not much older than her own children.

I can't say that my mother ever developed any closeness with Karen either. I don't remember the two of them ever going shopping or out to eat or anything else that adult women do as friends, but at least the former tension on my mother's end had diminished, probably now that the financial burden of child support had decreased by half. From what I saw, she seemed sociable enough to Karen.

Yet, evidently, my father still felt that he needed to hide from my mother the fact that he saw Karen more frequently than the family visits. Years later, Karen told me that Dad took her out to lunch once a week, right up until he died. I'm sure my mother never knew that.

Most of the things about Karen discussed in my presence had to do with her and Franny as a couple. Money issues seemed to follow them, and they had bad luck with cars. Dad often remarked that they changed one junk for another as often as Karen changed her hair color. The biggest issue for him, though, and one he voiced on many occasions, had to do with the naming of his first grandchild. Dad accepted "Francis" as the first name; one can hardly begrudge naming a son after his father. However, Dad resented the baby's middle name: "Cosmos," the first name of the paternal grandfather. Whenever he told the news of the birth of his first grandchild, Dad made a point of stating the baby's full name and rolling his eyes. His resentment became so obvious to me that I asked my mother if it would make him feel better if I gave our dog the middle name "Ralph," after him. She smiled and said she didn't think so. I made a silent promise then to name my first son Ralph, a promise I never had to keep since my only child, born years after my father's death, is female. Karen's second and last baby is also female, and Bruce never had any children.

My early memories of Bruce are few since he still lived at home with his mother. I hazily remember a couple of summers when he spent a few days with us, sleeping on the couch; however, apart from watching television together, I don't recall much time spent with him. Yet, somehow or other, I developed a fixation on Bruce as I got older. He became my hero, based on nothing but the stories I played out in my head. I wanted him to be my big brother, the way Wally was to the Beaver, and I fantasized that, at some point in the future, we would find a way to connect, that he would be the doting big brother and I the adoring little sister.

Somewhere around junior high school age, I asked Dad for Bruce's picture, and when I finally got one I placed it on the built-in cupboard in my bedroom. That way, when friends saw the photograph of the handsome boy with thick hair and Dad's startlingly blue eyes and asked, I could say, "Oh, that's Brucie. My brother." However, I never referred to Bruce as my brother when Ma could overhear. She made no comment about his picture on display in my bedroom, but every year on Dad's birthday and on Father's Day, she pointed out to me the absence of a card, gift, or phone call from Bruce, even though Dad himself never mentioned it.

Just as Dad hid from my mother and me his private lunches with

Karen, he also hid from us the father-son time he spent with Bruce. Only years later, did I hear about the ballgames and the rides on the Harley, and I hugged Bruce when he told me and said I was glad that he'd had that time with Dad.

Somehow I thought that after Dad's funeral, Karen and Bruce and I would become closer, but at sixteen years old, I didn't know how to make that happen, especially with Bruce. At twenty one, Bruce struck me as shy and quiet, almost painfully so. When he chose to walk back to the house from the cemetery, I decided to walk with him, hoping he would open up to me about his past, his future, Dad – about anything, but he said little, and I found myself filling in the silence. Throughout the calling hours and the Mass, Bruce had pretty much kept to himself, still in shock I reasoned, although I overheard unkind comments whispered by other mourners who wondered if "Buck's son" was stoned because, though he wasn't crying, his eyes were red. Those comments made me angry and all the more determined to reach out to Bruce.

Back at the house, Bruce drifted off among the throngs of people who seemed to fill every corner of the downstairs, while I searched through some of Dad's things. I thought that maybe I could find something special to give to Bruce in remembrance of our father. I had already taken Dad's gold and jade "owl" pinkie ring for myself the night he had been killed at work in the steel plant. Now I looked for his watch. I found the Bulova that Dad had regularly worn prior to his first gambling junket to Las Vegas, but I could not find the pricy newer digital watch that lit up at the touch of a button. After a brief winning streak at the craps table, Dad had bought the pinkie ring and the digital watch in the hotel jewelry shop, along with a Gucci watch for Ma and a pair of tri-colored gold earrings for me before heading back to the table and losing the rest of his winnings and more. I picked up the Bulova and went back through the crowd to find my mother.

"Ma, where's Dad's new watch?" I had pulled her aside.

"Why?"

"I want to give it to Brucie."

My mother turned to face me dead-on.

"I gave it to Jay," she said. "You can give Bruce that one." She motioned toward the watch in my hand, then turned away. I didn't know until days later that my mother had already received a registered letter from an attorney representing both Karen and Bruce and inquiring about my father's "estate." Other letters and phone calls would follow, rekindling a deep resentment in my mother regarding her husband's first family. Before long she would be forced to prove that her family home, inherited from her parents, had remained in her name alone and therefore was not part of my father's estate. Dad died deeply in debt because of his gambling addiction, much of the debt hidden (along with his other indiscretions) from my mother, who would find out its extent during the weeks following the funeral. The Ambassador station wagon, the only item of his with any real value, had to be sold to pay off his credit card, which she'd just discovered and whose statement listed jewelry and small appliance purchases she'd never made nor received.

My mother did not confront Bruce about the attorney's letter, assuming Karen to have been the one initiating the legal move, but she did confront Karen, right there in our home as family, friends and acquaintances helped themselves to various casseroles and desserts.

As my sister and her husband prepared to leave, my mother approached Karen and asked to speak to her alone. Ma handed this twenty-six year old woman who had just lost her father a pack of cigarettes – Dad's – and said, "Here. That's all there is." Without another word, Ma turned and walked away from her stunned step-daughter. I didn't see this incident, and Ma did not tell me about it. Over twenty five years after our Dad's death, Karen told me how her own mother, Flo, had talked her into retaining an attorney and how embarrassed and guilty she felt when confronted by my mother.

As the weeks passed after the funeral, my mother found herself dealing with more than just the newly acquired knowledge of my father's indebtedness. A mysterious package containing several of Dad's clothes arrived by mail, and the parish priest told her that a woman had inquired about the location of Dad's plot but would not give her name, confirmation (as far as Ma was concerned) of her suspicions regarding Dad's infidelity. Meanwhile, since my mother's heart condition had long since prevented her from working, the absence of my father's regular paycheck meant struggling to make ends meet while waiting for the paperwork for my claim on his death benefits to be processed. Funeral expenses had to be paid, and the Veterans' Administration decided to pay for the flat stone to mark the grave and nothing more.

Everyone assumed that big money would be coming because Dad had been killed at the shop, crushed by a 5,000 pound piece of steel that had fallen on him during on overtime shift, so questions regarding the lawsuit that surely had already been filed peppered seemingly every conversation with well-meaning friends and extended family members until my mother confessed to me that she wished people would just stop asking. When the only witness to the accident quit his job, moved from the area without leaving a forwarding address, and could not be located, Melvyn Glickman, the attorney Jay had hired to represent my mother, advised her to accept the amount offered by the factory's insurance rather than go to court, and she seemed reluctant to discuss the details.

Meanwhile a letter from the Social Security Administration arrived, indicating that Bruce had filed a claim under Dad's death benefits. My mother was livid.

"This is what kind of 'brother' he is!"

"He's still only twenty one. He's eligible," I said. "He has a right to file."

"He's taking food out of your mouth!" she yelled, waving the letter.

I hadn't seen or heard from Bruce since I'd given him Dad's watch after the funeral. Because the house had still been full of guests that day, I had pulled him into the hallway for privacy, and he'd hugged me and promised to stay in touch. I don't remember how much time passed between receiving news of the additional Social Security claim and the day that Bruce called to tell me he'd enlisted in the Army, but I do remember that my mother didn't even hand me the phone; she just plunked it down on the table, saying "It's Bruce."

I was thrilled! Bruce had actually called me for the first time ever! I didn't care that Ma stalked out of the room fuming. I practically gushed into the phone. I didn't care about how brief – a minute perhaps? – the call was. Even the news about his joining the Army didn't bother me because, at my urging, Bruce promised he would write, and I believed him.

As I neared the end of my junior year of high school, I became so caught up with dating, visiting and applying to area colleges, studying, and socializing with my friends that I hardly noticed that months had gone by with no word from either Karen or Bruce. By the time Pepere told me that he'd heard from Karen that Bruce was stationed somewhere in Germany, I had become as wrapped up in my own world as my father's children were in theirs. It simply never occurred to me to miss them.

I found Karen first.

Several years had passed since my mother had died and I'd moved from Florida, back to my family home in North Brookfield with my daughter, determined to start over after my divorce. I realize now that one does not "start over" by turning to the past, but at the time I sought its comfort, trying to recreate what I inaccurately remembered as an idyllic childhood. Unfortunately, marrying "the boy next door" and settling into the drafty one-hundred-and-thirty-year-old house my grandparents had bought in 1920 (and that hadn't seen a major renovation since the 1960s) had not proved the key to my happiness. After my mother's only sister died, I felt rootless. No immediate family (except my child) now remained in my life. My brother Jay and I had been estranged since the week Ma died, and though at first I'd hoped that, with time, he would realize that he had not been cheated out of an inheritance, his lack of interest even in his only niece indicated otherwise. I decided that the time had come to search for my other two siblings.

A cousin of my father's still lived in the same house in nearby Spencer where the Girouard family Christmas get-togethers took place each year after my Memere died. I had lost touch with Jeanette after I left for college, but a quick call to her, and I now had contact information for Karen. I wrote a long letter and waited.

The morning Karen called me, we talked for over an hour, catching up. As the conversation neared its end, I asked, "So . . . do you want a sister in your life?"

"I sure do," she said.

When I met Karen for our first of many lunches, I was immediately struck by how much she looked and sounded like my father's deceased only sister, Eleanor. The Karen from my childhood had all but disappeared. Not only had she aged, but time seemed to have tamed her. Where was the rebel who had seemed so wild, so dangerous, so on the edge? Gone were the boots and the slim figure; Karen had gained weight, wore glasses secured by a chain that hung around her neck, and got regular manicures and pedicures. I wondered how someone who had been so unconventional as a teenager and young adult had become so strait-laced. She bowled and golfed and worked in retail. She wore bold synthetic prints and chunky jewelry. She had become matronly, both in mind and appearance.

Still, I felt a connection; I lapped up being the "little sister," and treasured the dinners and holiday gatherings spent with her and Franny (now "Frank") and getting to know my nephew and niece, who'd been too young when Dad died even to remember me.

When Karen told me that the only thing of Dad's she'd received after his death was the pack of cigarettes, I found a couple of things to give to her: one of his trophies from the motorcycle races he'd been in when I was a baby and a gold lighter with his initial on

it. I also found a photograph of the two of them with Pepere and Karen's

infant son; I made a copy and framed it to give to Karen at lunch one day.

Our lunches often lasted for hours because we found so much to talk about. We now were able to relate to each other as adults, and we quickly became close. Karen also proved to be a sympathetic ear and patiently listened while I vented to her about my failing second marriage. She built up my self-confidence, convincing me that I had the strength to turn my back on an emotionally abusive husband. She made me realize that I had lost myself to the point where I no longer even cared about how I looked. Together, we went through my wardrobe, shopped for more flattering clothes, discussed make-up, and chose hair color to cover my gray.

Actually, Karen chose the color: light brown with auburn highlights. I sat in her kitchen, an old towel covering my shoulders, while she mixed the solution.

"Why did you let your hair go like this?" she asked. "You're way too young to be gray."

I looked at her pedicured feet as she flipped-flopped over to me from the sink.

"Cost, time, effort. I don't know." I did not ask her why she had let her once slender figure go.

"Well, after your hair is done, we'll try out your new make-up. You're gonna be a knock-out."

I loved her hands in my hair, the smell of her skin as she bent over me. I missed my mother, and I loved being mothered by Karen.

A while later, as she toweled my hair, Frank walked in and grinned at us.

"Look at you two sisters! One would lie and the other swear to it!"

"Yup," Karen said, grinning back.

Many of our private conversations focused on the past. I'd been too young and timid to approach my father about his first marriage, so I'd gotten only my mother's biased perspective and limited knowledge. I had lots of questions, and Karen filled in many of the blanks. I discovered that while my mother fumed over the money being sent each month to Flo, Karen and Bruce lived on hot dogs and beans until Flo remarried. Karen also substantiated my mother's voiced suspicions that debt had followed my father from his first marriage to his second, but as a result of his gambling addiction rather than Flo's spending.

I filled in blanks for Karen too. I assured her that money was always tight in our house as well, that Dad gave my mother a fixed amount each week from his paycheck with which she had to manage the bills. Ma always had to work, even when I was small, to make ends meet. During the last few years of their marriage, when Ma became disabled and could no longer work, Dad's addiction worsened. Many of their arguments were about money and where it was needed versus where it went, especially after the Las Vegas junkets began with Jay and Jay's former father-in-law, Frank. Losses in Vegas added up much faster than those from a few bad hands of poker at Duke's. Although he tried not to appear concerned, Dad did mention how a guy a couple of towns over had been run off the road and pulled from his car, both his legs broken by two men over money owed to the wrong people. Dad sold some of his things to pay off gambling debts - hunting and fishing equipment, tools – and prowled the house and garage looking for more items. He asked my mother if she could possibly budget with less money, and when she refused, he began working overtime. Meanwhile, he hounded her about putting his name on our house because, he argued, taking out a second mortgage would lighten their financial burden. Fortunately for us, Ma resisted the pressure he put on her; she was still paying for the badly needed renovations from years earlier and was not about to risk her house to cover his vices. I assured Karen that there had been no estate, only bills, left behind after Dad's death. The settlement that eventually came from the shop where he'd been killed had been pitiful, not even amounting to a year's salary once the attorney had been paid. My mother had needed it to live on.

Over the year or so of my reconnecting with my sister, she fascinated me with tales of family members I never knew, who had died when she was young, and she painted vivid pictures of places I barely remembered, where Pepere and Memere had lived before Memere died. One story my mother once told me had bothered me for years, and I felt that Karen and I had reached the point where I could bring it up.

"Ma told me that you were molested as a child, by an uncle, and that when Dad found out, he beat him up and threw him out. Is all that true?" Karen and I were on our way somewhere, and she was driving.

Karen sighed. "It wasn't an uncle. It was Pepere's father Amos."

"-and?" I prompted.

Karen sighed again. "How did *that* come up?"

I briefly told her how my Uncle Chuck had tried to molest me when I was twelve or so and how, when I went to Ma about it, she warned me not to tell my father. Based on hearsay of how he'd reacted to Karen's molestation, Ma worried that Dad might harm Chuck, causing irreparable damage to her relationship with her only sister, Ruth.

"Yeah, it was Amos. He was living with us for a while. Dad hit him and threw him out the front door. But it never really happened."

I stared at my sister whose eyes had not left the road during this conversation.

"What never happened?"

"I wasn't molested."

"You mean you made it up? But Ma said there were marks on your chest. That your mother saw them when you got out of the tub and called Dad in to see them."

"It was just childish fantasy," Karen said, still not looking at me.

"I don't get it, were there marks or not? What happened?"

"I was never molested," Karen said, her tone of finality ending the conversation.

More than once, I called my sister from my car, in tears over something my husband had said or done, because I needed a sympathetic ear and valued her perspective. However, the day I turned to her, sobbing and almost incoherent in a medical center's parking lot, she gave me much more than I bargained for. This incident had nothing to do with my husband Bob. I had just stumbled onto proof of my father's infidelity by inadvertently striking up a conversation with the best friend of his former mistress.

"Ma's suspicions were right," I cried into the phone to Karen. "This woman, Loretta, is now married to Chill. Remember Chill? He was Dad's best man when my parents got married. She just told me that her best friend, Rita, used to 'go with' Dad! This Rita person must have been the one who sent the box of clothes to my mother after the funeral."

"Okay, slow down," said Karen, "You're hysterical."

"I ran out of the clinic, but she's still in there. I bet Chill still lives in the same place, right here in Spencer, where he lived with his first wife. I could call. Or I could go to their house."

"Why would you want to do that, Donna?" Karen's voice was low and calm.

"They could lead me to this Rita! I could talk to her, ask her about Dad. Find out how and when it all started and what their plans were."

"What possible good would that do now?" she asked.

"I want to *know*, Karen. If she knew he was married or if he lied to her. If they were in love. If he was planning on leaving us. I have so many questions." Why couldn't she understand? I wanted explanations.

"Donna, that was over twenty years ago. Leave it alone." She sounded exasperated.

"Karen, he cheated on my mother!"

"Well, he cheated on mine, too. With your mother."

What? I felt the world tilt.

"I didn't want to tell you, but it's true. That's why my mother threw him out."

"My mother couldn't have known." Could she? "She would never have gotten involved with a married man." I could believe my father's duplicity, but I could never imagine my mother as being so deceitful.

"I wouldn't know about that."

Something clicked in my head. "No, she didn't know. That explains the two marriage certificates. I found them just before she died. She said the first was invalid because his divorce had not been final. She said she was furious when she found out, and ashamed, so she never told anyone. Once his waiting period ended, they had another ceremony, to make it legal, but she never forgave him for lying to her."

"Well, there you go."

"But you knew, and you forgave him? For cheating on your mother and leaving you and Bruce?"

"Dad was a 'good-time-Charlie;' it's just who he was, you know that. Life of the party, center of attention. He had his faults, but he was still Dad."

"I don't care," I said, "I will never forgive him."

Bruce was harder to find. No one seemed to know where he ended up – not even Karen, who had lost touch with him years earlier over something said that led to anger and hurt feelings. Internet searches led me to two Bruce Girouards of the same age. I wrote tentative inquiring letters to both. One sent a note saying, nope, sorry. The other one called me, and now he was parking his car in front of my house. An unimpressive dark green, four-door Pontiac sedan. Really? What happened to the blindingly yellow Camaro with the black racing stripe? I hadn't actually expected the same car, but certainly something similar. Something sporty. Something cool.

I held my breath as the door opened and a man stepped out. Yup, bald. That, I expected, since Dad had been nearly bald when he died. I sighed for Bruce's long-lost thick curly hair. Tall as I remembered, but stocky and, well, paunchy, is the word that

now fit Bruce. But the eyes, yes, still those bright blue eyes of Dad's that lit up as I opened my front door and then opened my arms.

"Let me tell you *my* 'Jay story,'" Bruce said.

Bruce had a "Jay story"?

We'd already finished lunch, and Bruce, at his initiative, had spent a half hour or so playing catch with my daughter out in the yard. He had briefly told me about his estrangement from Karen, and I filled him in about my estrangement from Jay.

"I didn't realize that you had any real contact with Jay," I said.

"I didn't, really. I barely knew him. But I have a story."

Still in shock after his father's sudden death, Bruce had accepted Jay's offer to go to the funeral home - not because he wanted to but because he didn't know what else to do. Sure, Jay was Dad's step-son and in charge of all the arrangements since Polly, Dad's wife, was pretty out of it, but Jay was not actually related to Bruce and had never made any attempt to get to know him. Why was he taking an interest now, or was he just being polite?

When the two men got to the funeral home, Jay led Bruce downstairs to the casket display room. The funeral director left them alone.

"So, what do you think?" Jay asked Bruce. "Which one do you like?"

Was he kidding? What difference did it make? Dad was dead, that's all Bruce could think about.

"I don't know," Bruce said, feeling somehow put off by this older man who acted as if everyone in the world worked for him.

"Come on, pick one. What about that one?" Jay pointed to an expensive mahogany casket with brass trim. "Do you think your father would like that one?"

"I don't know. I guess so." Bruce shrugged.

"Or how about that one?" Jay said, pointing to another of oak. "Do you think he'd like that one?"

"I guess, sure," said Bruce, not caring but trying to be agreeable. If Jay wanted his help, he'd try, even though his heart wasn't in it.

"Okay, so that one. That's the one you like?"

"Yeah, sure."

"Well, that one over there," Jay pointed across the room to a completely different casket of sleek steel with a gleaming black finish and flashy platinum trim, "that's the one I chose for him." He abruptly turned and headed for the stairs.

"I didn't know what to do," Bruce said to me now, "so I just followed Jay out the door."

"That's terrible!" I said. "God, I'm so sorry!" What a dick.

"Twenty one – still a kid really - and I'd just lost my father. But that was a long time ago. It doesn't matter now."

I drove. By the time we got to the cemetery, the sun had set. Despite its being his idea, Bruce still seemed squeamish about visiting Dad's grave; he'd put it off for weeks. But during this visit, another lunch at my house, we'd talked more about Dad and his death.

"This may sound crazy to you - Karen certainly thought so - but I always felt that Dad's accident at the shop was no accident," he'd said over pie.

"Really? You too?"

"Okay, so it's not just me. He owed a lot of money, didn't he?"

"Thousands in gambling debts. We never found out just how much."

Bruce looked thoughtful. "I assumed Krock was involved somehow."

I shook my head. "Nah, I don't think so. Dad hadn't chauffeured for him in years. Plus, Krock was already out of the country by then, evading the IRS." I leaned closer. "I think if anyone knows the real story, it's Jay."

As Bruce wordlessly stared at me, I listed all the reasons why, in my mind at least, our Dad's death had not been a work-related accident.

In addition to the gambling debts resulting from the Vegas trips arranged by Jay and Frank Kretchmar, Jay's bookie ex-father-in-law; the implausibility of a 5,000 pound piece of steel tipping over by itself onto Dad just as he passed during an overtime shift with only one witness on the floor; the disappearance of that witness before a hearing could be scheduled; the lack of a proper police investigation; and the paltry settlement my mother had been coerced to accept by the attorney Jay had hired for her; there'd been Frank's offer to me of college money.

"He told me not to worry, that if I still wanted to go to Clark or Assumption instead of to a state college, he would take care of it. I'm not saying Frank or Jay was involved, but why would Frank make an offer like that unless he knew something and felt guilty?"

Bruce shook his head, dessert forgotten. "Did you take the money?"

"I politely thanked him, but no. Hell, no. I ended up going to Westfield on scholarships, grants, work study, and my share of Dad's death benefits. And there's one more thing."

I told Bruce how a couple of years after I'd moved out, my mother had needed a new roof on the house, and had mentioned how tight money was and that she needed to borrow from Jay to cover the extra expense.

"That's when I asked about the settlement – the actual amount, I mean. And when she finally told me she'd gotten only around twenty thousand, I got angry. I started talking about reopening the case. Supposedly, Glickman, her attorney – hired by Jay I might add – had told her she didn't have a case, that CPC Engineering would find a way to turn it back on Dad, making it his fault. Tell me how a man could single-handedly tip a five thousand pound hunk of steel over on himself."

Bruce just shook his head.

"Furthermore," I continued, "the company's owner, Ciaffone was his name, was some kind of rich philanthropist. He came to the hospital that night Dad was killed. Approached me to tell me how sorry he was. Given his public image and reputation, it seems to me that the media should have been all over the incident. And where was OSHA? As I persisted with my questions, Ma got hysterical. She told me I couldn't pursue this, that she'd 'promised.' When I asked who she'd promised, she hung up on me. Next thing I knew, my phone was ringing and it was Jay."

Bruce said nothing, but his eyes opened wider.

I could feel myself becoming angry again, even after all the years that had passed.

"Jay reamed me out. He accused me of only wanting money for myself. Said I didn't give a shit about how this kind of stress would affect Ma's health, and on and on. I couldn't even get a word in. Then *he* hung up on me too."

"So you dropped it," Bruce said.

"What else could I do? Ma called back a little while later, crying, asking me to promise her that I would leave it alone, just like she promised whomever she promised. The only one still alive who might know anything about this is Jay, and he and I are not exactly on good terms."

When we passed through the St. Joseph's Cemetery gate, I could feel Bruce tense up.

"I haven't been back since the funeral," he said as we pulled up to the gravesite.

"Well, as I told you, I moved back home the year my mother died, and since then, I've been keeping it up. I plant portulacas every spring." I tried to keep my voice even.

At first we were quiet, just standing over the stone. Crows cawed their way back to their nests as the shadows of twilight lengthened. Mosquitoes began to whine around our heads. Finally Bruce looked down at me, and we stared at each other. I could barely see his features, but I could feel the sadness that matched my own. I broke the silence.

"I knew that somehow I would find you. I had a dream. I was walking out of the funeral home after Uncle George's service, and I heard my name whispered from the bushes. It was you, hiding. When I woke up, I felt that you were near. I knew then that we would meet again, that you would come back into my life." I started to cry.

Bruce said nothing, just stared at me. Then he walked the few steps to put his arms around me, and we hugged each other.

"I want to bake you a cake," Bruce told me over the phone.

"Are you serious?" My birthday was approaching and we'd discussed going out to lunch for a change.

"Yes. In your kitchen. I'll bring the ingredients. I'll make my specialty, pineapple upside-down cake, for your birthday."

A few days later, I sat and watched while Bruce arranged pineapple slices on the bottom of a rectangular baking pan he'd lined with wax paper. He sang - Creedence's "Green River," I think - as he worked.

I'd never liked my mother's galley kitchen. Long and narrow, it had been a bedroom once upon a time. My grandfather himself had cut the opening for the door at the room's back end after he and my grandmother bought the house, before my mother was born. According to her, a hand pump had once drawn water from the well into a porcelain tub that sat in the same spot as my stainless sink, and an ice box once stood where my refrigerator now stood. Gas lights once lit this room where Homer used to shave every morning because there was no bathroom yet, and Annie used to brew beer in big kettles on the same stove into which my brother now set his baking pan. The scent of cinnamon mingled with the grassy-earthy tang from the side yard garden as the summer breeze drifted through the room's only window. I sighed, contented.

Bruce turned to me, the oven mitts still on his hands.

"You have pretty blue eyes," he said.

I laughed. "So do you. Dad's eyes."

He took off the mitts and sat down at the table. "I need you to do something for me. When you get a chance."

"Sure."

"I'm almost as old as Dad was when he was killed. I'd like you to calculate for me the exact date when I will be the same age as he was that day. When that day comes, you and I will get together and do something special. Okay?"

"Well, okay, but you could do the math," I teased, trying to keep the mood light, "You're an accountant." I still couldn't believe that Brucie had become an accountant, of all things.

"I know I could, but I'd like you to do it."

I followed through with my brother's request, but he and I would not spend that day together.

I'll admit I made mistakes. With Bruce, I pushed too hard, although I didn't realize it at the time. He seemed genuinely pleased to extend his hand to my daughter, Chloe, at first, but when I invited him to her high school graduation, he balked. He assured me that his resistance resulted only from an unwillingness to mix with Karen, whom I'd also invited. He insisted that Karen was potentially "a bad influence" on me as well as on Chloe and ended up reciting a litany of her past misdeeds, many of which had occurred while Bruce had still been a child.

I also made the mistake of extending an invitation to Bruce for the annual family Christmas event that Dad's cousin, Jeanette, still organized and which I'd begun attending. Bruce wrote me an angry letter, informing me that he had no interest in any other family members, that "'our relationship' is 'our relationship' . . . I came to see you!" He signed the letter "Love, your brother, Bruce."

Somewhere around this time, he also informed me that he'd decided to take legal steps to change his name.

". . . although I'll always be 'Bruce Girouard' to you," he said.

"I don't understand why," I later said to Karen. "His reasons were so vague."

"He's weird," she shrugged. "Always was."

Shortly thereafter, when Chloe expressed disappointment in having "lost another uncle," I asked Bruce if he would consider including her in one of his visits, which had turned into meeting for lunch in restaurants since I had not yet been invited to his home and he had stopped

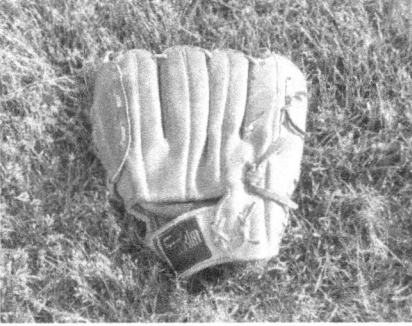

coming to mine. Although he had initially seemed genuinely pleased to be part of Chloe's life, even handing down to her his baseball glove since they were both "lefties," Bruce now balked and felt I was pushing. He sent me a very stern letter expressing doubt over whether or not he was "prepared to take on any meaningful relationship" with me, partly because of my "reverence for death" and "longing for the afterlife." I responded in an angry letter of my own in which I accused him of having sent me mixed signals from the beginning and of his being the one with the obsession for death. However, despite my private disappointment in Bruce's failure to live up to my childhood fantasies of him, I assured him that I still wanted to be in his life because, after all, "I am still your sister." Bruce's final letter was a methodical critique of my letter, each statement bracketed, numbered, and separately answered on the back of the paper. He ended by wondering if he should even have responded to my initial letter to him a year or so earlier because he "suspected it would come down to something like this." My typed word "sister" was bracketed and numbered "(25)" and corrected as "half-sister."

Bruce's death from pancreatic cancer a few years later was a quiet one. He'd told none of his friends and no one from our Dad's side of the family about his illness. As I understand it, two people were with him when he passed: the adult son and daughter from his mother's second marriage, the only people with whom he'd managed to sustain a lasting relationship. No obituary was posted. Bruce had been dead nearly six months before I heard of it.

I made mistakes with Karen too. As my marriage disintegrated, my issues with my husband, Bob, became so overwhelming that I allowed them and my overall unhappiness to overshadow everything else in my life and to cloud my judgment. I began drinking too much, to Karen's disapproval and often in her presence. My biggest mistake, however, involved my niece, who had expressed her own marital unhappiness to me. Cathy and I became confidantes. After a while, I began to sense Karen's resentment, although I was unprepared for her reaction when she finally found out, by accident, that Cathy's marriage was over. My sister blamed me, insisting in an angry email that keeping her daughter's secrets prevented saving a marriage she claimed she could have saved.

"Your loyalty should have been to me," the email said, "not to my daughter."

Her final words, despite my attempt to apologize and reason with her, were "Goodbye. Karen."

My twenty year old daughter Chloe, knowing how much my new-found relationship with my sister meant to me and upset over the prospect of being abandoned by yet another family member, tried to appeal to her Aunt Karen on my behalf in a teary phone call. Unmoved, my sister reaffirmed her position regarding me, and, furthermore, informed Chloe that any future contact between the two of them would have to come from Chloe.

"It'll be up to you," Karen said as she ended the conversation.

"I hate her," Chloe sobbed in her phone call to me that immediately followed. "She's a cunt."

13

Adultery

Driving from North Brookfield to the seminary in Cheshire, Connecticut, should take no more than a couple of hours, but I knew that, the way my mother drove, the trip would be closer to three. I watched her take a ticket from the toll collector at the Palmer entrance to the Mass Pike, flip on her blinker, and hesitantly merge into traffic.

I dreaded the long drive, dreaded the whole long, boring weekend ahead, but I did not offer to take her place behind the wheel, even as a diversion. Although, at sixteen, I'd just started Drivers' Ed with my English teacher, Mr. Boucher, I hated driving the Matador my mother had just bought after selling her carefully maintained 1965 Rambler for $150 to Jay Buckmaster up the street from us. Buckmaster thought the Rambler would be the perfect starter car for his daughter, who had just gotten her license. I agreed – the perfect starter car in which *I* had learned to drive, but *I* couldn't have it. When the Rambler's fan snapped, putting a large dent in the hood from underneath, Ma became wary of her eleven year old car, but the day one of the wheels fell off and rolled down the street as she backed out of our driveway, she decided the car that she'd had for its entire life (and most of mine) had to go despite my pleas to buy it. Now I had to see the car I'd hoped to own driven past my house nearly every day by another girl just about my age. The Matador only reinforced the sense of loss I'd been feeling since my father's death.

Our Lady of La Salette Seminary in Cheshire used to be a school but had just recently closed its doors to the public except for occasional retreat weekends and couples' counseling sessions. Ma and I had been invited by one of the brothers, a former classmate of hers from St. Joseph's School, to spend a day and night visiting and touring the grounds. The whole idea had been sprung on me last minute, and, though I tried to get out of it, Ma insisted that sixteen was still too young to be left home alone overnight. She talked up the relaxing weekend ahead and the beautiful gardens and buildings of La Salette, but I most definitely did not want to spend part of my spring vacation there just to see where Brother Jerome lived.

Aside from the fact that I'd already begun having major doubts about my affiliation with Catholicism, Brother Jerome was just weird. Even though he and my mother were the same age, his thinning hair had already completely grayed. He had a very soft voice, too soft, I thought, and when he spoke, his tongue made clicking sounds in his dry mouth. He licked his lips a lot, which I found distracting. Ma said the medicine he took for his nerves had side effects. I couldn't understand what about his cushy life made him so nervous.

During the last few years, Brother Jerome had started dropping by the house every few months when he came to town to visit his family in Little Canada. After the first few times, I'd say hi to him and stick around only long enough to be polite, then slip away to my room and stereo. Every visit went pretty much the same way: Ma caught him up on town gossip, and Brother Jerome talked about God and his wonderful life as a brother. He had his own car, spending money, paid vacations to tropical islands - all courtesy of the Catholic Church, and all he had to do in return was tend the gardens of a pretty much defunct seminary where he lived for free. He repeatedly told my mother how good God was to give him this life that he loved, even though, despite his medication, he occasionally had to be admitted to some sort of hospital for his nerves. His visits to North Brookfield usually occurred right after being discharged, so he always seemed pumped about his life and God and his gardens back at the seminary. I had nothing to contribute to these conversations beyond answering the typical questions of how I was and how I was doing in school. The one time he'd shown more interest, I must have been eleven or twelve.

"So what do you want to be when you grow up?" he'd asked, peering through his wire-rimmed glasses and sipping from a second glass of wine, his hands only slightly shaking.

"A veterinarian." Honestly, I had no idea, but adults always expected an answer, and a veterinarian sounded good to me at the moment.

Brother Jerome looked thoughtful. "There are so many careers that help *people*. Why a veterinarian?"

I hadn't expected that kind of reaction, so I blurted the first thing that came to me. "Because I like animals better than people."

Wrong answer number two. Brother Jerome frowned, obvious disapproval in his eyes.

"You don't mean that," he said, and at the same time I heard "She doesn't mean it that way" from my mother.

I looked from one to the other. Didn't they want me to be honest? I couldn't lie to a brother, and right then I passionately wanted to be a veterinarian because I loved animals - and as for people in general, not so much.

"Yes, I do," I said then got up to leave when he began reaffirming the wonderful life as a servant of God.

A whole weekend of gardens and God-talk and Brother Jerome licking his lips. Wicked. I scrunched down in the Matador's back seat and stared at the trucks passing us on the highway. Reading made me carsick, so I had nothing to do but brood, something I'd become great at lately.

I couldn't accurately say I missed my father because over the last few years he'd spent increasingly more time away from home. My mother had occasionally wryly commented that he came home only to sleep and change clothes – and sometimes not even for that. His second shift job at the steel plant along with all the overtime he worked meant that I rarely saw him during the week anyway, but he'd no longer spent much time at home during the weekends either. Typically, he'd leave the house on Saturday late morning (having worked Friday night) and return sometime Monday just before work. After years of picking fights over his whereabouts, my mother had given up the battle, finally realizing that nothing she said or did would change his ways.

Dad had missed so many family occasions, holidays, and even birthdays that you'd think I wouldn't feel his absence as much as I now did, especially since his presence at any event usually meant that either my mother or I ended up in tears. Yet, I still imagined I heard his voice

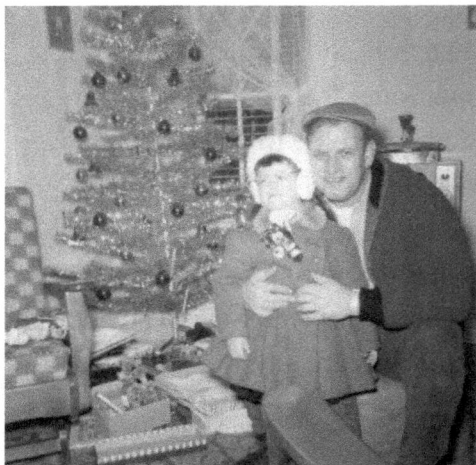

downstairs over the stereo from up in my room. I still caught myself glancing at the back door, expecting him to walk in. Before long, I realized that the loss I felt was one I'd gradually felt for years: I grieved not so much for the man who had virtually deserted my mother and me but for the father from my early childhood. I missed my Daddy, who'd held me, his "Chick-Chick," in his lap and told me stories; who'd made for just the two of us on Saturday mornings the most perfect eggs and oatmeal that my mother could never get quite right; who'd taught me air guitar and Yahtzee and the correct way to section a grapefruit.

Daddy let me ride in the bed of his truck, even on I-495, and took me on roller coasters. On summer nights, we drove into The Dump, slowly and with the headlights off, and, after he killed the engine, we sat for a few minutes until he flicked on the brights so I could watch all the rats scuttle around the blackened skeletons of discarded furniture and

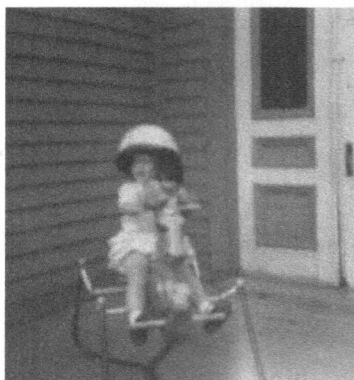

through the charred remains of trash. During elementary school, when I'd come home talking about this or that boy, Daddy always made me laugh by teasing, "Invite him over so I can run him down with my car."

Once upon a time, my Dad was my hero, and I clung to that for as long as I could lie to myself. One Halloween, in sixth grade, I threw a party in our new garage that he had just built. I dressed up as Dad, having borrowed his baggy sweatshirt, workpants cinched around my waist, clunky work boots, and driving cap, and I felt only mild regret when I saw the lovely Dani Ballard, a class-mate and rival, dressed as a dancer. No one thought to pull out a camera, and Dad worked that night, so he never saw my impersonation.

As a child, I wanted to please him, even to impress him. In my fantasies, I saw myself as the tomboy to compensate for the second son I thought he wanted, but, in reality, I felt as though I always fell short. My poor eyesight and lack of coordination meant failure at sports, and though I excelled in school, I never saw the approval and pride in his eyes that I saw in my mother's. Only after his funeral, with friends and family gathered at our house, did I hear that he'd often said to others the words he'd never been able to say to me.

"Your father was so proud of you," said the wife of one of his close friends as she gave me a hug.

I stared then said, "He was?"

"He talked about you all the time, how smart you are."

"He never told me."

As I matured, Dad became more awkward with me or I became more awkward with him or a combination of both, as if we couldn't fig-ure out what to say to each other. I blamed myself, although the continu-ous strife between my parents could have been the cause. I tried not to get involved but when I occasionally had to choose sides, I generally chose my moth-er's because she was the one I'd have to deal with after he inevitably stormed out of the house. I chose Dad's side only when I thought I could safely do so, like when he decided to grow a beard, when he bought a stupid-looking Beatles-style wig to cover his balding head, and when he started wearing a large silver peace medal-lion that dangled over his turtlenecks. Part of me admired Dad for being such a free spirit, yet I gradually began to acknowledge (if only privately) the flaws in him as a husband and father.

The morning I turned thirteen, however, he'd clearly made plans to please me. I'd asked to spend the day in Salem, touring "witch muse-ums," and Dad had taken the day off from work to go with me, my moth-er, and a friend of mine from school. A few weeks earlier, he had brought home a portable plastic table organ that my mother set up on a stand in the dining room. Dad started teaching himself a few songs on the num-bered keys, practicing here and there, "My Wild Irish Rose," "The Wed-ding March," and other outdated selections from the *Easy Organ Song-book.*

The morning of my birthday, as I descended the first couple of stairs, still in my pajamas, still rubbing sleep out of my eyes, I heard the organ, and his rich voice as he sang "I love you as I never loved before . . ."

Then my mother's voice, speaking low, "Buck, she's not six-teen."

My father, ignoring her, continued to play and sing so that as I emerged from the hallway into the dining room, I saw him in his bath-robe at the organ, his back to me but his head turned to see my expres-sion when he sang, ". . . when you were sweet, when you were sweet thirteen," emphasizing the last word because of course he had planned that all along, and even my mother had to smile. Later, as he made his special eggs, she privately told me that he had been practically pacing, intermittently glancing up the stairs, impatient for me to wake so that he could serenade me on my special day.

I barely noticed as Ma paid the toll in Springfield and turned onto I-91 South, headed toward Connecticut. Then I could feel her eyes on me in the rearview mirror.

"How you doin' hon?" she asked, in a tone that sounded like she was speaking to a child.

God, I hated that. I knew she meant well and was just trying to cheer me up, but I just wanted to be left alone.

"Fine." I faked nonchalance, hoping she wouldn't want to chit chat. I just wanted to wallow in my thoughts.

As Dad spent less time at home, I tried to make the most of whatever father-daughter time we had, even if doing so caused me physical discomfort. In fifth grade, I started getting occasional dizzy spells, and when they didn't go away on their own, our doctor admitted me to St. Vincent's Hospital the following year for tests. The night of my arrival, I experienced my first spinal tap, and, afterwards, the nurse mistakenly propped up my head with a couple of pillows. The result was a searing headache that intensified if I raised my head and persisted for the rest of my stay. My mother had brought me in and had been in every day since to see me, but my father surprised me by simply appearing next to my hospital bed one afternoon while my mother worked. After only a few minutes of awkward small talk, I could see that he was losing interest, so when he suggested a game of cards, I agreed, sort of half sitting up to play. Unfortunately, we hadn't even finished one game of Hearts when I had to stop.

"I'm sorry, Dad," I said, nearly in tears from both the disappointment and the pounding behind my eyes. "I have to stop. My head is killing me."

"It's okay," he said, gathering up the cards and putting them back in his pocket.

Dad sat with me while I tried to gather enough strength for another go at it, but after a few minutes of neither of us having anything to say, he kissed me and went out the door. I cried, feeling as if I'd failed to measure up yet again.

Dad and I spent so little time together as I got older that even ordinary errands became special memories for me. Although I would miss his pickup, I happily tagged along when Dad decided to shop for a new vehicle. At fourteen, I had already begun eyeing the cars in Buddy Lane's AMC lot when I took the long way home from school, and I thought that just maybe I could convince Dad to test drive the purple Javelin AMX parked on the end.

Dad pulled into the lot and parked his truck off to the side. Together, we strolled over to the selection of new cars, passing by the Beetle ragtop, the Spitfire and the other trade-ins. I tried to contain myself as he ignored the Jeeps, barely glanced at the Gremlins, and approached a fluorescent green Hornet. He bent down to peer in, then opened the driver's side door.

"What do you think?" he asked.

"Uh. Well. I think Ma would like it," I said, hoping he'd get the hint.

He climbed in and felt his head brush against the headliner.

"Yeah, well, she has the Rambler. This one's for me."

Now was my chance.

He let me lead him to the Javelin and gave it the onceover. I fairly drooled over the gleaming deep purple, the black T-stripe and interior, the wide tires. In another year or so, I would be learning to drive, and I could imagine no cooler car for my Dad to take me out in. He grinned at Buddy, who approached, dangling the keys. With a roar that made my stomach vibrate, the Javelin leapt to life.

After a few minutes, Dad turned off the ignition and tossed the keys back to Buddy.

"*Aw, Dad!*"

"Your mother would kill me," he said.

Dad's choice that day, to my utter embarrassment, was an Ambassador station wagon with fake wood grain along its sides, air conditioning and power everything. I could not see how a guy as cool as Dad could sink from a motorcycle to a truck, to another truck, to a station wagon, and I could not see myself ever driving it.

Though my mother had secretly taken me out in her Rambler before I'd gotten my permit, Dad was killed at work the week after my sixteenth birthday, before he'd had the chance to give me any driving lessons. He'd taught me to ride a bicycle, but he would never teach me to drive. He would never see me graduate from high school. He would never walk me down the aisle or dance with me to "Daddy's Little Girl" as I had fantasized when planning the perfect someday-wedding with my friends. As my mother's Matador crossed the Connecticut line on that April morning in 1976, I felt the permanent loss not only of the hero-Daddy of my childhood but of any chance that he and I could ever again get it right, and the scenery outside the car window blurred.

And then there was the guilt. I loved my father but sometimes I didn't like him very much. Now I agonized over all those times I'd felt relief when he walked out because it meant a reprieve from the arguing. I thought of my parents' separate, tension-free vacations I'd come to prefer and felt a lump of shame in my throat. Dad could be critical, and some-times days without him were just easier. Also, though I realized money would be tight without his income, I tortured myself over sharing my mother's relief at the regularly paid death benefits from the government that no one would lose at cards or at a Craps table in Vegas.

A recurring dream I'd had over the years was of my parents in the front seat of the Rambler - my father driving - and me in the back. Each trip began pleasantly, sunlight shining through the brilliant autumn foli-age and flooding the car as we sailed along country roads. I noticed wa-ter, a lake alongside, and as we passed, the road narrowed, then bore sharply left toward the stretch of shimmering blue. When I felt the car begin its descent, I leaned forward, over the top of the bench seat to get a better view through the windshield and could clearly see the road disap-pearing just ahead into the lake. I panicked and, each time, yelled at my father to stop, to back up, but, though I pounded and grabbed at his shoulder, he always blithely continued forward, my mother sitting pas-sively next to him, until the Rambler's nose met the water, ending the dream. I didn't have to be Freud to understand my subconscious fear that Dad's gambling addiction would sink our family, and now I didn't have to worry about that. The dreams had stopped after his death, and so I felt guilty.

I also felt guilt over the previous Father's Day's gift and card that I'd resentfully withheld after waiting all day for him to show up from who-knew-where and how the next day, when he finally appeared, I ig-nored his hints and, despite the hurt look in his eyes, never even wished him a belated Happy Father's Day. I ran across the wrapped gift a few months later and cried, wishing I could replay that scene.

I felt guilty over the bulls' eyes candies I'd hidden under the chair while watching t.v. one day when I heard Dad's car pull up. He loved them, and I was afraid he'd eat too many, perhaps even finish the bag. I felt guilty for my squeamishness when he asked me to knot pieces of string around the skin tags he couldn't reach on his back.

I felt guilty for not having been a better daughter.

The Matador turned into the entrance at La Salette Seminary, and as it rounded the bend, I could see Brother Jerome knee-deep in a patch of flowers, a running hose in his hand. My mother slowed the car and waved. He waved back and pointed to the entrance of what looked to be the main building. I wiped my eyes and tried not to think about how the tang of the freshly mowed lawn brought to my mind the image of my father, shirtless, his broad shoulders sunburned, his stomach overlapping the waist of his plaid knee-length shorts as his muscled arms pushed the mower in our yard - before he'd lost interest in our house and in us.

Years later, I would try to recall details of that weekend in Cheshire, the buildings and gardens we toured, the people we met, but found that I had blocked most of it out. Of all the structures, only the chapel impressed me, mainly because of all the blond wood – so modern looking compared to the dark pews in the more traditionally-styled Catholic churches I'd previously seen. The stained glass in the La Salette chapel was cut in geometric designs of primary colors instead of in complex renditions of famous religious paintings or Stations of the Cross. The nave itself seemed lower and wider to me and very open. I could hear the breezes shushing through the rafters, and wondered, even then, if there was a God after all - or was it Nature trying to speak to me.

Brother Jerome and my mother and I ate in the service kitchen. The cook made sandwiches of some sort, but all I would later remember about her is that she had had impressions taken for false teeth and that the plaster, or whatever had been used, kept breaking off in her mouth so that she had to keep reaching in to pull out the pieces. Fascinated, I alternated watching her and the giant pot of something she stirred on the stove, to be served that evening for the brothers' dinner, and wondered whether it contained any of the residue.

I would remember Brother Edmund, too, and not because he impressed me but because I had to spend several evening hours with him in his room when my mother disappeared. Brother Jerome had introduced Brother Edmund to us right after our arrival as his closest friend at the seminary. Younger, with dark hair and sideburns nearly to his chin, Brother Edmund looked to me like he should have been singing in a rock band like the Kinks or the Raiders. In fact, he reminded me of Mark Lindsay, except Brother Edmund's eyebrows were not as bushy. You'd think someone who looked like a rock star would have at least a mildly interesting personality, but Brother Edmund couldn't have been more dry if he'd tried.

Somehow or other, my mother and I got separated after supper. Ma liked to meet new priests, so every time she and I attended Mass in a different church, she always made a point of introducing herself. She had mentioned that she planned to speak to the La Salette priest as soon as he was free to see her, so when Brother Jerome escorted me to Brother Edmund's room, I just assumed my stay there would be minimal. Brother Edmund didn't even attempt conversation with me after Brother Jerome went out the door, leaving it ajar; he immediately turned on his television, looking for something I "might like" until The Sound of Music started.

As Brother Edmund and I sat in his room watching the movie, he on his bed and I on his desk chair, I kept glancing at my watch. I would have preferred a Charles Bronson or Clint Eastwood movie to this sappy musical, but Brother Edmund's eyes stayed glued to the screen. Where was my mother? And why was her visit with the priest taking so long? The credits were rolling when Brother Jerome finally returned. When I saw my mother a few minutes later, her eyes were red and puffy, but I didn't think much of it. After all, she teared up over birthday cards.

On the way back to Massachusetts in the car the next morning after Sunday Mass, my mother glanced several times at me in the rearview mirror before she spoke, as if she needed to tell me something but couldn't figure out how to phrase it.

"I'll be able to receive communion from now on," she finally said.

I looked up. "How?"

My mother had been unable to receive any of the Blessed Sacraments since her divorce from her first husband and remarriage to my father – one of the rules of the Catholic Church with which she disagreed yet observed even when we attended Mass out of town. I'd been aware of this fact since I became old enough to notice and ask why she always stayed in the pew when the other parishioners approached the altar.

"I went to confession. That's where I was last night, talking to the priest," she said, alternately glancing from the road to the rearview mirror.

"Confession?" Anyone could confess to a priest, but Ma had not seen the point since absolution, another of the Blessed Sacraments, had likewise been denied to her. Unless.

"Wait, what did you confess?" My voice had risen, and I could hear the mixture of anger and incredulity creeping in at the realization of what my mother had done.

She didn't answer right away. I knew what I was about to hear, but I wanted to make her say the words, so I waited, glaring at her.

"Well, I had to, you know, confess to adultery, so that I could receive the Sacraments again." She spoke haltingly, in an apologetic tone.

"How could you do that? How could you do that to *Dad*?" I no longer cared how hysterical I sounded.

"Donna, your father is dead. It doesn't matter to him." Her eyes pleaded with me. "And my faith is important to me. You know that your father and I haven't had a real marriage for a long time."

Of course I knew that. The bickering I'd heard virtually all of my life, their separate sleeping arrangements from around the time I turned nine, their separate vacations beginning shortly thereafter, his weekend disappearances – clearly, their marriage had steadily deteriorated over the years. She'd also once confided in me that the passion had gone out of their relationship - not that I wanted or needed to know that - and that the lack of interest had been solely his.

"When a woman is rejected by her husband, it's an awful blow to her ego," she'd said, surprising me. I'd just assumed that her resentments and hostilities over habitually being disappointed and lied to had killed her attraction for him. Additionally, though both my parents looked younger than their years, my mother had maintained her slim figure while my father had put on a few extra pounds around his middle. The fact that she still wanted him but that he no longer wanted her fed her suspicions of there being a third party involved. "If a man doesn't want sex at home, he's getting it somewhere else," she'd continued. I'd held up my hand in protest, not wanting to hear anymore.

Yes, I knew that their marriage had virtually ended, but I also knew that she had still loved him and had tried to hold our family together as much as she could when faced with his indifference to her accusations. And I knew that she still missed him, or at least an earlier version of him. A few weeks after Dad's death, Pepere had come to visit, and I heard him say to my mother, "I miss that boy." My mother's voice sounded so sad when she said, "I keep hearing his Harley pulling into the driveway." I realized then that, just as I was missing the hero-Daddy from my early childhood, she was actually missing not her husband of seventeen years but the dashing, reckless young man in the leather jacket who used to race his motorcycle at Watkins Glen, the man with whom she had fallen in love.

They'd met at a dance in Connecticut. Completely self-sufficient and self-reliant since her divorce a few years earlier, my mother had no interest in finding a husband. She had a good job at Gavitt Wire & Cable and had raised her son Jay, now a Marine, with no financial help. Going to dances with Clara, Lorraine, or Aurore simply meant an evening out and no more. However there was just something about "Buck" - perhaps the bike and the leather, perhaps the way his dark hair curled over his forehead when his brilliant blue eyes fixed on hers, or his polished charm despite his tough exterior. Despite her resolve, Polly fell hard.

Almost from the start, Buck and Polly had their minor disagreements, but didn't all couples? Even while dating, she had had her doubts about whether or not they were suited to each other because, while Polly was somewhat reserved in a crowd, Buck liked being the center of attention, perhaps a bit too much. Like that time at the Sportsman's Club when, oblivious to her embarrassment, he began heckling the band just to call attention to himself. She'd sunk into her seat when the frustrated singer dared him to do a better job. Without hesitation, Buck took the microphone and started singing "I Left My Heart in San Francisco," and, at the end of the song, she whistled and applauded along with the rest of the audience, relieved when the singer clapped him on the back and bought him a drink.

Polly could see a bit of a wild side to Buck, but tried to convince herself that they would balance each other out, in contrast to him and his ex-wife who, according to him, had been too irresponsible and unreliable. However, when Buck took her along on a motorcycle run, Polly had not enjoyed the thrill of clinging to his waist while simultaneously trying to keep her seat on the back of his Harley. As they wound through narrow trails, the low-hanging twigs he'd ducked slapping her in the face, she decided that separate hobbies surely couldn't hurt a couple. She could stay home, she reasoned, and he could have his time with his biker friends once in a while.

One afternoon, though, they did quarrel, over something that began as insignificant but that somehow blew way out of proportion. Her doubts kicked in and took over; she broke off their engagement. Later that night, just as she wound her alarm clock and sat down on the edge of the bed, she heard music outside. When she opened her window and looked down, there stood Buck in the glow of the streetlight, his arms full of the accordion he'd learned to play years earlier, serenading her and not caring who saw or heard. She sat at the window, crying all through "Let Me Call You Sweetheart" and, when he finished, ran down the stairs and out the door to throw her arms around his neck.

I knew about their courtship and the early years of their marriage only through my mother's stories to me as a child and the way her eyes got that dreamy look when she'd told them to me. I thought I knew everything about their history when, as I glared at her from the back seat of the Matador, I said, "But you *loved* him" in a tone meant to sound accusatory.

I couldn't put into words how I felt that by confessing to adultery, she had demeaned their entire relationship from start to finish as sinful and dirty and denounced their marriage as something that never should have happened. A huge mistake that she regretted. Also if, in the eyes of the Catholic Church at least, her marriage to my father was considered adulterous, where did that leave me? A bastard?

But if I had then known the whole story, would I have felt any different?

I knew about the initial lies my father had told my mother regarding his finances: that his money was tight - supposedly because his first wife had been a spendthrift. Shortly after their marriage, Ma had discovered his lies of omission: the enormous credit card debt and the payments still owed on the gleaming white Harley that he'd earlier claimed had been paid off. Ma insisted he sell the bike to offset his indebtedness. He did, but he never forgave her. Ma also quickly realized that his gambling was not merely the diversion he'd made it seem but a growing addiction. Dad's biggest lie of omission, however, was one that my mother kept hidden from me until just a few weeks before her own death.

I'd sat on her bed and together we dug through the contents of her strongbox. I didn't know what documents she needed, but since I'd never before had access to the red metal container that looked very much like a tackle box, I was curious. I leafed through receipts and records of bills paid years earlier and briefly scanned old papers pertaining to the house, including the original bill of sale made out to Homer and Annie Martin in 1920. When I came across my parents' marriage certificate, I paused to read it.

"Uh, why does it say 1960?" I was born in 1959.

"Keep looking and you'll find the other one," Ma said, her tone neutral.

Other one?

Seconds later, I held a marriage certificate in each hand, one dated 1960 as well as the original one from 1958, which had a neat cigarette burn in its corner. Ma then explained how she had been confused when Dad insisted they marry out of state and that the wedding be kept quiet even though they'd been dating well over a year, but she'd agreed since, after all, they'd both been married before and didn't need a

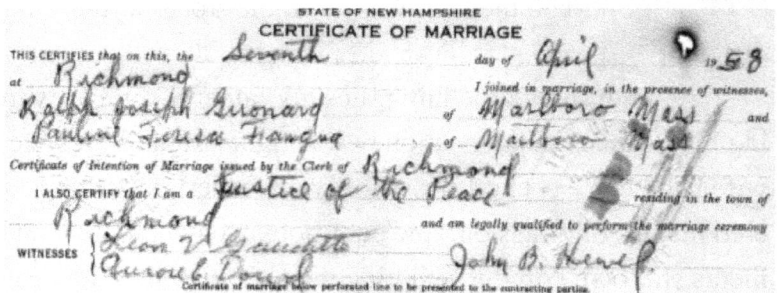

big to-do. They'd gone to a Justice of the Peace in New Hampshire with only Chill and Aurore as witnesses and afterwards had all gone out to dinner before the newly married couple headed for the Poconos. Nearly a year had passed when she got the phone call from her new mother-in-law who said she'd just that day run into their family attorney and happened to mention her son's marriage.

"He told your Memere the state's two-year waiting period for re-marriage had not ended and that our marriage was invalid," she said. "Apparently, your father had not filed for his divorce from Flo until just before our wedding. So we had to get married again, for real. I was tear-ass."

I stared at her, shaking my head and trying to imagine my mother waiting for my father to come home from work *that* night. I looked over at the framed wedding photograph still displayed on her dresser even

though my father had been dead for over twenty years. Ma's pretty young face grinned at the camera as she stood next to my father, her royal blue hat with its little veil matching her suit, gloves and high heels. I knew she'd even kept the hat in a trunk in the attic.

Ma caught my glance. "That picture is from the first ceremony. The second time, the four of us went to Connecticut, and I was so mad I wore brown. I wouldn't let anybody take any pictures."

I looked again at the cigarette burn in the original certificate. "I'm surprised you still married him after finding out he'd lied to you."

"I don't know." She sighed. "Your father lied about so many things. Besides, what was I going to do at that point? By the time I found out, I was already pregnant with you."

However, I knew nothing about that bogus first ceremony when I was sixteen and sitting in the Matador on the way home from Cheshire, furious at my mother for having turned against my father and dishonoring his memory. Just as I didn't then know that I would someday confirm my mother's suspicions of his infidelity during an accidental encounter with his mistress' best friend and that just as my father and Chill, both married, had cheated *with* my mother and Aurore, they would, years later, cheat *on* my mother and Aurora with two women named Rita and Loretta. In my grief and my ignorance of the extent of my father's duplicity, perhaps I could afford to be self-righteous at my mother's expense. I certainly thought so.

During the rest of the drive home, I wouldn't speak to her. I wouldn't even look at her.

IN AN UNDEVELOPED, PRIVATELY OWNED FIELD NEAR CIDER MILL ROAD, THE CROW LANDS ON ONE OF HER FAVORITE SPOTS, AN OUTCROPPING OF ROCKS THAT WERE ONCE THE BACK WALLS OF CAVES WHERE, DURING THE SMALLPOX EPIDEMIC AT THE END OF THE EIGHTEENTH CENTURY, THE SICK WOULD STAY TO TRY TO RECOVER WHILE NOT ENDANGERING THEIR FAMILIES. LEGEND HAS IT THAT TOWNSPEOPLE WOULD LEAVE FOOD AND SUPPLIES AT REGULAR INTERVALS IN A DESIGNATED SAFE DISTANCE FROM THE INFECTED. MOST OF THE CURRENT POPULATION HAS ONLY A VAGUE IDEA OF THE RUINS' LOCATION BECAUSE THE AREA IS POSTED TO KEEP OUT TRESPASSERS, BUT, SUPPOSEDLY, ON ONE OF THE ROCKS, A MESSAGE CARVED OVER TWO CENTURIES AGO CAN STILL BE READ: "I HAVE SMALLPOX – APRIL 12, 1782." IF THE DAY WERE SUNNY, THE OLD CROW WOULD BE CONTENT ON THE COOL, SEMI-SHADED ROCKS, BUT THE CONTINUOUS DRIZZLE URGES HER ON.

THE OLD CROW FLIES EAST, STAYING FAIRLY CLOSE TO THE NORTH BROOKFIELD TOWN LINE, NOT STOPPING UNTIL SHE REACHES THE ANTIQUE BARN AT THE END OF THE EAST BROOKFIELD ROAD. THE BARN HAS A LARGE "FOR SALE" SIGN ON ITS FRONT AND HAS BEEN EMPTY FOR YEARS, ITS DECAY AND NEGLECT BECOMING MORE OBVIOUS WITH EACH WINTER THAT PASSES. SOMEONE BROKE A WINDOW, SO NOW BOARDS HAVE BEEN NAILED UP TO DISCOURAGE ANY FURTHER VANDALISM. THE OLD CROW LANDS ON THE BARN'S ROOF AND LOOKS ACROSS TO WHERE THE HIGHWAY MEETS BRICKYARD ROAD, WHICH, FARTHER DOWN, HAD BEEN A POPULAR PARKING SPOT FOR 1970S TEENAGERS WHO WANTED PRIVACY. ANOTHER OF HER STAGING AREAS, THE LAND WHERE THE TWO ROADS JOIN IS LOW AND MARSHY. THE TREE STUMPS THIN AND BRITTLE. DEAD BRANCHES CRISS-CROSS OVER THE MUCK WHERE NO FISH COULD LIVE BUT WHERE WORMS, SLUGS AND MANY VARIETIES OF BUGS CAN BE FOUND, ESPECIALLY DURING THE LIGHT RAIN OF A CHILLY GRAY DAY.

14

To the Left at the Top of the Stairs

(1920s)

It's the spare bedroom in Annie's house, rarely used except when one of her younger bachelor brothers is on a toot, needs a place to dry out and has nowhere else to go. Stern but good-hearted Annie will always take them in, sometimes for days at a time, providing fresh sheets, clean clothes and hot home-cooked meals, not to mention a bit of her home-made brew for the morning-after shakes. Medicinal purposes only. Hair o' the dog, you might say.

One brother, Henry, lives alone just next door, on the first floor of a tenement he owns, but for some reason he climbs the stairs past his widowed sister Molly's apartment to the empty third floor, where a fire of unknown origin killed old Mrs. Belrose, and up there all alone, he quietly drinks for days, drinks himself sick, until eventually he finds the strength to wander over to Annie's to begin yet another period of drying out until the thirst starts up again. The fire on the third floor was the second one on his property. The barn had already burned down, and rumor has it that Henry himself had set that fire for the insurance money. Blarney. Henry sells Pontiacs for a living and collects money from the state for Molly's rent; he doesn't need to be setting his own buildings on fire. Eventually, he will die in that third floor room where he drinks, from the burst appendix that will poison his already poisoned system while he sits slumped over, unconscious and unaware. It will occur to Annie, or maybe Molly, that too many days have passed since Henry's last appearance, and one of the sisters will find him dead on the floor.

Perhaps, this week, 'tis Bob who will be occupying his sister Annie's spare bedroom to the left at the top of the stairs. Bob served in World War I and claims to have swallowed the gas while over there. He still has the gas mask to prove it. It hangs in the little closet in Annie's spare bedroom along with his uniform even though Bob still lives at home with Ma and the youngest girl, Lizzie. Bob collects the disability and walks the two doors down to Hart's Café to do his drinking. He knows that if he gets carried away with a bit too much of the beverage, Lizzie will turn him away. His Ma's rapidly declining health has put Lizzie in charge and made her bossy. She has recently threatened to lock him out for good, the way she locked out their Da, if he doesn't change his ways. Bob resents his younger sister's new authority but fears her thunderous self-righteousness. Ah, bless Annie for always being there in a brother's time of need.

Long after dark, Annie and her husband Homer hear the clear but teary tenor Irish lilt "...Tell me this before I die, shall my soul pass through Ireland..." and here comes Bob down the street, staggering or perhaps being half carried by one of his hooligan friends. Once, he arrived barely conscious in a wheelbarrow that its driver dumped at the bottom of Annie's porch steps. Homer says nothing; he has become used to the unannounced visits from his wife's rowdy Irish family. Annie always meets Bob on the front porch in case he has forgotten her rules. The price for a few days in the spare room is that he must sleep off some of his drunk on the porch swing. Annie keeps a spotless house and will not tolerate any hung-over vomiting, even in the thunder pot under the bed. As dawn begins to streak the sky, Bob wakes, vomits over the porch railing into the lilacs, and only then enters the house through the front door. He must tread lightly if he can; Annie's wrath will be fearsome if he wakes little Pauline. Bob climbs the stairs, then turns to the left to enter the small sparsely furnished spare bedroom with its pale green horsehair plaster walls and bare wide board floor. Through the far wall, a slightly darker green plank door, narrow and only about four feet high, with an ornate black wrought iron latch leads to the little attic room where Annie keeps trunks of seasonal clothing, discarded baby furniture, and other items not needed on a regular basis. Her considerable girth, nearing three hundred pounds, makes access to the attic difficult and frustrating, so now it's become Pauline's job to fetch an extra blanket or winter overcoat while Annie waits just outside the door.

No kerosene lamp has been left out for Bob in the bedroom for fear that the tremors may knock it over, but just enough light seeps through the single curtained window for him to make his way shakily past Annie's Singer treadle sewing machine to collapse onto the small quilted bed in the far corner.

When Daniel Kelley visits from the city, he also stays in the spare room. Even now that he is remarried (for the second time), he comes to North Brookfield alone and unannounced and only to see Annie, his eldest daughter. True it may be that he should not have kept company with the ladies while his wife lay at home sick and possibly dying, the excess fluid seeping out of the pores in her puffy ankles, yet he can't forgive Lizzie, his youngest, for ordering him out of his own house. Well, if she was hell-bent on doing without him, then she could do without any of his money too. In his occasional self-righteous rants about ungrateful children, Daniel forgets that he has spent most of his money on clothes, expensive cigars, and trips to New York City to see Cousin Georgie Cohan perform on Broadway. Quite dapper in his spats and top coat, his hat sitting at a jaunty angle on his balding head, his cane twirling from his fingers, Daniel doesn't bother to knock. "Annie, girl, where are ye?" he bellows, and the answer is typically "In the kitchen, Da."

Pauline, born to Annie late in life, is Daniel's favorite grandchild and comes running to throw herself into his outstretched arms. "Grampa Kelley" will be the one to give Pauline her first grown up gift on her fourteenth birthday: black high heels bought in New York that she will always remember as her "Joan Crawford shoes."

Homer nods to Daniel from his overstuffed chair, where he coughs up that day's asbestos from the factory where he has worked all of his life into the

nearby brass spittoon. During the years to come, his lungs will completely fill, and he will die of the asbestosis, but until then, except for the few
minutes of rest he allows himself after work, he stays in motion: building, fixing, cleaning, so much so that he has earned the nickname "Uncle
Shine and Polish" from his giggling nieces and nephews. Although he
would never admit it, most of Homer's activities give him an excuse to
lay low amid the almost constant comings and goings of his sisters and
brothers-in-law and there many many children. Of French Canadian descent, shy and quiet Homer Martin is often represented in old family photographs as a figure in the background, caught mid-sweep, broom in
hand, his presence a mere whisper in the hub of activity around him. Perhaps it is his unassuming air, his tepidness amid the stormy Irish tempers,
which always provokes his father-in-law to begin an impassioned tirade
about politics or, worse, religion in Homer's presence. A self-professed
atheist, Daniel Kelley reaches for the family Bible, reads aloud a random
passage, then proceeds to harangue his reluctant son-in-law into a debate
on God, the Pope, and Catholicism: "Why should I believe an Italian?!"
Voices rise as Homer gets drawn in by Daniel's persistence only to be
shouted down every time.

Though religious, Annie is unfazed by her father's blasphemes,
but years later they will provide the excuse for fiercely Catholic Lizzie to
bully her siblings into agreeing that Daniel's body be banished from the
family plots in St. Joseph's Cemetery. "He didn't care for the church
while he lived; why would he care now?" Lizzie will reason and arrange
for burial across town in an unmarked grave in Protestant Walnut Grove
Cemetery.

When her husband and father argue, Annie wisely stays out of the
commotion except to move Daniel aside when she needs to get her roast
from the oven where he stands to warm his backside: "Will you please
move your arse, Da?!"

Even though he fully expects to win all of the arguments, Daniel
does not take his cigars with him at the end of the day when he climbs
the stairs and turns left. He, too, knows Annie's rules.

(1960s)

It is a sewing room in Pauline's house, and as I climb the stairs and turn to the left I can hear the clackety clack of my Grandmother Annie's Singer responding to my mother's right foot rhythmically working the treadle. When I was very young, I would sit nearly hypnotized at her feet on the bare board floors while, above me, her fingers, not yet crippled from arthritis, would deftly maneuver a skirt hem or pant cuff under and around the machine's presser foot. Occasionally, to backstitch, she turns the wheel, and she hums to herself. My mother does not sew clothing from whole cloth, as her mother did; she mends and re-sizes, but her stitches are accurate and confident from years of practice.

Around the time I begin Junior High School, she and I will take sewing lessons from a woman up the hill. My mother will make only one pair of slacks for herself out of double knit polyester and then quit, but I will continue through high school to make many of my own clothes on the new electric Singer bought by my father to replace Annie's treadle machine. My mother will force herself to learn to operate the updated model, though she will frequently voice complaints of its complexity compared to the antique which spends the rest of its days in my mother's house folded down into its cabinet underneath its replacement.

Because she works as a waitress during the day, Ma's time spent with Annie's Singer occurs only in the evenings; otherwise, the sewing room door stays closed. Not yet wired for electricity, the room sits in shadows, its only artificial light a bright circle from a desk lamp carefully balanced on the edge of the sewing cabinet's hinged top and connected by an extension cord to an outlet in the bathroom down the hall. Against one pale green wall towers an oak drop-front desk that stores letters and cards and other documents important enough to save but not important enough for the strong box in the attic. Next to the desk squats a mahogany record cabinet full of 78s, its companion Victrola long since gone. Leaning against the wall by the door, too heavy to hang from the horse hair plaster, is a framed landmark and residential map of North Brookfield dated 1880. An oak dresser is stuffed with gloves, scarves, and handbags. The cherry rocker, a wedding gift to my grandparents, sits unused in the far corner by the window where, years ago I am told, a bed used to be. Coat and suit boxes nesting still more boxes of decreasing size balance themselves on the rocker's arms. The very top box holds an assortment of all-occasion cards, spools of ribbon, and small pieces of wrapping paper. No one has sat in the cherry rocker since Annie died in 1943.

Miscellaneous boxes of Christmas paper rolls, years of carefully dated and catalogued receipts, and generic gifts to be re-gifted are arranged here and there, their placement and exact contents controlled and carefully monitored by my mother. "Were you looking for something upstairs?" she will ask my father (or me when I am older) because she has noticed a slight disarray or a box not quite where she left it no matter how carefully he (or later, I) try to replace it. One Memorial Day when she and I accompany my Aunt Ruth to the cemetery to place flowers on their parents' graves, Uncle Chuck will stay behind claiming he doesn't feel good. That evening, my mother will make an angry phone call to her older sister about Chuck's obvious snooping only to be calmly told that privacy is unnecessary if one has nothing to hide. Chuck will never again be left alone in my mother's house.

I am not allowed in the sewing room, unless my mother is already in there, and the little attic room beyond, with all of its secrets and stories hidden among the trunks and antiques, is likewise forbidden until I am much older. I have asked my mother to promise me that she will announce when she plans to sew, or better yet, when something needs to be stored in or retrieved from the attic, so that I may accompany her through the miniature doorway into the stark, unfinished room where even I, still a child, have to stoop except under those rafters that meet at the center peak. Often, so intent on her task, Ma will forget the proximity of the low exposed beams and straighten up suddenly, whacking her head. "Bitch!" I hide my snickering, unaware that, years later, I will be the one cursing.

Roofing nails poke through the rough boards and sometimes snag my hair. The tiny window at the room's far end lets in minimal light, so a flashlight is required, even during the day, to see anything but the largest and most obvious objects: my Grandfather Homer's rickety wooden high chair and baby crib; the metal high chair and wooden playpen that were first my brother Jay's then mine (and years later will be my daughter Chloe's); and my mother's wicker baby carriage, from which, if I bend down very close and squint through the gloom, her "Baby Alice" doll's cracked and peeling face can be seen peering out.

My mother shines the flashlight into this or that box or trunk while I carefully tip toe through the dim corners, my hands clasped behind my back, making sure not to knock over or dislodge any of the precious items. "Tell me again about this one," I'll beg, pointing. My favorite story is about how she saved her pennies for weeks to buy Baby Alice from the Sears Roebuck catalogue and how she filled out and mailed the order form herself. Sometimes, at my request, she pulls out Annie's small brown photograph album, the black and white pictures secured on its thick black paper pages by tiny black paper photo corners. My mother does not look through the album, however, but carefully hands it to me to browse. I may ask for a name I've forgotten since last time ("Which one is Uncle Bob?"), but I know better than to ask her to look at any pictures with Annie in them. Even after over twenty five years, she cannot see her mother's image without crying. Years later, when I am an adult and she is elderly, Ma will be able to handle pictures of Annie only in her youth but still not as she herself remembered her.

The downstairs phone rings. Ma answers, but I'm close enough to hear Jay's voice, "Ma…what's mine that I can have?" Occasionally short on cash, my brother calls to ask for an item from the sewing room or attic that he can sell. At first, my mother steers him away from the family heirlooms toward items that were left behind when she and her first husband Johnny divorced. "Here, you can take these chairs," she tells Jay, pointing to a set of six antique dining chairs, the style of which I have never seen displayed in our house, "your father brought them home one by one when he worked at the farm. They were being stored in their barn." Even at nine or ten, I am stunned. I knew Jay's father had once worked as a groundskeeper at nearby Elm Hill Farm, the birthplace of "Elsie the Cow," but I had no idea he had stolen from Mr. and Mrs. Means, his employers. "No kidding," Jay laughs, apparently delighted by his father's dishonesty, "I guess they never missed 'em." He grabs the first two as my mother already begins rearranging to fill in the space.

Before long, only furniture from my mother's family remains to be picked over. The next time my brother announces his intentions, Ma ushers me upstairs and to the left. "Jay is on his way. Before he gets here, I need to know what you want to keep." From as far back as I can re-member, Ma always said that when she dies, I will get the house and Jay will get "the things in it," meaning the furniture currently in use as well as the stored antiques, except for whatever items remained from my fa-ther's family and those that have been bought for or given specifically to me.

It is daytime, and my mother and I stand in her sewing room wait-ing for Jay. She has opened the little attic door, but I already know that nothing in there interests me.

"You can pick one thing," she informs me.

I consider my options. Ma has already given me the pine Shaker hutch, found in the house when my grandparents bought it in 1920 as well as her first kitchen table bought in 1938, maple with an enamel top and leaves that slide out and pop up to lock into place. The table and the hutch are both safely tucked away in the attached shed, which I have tak-en over as my summer clubhouse. Both will be prominent pieces in my own kitchen after I marry.

I point to the cherry rocker. "I want that." Ma smiles. She now knows that her mother's rocker will stay in the family through at least one more generation.

When Jay leaves that afternoon, the oak desk goes with him. Next time, it will be the record cabinet. When he asks about the rocker, Ma just silently shakes her head.

(1980s)

It is the haunted storage room in the nightmares that begin once I marry and move away, the room beyond which the smoky green light lives. Sometimes I climb the stairs and turn to the left, but other times the dreams begin when I am already standing in the room. It may be either daytime or nighttime, but even in daylight the room is shadowed. I may notice Annie's treadle sewing machine against the wall directly in front of me, the only piece of furniture I ever recognize. There are always boxes, so many boxes, piles of boxes in this outer room, the room that, in reality, is still my mother's sewing room. Sometimes the little attic door is wide open or missing, but usually in these dreams it is only cracked open. I understand that my very presence in this storage room is unwelcome and will ultimately disturb what lies in wait in the attic, yet if the inner attic room is clearly visible, I enter, knowing I am briefly safe to do so and hoping even in my dream state for an alternate ending. Unlike the cluttered storage room, the attic yawns nearly empty and is somehow brighter and many times larger than its actual size. Even before the atmosphere begins to thicken and change color, I can see the treachery in front of me but not low rafters and sharp roofing nails because the dream-attic is not only wider and longer but higher than the real one. These floor boards are brittle and rotted; some are missing, and I have to navigate around gaps and weaknesses that threaten to send me plummeting into the abyss below. In reality, the attic is situated directly above the Other Side, another storage room that was once my grandmother's dry goods store, but even by the window's light, I can't ever see through the boards to what lies below. The space drops into murky nothingness. As I carefully pick my way through and around the pitfalls, the light always dims, the signal for me to retreat.

If the little attic door is closed or only cracked open, I do not attempt to enter. I hurry through whatever has brought me into the sewing room because I know in these dreams my time is shorter. Too soon, the little plank door creaks, slowly, slowly, and the air thickens, the light dims. My chest tightens; my heart pounds, but I must appear calm because "it" can sense fear. I mustn't look towards the attic or in any way acknowledge "its" presence because to do so will increase its speed and power. Peripherally, I see the low greenish light curling around the plank door, silently snaking its way into the sewing room as I head for the hallway. I can't hurry until I am descending the stairs; only then, acutely aware of its pursuit and its increasing speed do I allow myself to break into a run.

Why do I always ignore the front door at the bottom of the stairs? I can only guess that I need to ensure that my mother is not in danger. Often, in these nightmares, I will call out to her: "Come on, we have to leave now!" and I make sure she follows me out the back door, taking her arm to assist her in those dreams when she is elderly and frail. However even during the few nightmares when I somehow know that I am alone in the house, I still ignore the front door. Instead I round the bottom of the stairs, dash through the dining room and kitchen and exit the house through the back door, knowing that, once outside, I'm safe from the greenish light.

(1996)

It is my private den in my house where I have returned to raise my daughter, Chloe, after my divorce and remarriage. True to her word, my mother bequeathed the house to me and left instructions for disbursement of most of its contents – along with $10,000 in cash in an envelope and an additional $20,000 to be paid by me - to my brother, Jay.

My den to the left at the top of the stairs has sunny yellow walls with darker yellow trim. Three coats of clear urethane bring out the golds and reds of the formerly unfinished maple wide board floor. A crystal-shaded ceiling light has been added, its wall switch just inside the door, and new wall outlets provide power to my computer, desk lamp, cordless phone, and my new sewing machine that sits on its cabinet against the same wall where my grandmother's treadle machine once sat. Three bookcases, one I'd bought while in college and two that are really just boards slapped together by my new husband Bob, hold most of my books. A small pine secretary that I bought unfinished and stained myself sits by the window where the oak drop-front desk used to be. Prisms and multi-colored sun catchers reflect slivers of light as they dangle inside the sheer curtain. Incense smoke of rose or sage curls toward the ceiling. Framed photographs of my parents and grandparents are displayed here and there along with trinkets and mementos of mine, my mother's and both grandmothers': a favorite stuffed bear, a music box, a vase, a vacation souvenir. A small table holds a ceramic Venus de Milo and other ritual items for my Esbat and Sabbat celebrations and faces north just next to the miniature plank door that leads into the inner attic room.

"It's a gnome's door!" Chloe delightedly exclaimed the first time she saw it. "Does 'David the Gnome' live in there?"

I smiled at her reference to one of her favorite Nickelodeon shows. Unaware of my nightmares, my child still regards the rough, un-finished inner attic as enchanted and laughs when I carelessly whack my head on one of its low, exposed beams. "Shit!"

No longer a keeper of family secrets, the attic now stores mostly practical items: camping equipment, trunks of blankets and pillows or of seasonal clothing, Christmas decorations, and miscellaneous dishes and other household objects. A single bare bulb is wired into the room's center peak, but a flashlight is still necessary to see under the eaves. Like my mother, I know exactly where everything is and mildly resent finding any evidence of another's search: "Just ask me, and I'll get whatever you need from there," I tell my husband and daughter.

My grandparents' cherry rocker, the one item I'd chosen once my brother had started sporadically raiding the family heirlooms, no longer serves as a repository for empty gift boxes but was moved down from Ma's sewing room to my new living room when I began renovations. Both the enamel-top kitchen table and the Shaker hutch promised to me as a child by my mother have returned home from my Florida apartment and occupy my newly painted kitchen. Only one other antique from my mother's family remains in my house.

"I've been thinking," my mother began one day during her dialysis. Three times a week during those final months, I had sat with her and we had chatted to make the hour pass more quickly. I always tried not to be obvious about keeping one eye on the heart monitor. As stubborn as her own mother had been when in decline, Ma had just decided to have both her pacemaker and her defibrillator disconnected and had filled out "DNR" papers. Far from being suicidal, she had simply decided to forgo any heroic efforts to prolong her steadily deteriorating condition. As difficult as it was for me not to intervene, I respected her wishes, insisting only that she continue with her medication and dialysis.

"Will you take Dad's chair?" Her father's chair? With its hard seat cushion and scratchy brown tweed fabric that had begun to fray on the arms? Just the week before, she had finally cancelled the registration on her Bonneville and asked that I transfer her plate to my car. She'd kept the

same tag number since her '48 Chevy and wanted to see it continue. Despite the cost, I promised I'd follow through. But the rough, unsightly, uncomfortable chair? I hesitated.

"I had it reupholstered when you were a baby, but it needs to be done again," she persisted, "Will you have it reupholstered and use it?" Ma rarely discussed her father except to say that he worked hard. Her reminiscences typically centered on Annie, her mother, with Homer in a supporting role. I suddenly realized that, apart from his wallet, his garnet ring, and his name tag from the asbestos factory, only the chair remained as being solely "his."

The heavy Indian cotton fabric in a flowered pattern of blue, lilac, and green; new springs; and a softer, plumper cushion cost me nearly $400. I'd had no idea that reupholstering would be so expensive. The chair's original brass upholstery tacks shine like

new, and the mahogany "ball" feet are carefully oiled. Saved from the same fate as Baby Alice, Annie's Singer, and the rest of the antiques left to Jay, Homer's chair is tucked into a corner of my den, too beautiful to risk being damaged by everyday family use but perfect for me to settle in with a good book.

Within days of my mother's funeral, I'd gathered the rest of the antiques and miscellaneous furniture from her side of the family and moved them out of the house and into the shed to be picked up by Jay at his convenience. He had already sold Ma's car. The last day Jay would ever set foot on my property, he and a friend of his filled a pickup truck ten times while I watched from inside the house. As they loaded the last few items, I saw Jay turn toward my father's garage, which still contained all the tools and lawn-care equipment.

"That Toro mower is mine!" he yelled over his shoulder. "I paid $750 for it!"

I'd expected as much. "Ma reimbursed you," I yelled back through the screen door. "She wrote it all down." One of the last things my mother had said to me was "No matter what anyone might have to say, I pay my own way. I always have." After her death, I'd gone through her detailed records and all her receipts dating back several years.

"You can go fuck yourself!" Jay screamed at the house as he got into the truck.

(2009)

It is the only room not yet emptied in the house that belongs to the bank. Just this morning, I signed over the Deed in Lieu of Foreclosure in Blaise Berthiume's office. Fed up with Massachusetts' rising cost of living and nasty weather, I'd relocated to North Carolina after ending my ten year marriage to Bob Mallon but had been unable to sell my "functionally obsolete" house in a neighborhood currently referred to as "economically depressed" because of its numerous foreclosures. For nearly a year, the house sat empty while I struggled to pay two mortgages. To offset the expense, I reluctantly attempted to rent out the property; however, despite careful screening and reference checks, I ended up with non-paying tenants who refused to vacate until finally ordered to do so months later in housing court. Out of both money and energy at that point, I accepted the bank's offer to buy back the house for what I still owed on it and arranged for the final trip to retrieve those items locked up in the garage and attic that I'd not yet been able to transport to my new house.

Nearly nine o'clock and still no sign of my daughter, Chloe. I stand out on the front porch and wave my arm back and forth, trying to get a signal on my cell phone.

"I'm on my way," Chloe informs me when I finally reach her, "I got hung up at work."

I pace while I wait. I have promised to drop off the keys to Blaise first thing in the morning. Gas and electricity have already been disconnected. The loaded U-Haul sits in the driveway ready to go, with just enough space left in it for the camp cots and sleeping bags from the little attic, on which my new husband Scott and I plan to spend this last night downstairs in the house. Whatever is left in the garage will stay behind: an extra porch post, some Bruce hardwood flooring, extra ceramic bathroom tiles, snow shovels. However, the room to the left at the top of the stairs is still full of things that belong to my daughter and need to be sorted through, things she'd been unable to take to her apartment when she'd moved out. When I made the trip back to interview perspective tenants several months earlier, I gathered all of Chloe's leftover books, dishes, clothes, aquarium supplies, and other non-essentials from the upstairs bedrooms where she had been living and secured them in my former den, hoping she'd find the time to pick through the items, take what she wanted to keep and throw out the rest.

"I really don't want to do this," Chloe announces as she steps out of her two-door Toyota.

"Chloe, you've had over a year. It's now or never. I thought you were coming in the Ranger."

"Bill's dad needed it. I'll just have to fit whatever I can in here. Is the rest of your stuff already out of the attic?"

I hand her a flashlight as we climb the stairs and turn left.

"Mom, I don't want to do this at all," Chloe complains. Even by the dim light of the kerosene lamp I set up on the floor, the clutter seems to fill the room. "I've lived without this stuff for over a year. I'm sure there's nothing here I need."

"You have to sort through it, Chloe. Look, there is the set of china that Aunt Ruth wanted you to have…" I start lighting and arranging candles here and there among the bins and boxes as Chloe squats down and begins randomly picking through the items.

"Where can I put what I don't want?" she sighs, already exasperated.

I scan the room. I'd brought no extra boxes. We make piles at first. Scott helps move things aside, but soon we all get confused in the dim light, so I open the little plank door to the inner attic. "For now, just put what you don't want in there."

I try to be helpful to Chloe by pointing out the things that I think might be useful or hold sentimental value, but my suggestions seem only to agitate her. Scott silently appears and disappears to move downstairs and out to her car whatever Chloe has decided to keep. When her car is full, he will turn to mine.

As I watch my daughter pick up, examine, and make a decision on this toy or that book,   the reality hits that this is the last time that she and I will be together in this house. As ambivalent as I have been over giving up my family home, I am fully aware that Chloe does not share my feelings. Perhaps because she was already ten years old when we moved back to Massachusetts from Florida, and my mother died less than a year later, but my daughter feels none of the attachment and responsibility that I had been raised to feel toward the house. If she did, I might have tried harder to hold on to it. For me, the house symbolizes my childhood and my family. Half of Chloe's childhood was spent in Florida, and most of her family is now deceased – even my brother Jay, dead of lung cancer a year and a half earlier. I think of him now and wonder what he would have said if he'd been around to see me trying to sell the house and failing. I'm sure he would have gloated.

Despite the open hostility shown toward me by my brother during and after our mother's funeral, I'd attempted to keep communication open between him and my child because I wanted her to have a sense of family, especially now that she had no grandparents at all and her father had stayed in Florida. Jay, however, seemed uninterested in pursuing any kind of meaningful relationship with his only niece. Although he did not outright reject her, he never initiated any meetings or phone calls but remained on the receiving end of her efforts, right up until their last meeting.

"I'll pick you up in an hour, okay? That will still give us plenty of time to get you to the airport." Clutching the little wrapped gift in her hand, Chloe had silently nodded.

I swung over in front of Jay's Barber Shop. I could see that she was nervous, but I couldn't tell whether her anxiety resulted from the prospect of seeing her uncle after not having heard from him in nearly two years or from the upcoming three hour flight alone to see her father with whom she'd be spending the summer. My fifteen year old daughter tended to keep her feelings to herself.

I did not get out of the car but swung back into traffic as soon as I saw her go through the Barber Shop door. I had not spoken to Jay since Ma's estate had been settled. He'd made it very clear that I would never again be a part of his life. No great loss, really, since he'd never been a real brother to me; anything he'd ever done with me or for me had always been at our mother's request. "I wish you and your brother were closer," I'd heard her sigh so many times over the years. I could never understand why Jay had always shown so little interest in a sister who so much wanted a big brother to look up to. I got my answer the day in the hospital after he disowned us both over her Will, the last day I saw my mother alive.

"He always resented you. From the day you were born," she'd sadly announced.

"I wish you'd told me," I'd replied, trying not to be angry, "I wouldn't have tried so hard."

As I drove back to the barber shop, I mentally ticked off my errands: Bank, Bookstore, Post Office. I glanced at my watch. Just about an hour had passed. I approached Jay's house, surprised to see Chloe already waiting outside, huddled under the spinning barber pole. She looked unhappy.

"How did it go?"

It was all I could do not to turn the car around as Chloe described the visit. At first Jay hadn't seemed to recognize her. She'd hugged him, both when she arrived and as she was leaving, but his response had been half-hearted. He thanked her for the gift but hadn't opened it. Though he had no customers, a couple of his cronies had stopped by to shoot the breeze. Jay pointed to a chair where Chloe was to wait. For several minutes, the men repeatedly glanced from her to Jay, visibly uncomfortable by Jay's rudeness until one of them finally wrapped up the small talk and they left the shop. Once alone with his niece, Jay launched into a tirade of complaints about his health and finances. Not once did he ask her how she was or what she'd been doing. Finally, the greatest insult of all, as soon as his tirade wound down, Jay thrust a fifty dollar bill in her hand and ushered her to the door. She'd been waiting outside for me for nearly half an hour.

"I don't want his money," Chloe wailed now, nearly in tears, "I just wanted an uncle."

"I'm sorry, honey. It's not you; that's just his way." How many times had Jay stuck money in a birthday card for me because he couldn't be bothered to shop for a gift? I hadn't known until I was older that he hadn't even bought the cards; my mother had picked them out for him to sign. All the old resentments I'd buried flared up, sparked by my brother's indifference to the pain he'd just caused my child. My fingers tightened on the wheel. Well, I'd be passing by his house on the way back from the airport too.

As if reading my mind, Chloe, turned to me and said, "No, Mom. No."

"Chloe—"

"Mom…" she blurted, then hesitated. I held my breath and waited for her to finish. "This visit was his last chance."

"I don't get it."

"I've been sending him tickets to stuff at school," she told me. "Every concert I was in, every play. I didn't want to tell you. I was afraid you'd be mad."

That bastard. I knew where this was headed. I tried to keep the anger from boiling over into my voice, "I wouldn't have been angry Chloe, only afraid for you. That you'd be disappointed and hurt."

"Yeah, I know that now. He never came. Not to any of them. But please don't say anything. Don't go near him. If he doesn't want to be my uncle, then fuck him. Fuck him, Mom."

Now as I watch my adult daughter determinedly going through the piles of her belongings in the room to the left at the top of the stairs, stacking some things, tossing aside others, I realize that I am still mourning the end of three generations of ownership of this house. There was a time, not too long ago, when I believed there'd be a fourth, but that dream ended with me. Chloe is not of my mindset.

"I don't care if I never see this place again," she'd declared when she moved out, her firm tone shocking me.

Have I been remiss, I wonder, at not instilling in her some sense of commitment to the family legacy, or, by not reinforcing those sentiments, have I instead done her a favor by freeing her of the guilt that I am feeling over leaving this house?

Chloe picks up a heavy, bound scrapbook given to her by my Aunt Ruth after the death of her son and rises from her crouched position.

"I don't need Bird Coins of the fucking World, Francis!" she suddenly yells. "Why do I have this?!" She tosses the volume in the corner, but the discovery of my dead older cousin's coin collection seems to have galvanized her into action. In a frenzy, she seizes ornaments, records, books, whatever she can reach and hurls them one by one into the pitch dark inner attic, where they smash as they hit the hardwood floor. "There!" Too horrified to react, I look for Scott, but he has left the room. I stand there, cringing at her triumph in each shattering of glass and metal. "And that!"

I can't breathe. How can she do this? These are her memories too. What would my mother say? And the mess. Who will clean all this up?

"Chloe, stop" is all I can say, but she is oblivious. In the murky light, her blond dreds swing as she stoops and rises, stoops and rises, and the muscles in her bare arms strain with the force of her anger.

And then she starts to laugh.

BEFORE THE OLD CROW CAN TOUCH OFF THE BARN ROOF IN PURSUIT OF HER LUNCH, SHE FEELS MORE THAN HEARS A DISTANT RUMBLING. SHE WAITS, MOTIONLESS, AS THE RUMBLE APPROACHES, AND THEN SHE SEES IT AS IT ROUNDS THE LAST BEND HEADED OUT OF TOWN ON THE EAST BROOKFIELD ROAD: THE LARGE YELLOW MOVING TRUCK THAT SHE'D EARLIER SPOTTED IN THE DRIVEWAY OF THE HOUSE IN LITTLE CANADA, (THE HOUSE ONCE OWNED BY ANNIE KELLEY, THEN BY HER DAUGHTER, PAULINE MARTIN, AND UNTIL RECENTLY BY HER DAUGHTER, DONNA GIROUARD). THE CROW, WHO HAS LIVED HER WHOLE LIFE IN NORTH BROOKFIELD, AS HAD HER PARENTS AND GRANDPARENTS AND THEIR PARENTS AND GRANDPARENTS, KNOWS IT IS THE SAME YELLOW TRUCK BECAUSE SHE RECOGNIZES THE DARK GREEN SUV FOLLOWING JUST BEHIND IT.

AS THE VEHICLES CROSS OVER THE TOWN LINE, THE CROW SCREAMS AT THEM AS IF IN REPROACH: **YOU'LL BE BACK.**

15

Going Home

(2009)

I decide to take Forest Street, to approach the house indirectly from its front corner, so I drive straight up School Street instead of turning left onto Grove and passing the Common. My decision is made spur of the moment, at the Rubber Shop where the train tracks ended when I was a child, having wound their way there from both Springfield and Boston. The train still ran back then but only for freight, although I would occasionally stand on those tracks and gaze just up the road at the rundown brick station, imagining women in bustles and button shoes and men with canes and top hats waiting for the only transportation in or out of North Brookfield, Massachusetts, to chug to a stop.

My grandmother would have met that train from Boston the day it brought the toddler (my Aunt Ruth) she and my grandfather had arranged to adopt after nearly six childless years together, and Annie would have stood on that platform, brushing away the soot and asbestos fibers that swirled through the air like a summer blizzard from the factory across the street, anxious to meet her new little girl.

The asbestos factory would have been running at full throttle, and in nice weather when its windows opened to let out the oppressive heat, the fibers swirled in the breeze to land in gardens and on damp laundry hung out to dry even blocks away in Little Canada, where Homer Martin and Annie Kelley began their married life in Phoebe Barrett's modified Cape on North Common Street. Homer made his living in the contaminated warrens of the massive multi-story brick and wood structure of Aztec Asbestos until the black he continuously coughed up filled his lungs so that he could no longer work. Designated an environmental hazard by the state during my youth, the asbestos factory finally fell to the bulldozer a generation later, so that only an empty five acre lot, fenced off with

chain link and barbed wire, now marks its existence across from the Rubber Shop as one of the town's once primary industries.

Perhaps I have chosen this route because the alternative would
take me past my ex-husband's house – not that there would be any
chance of running into Bob since he was eaten up by cancer a couple of
years after our bitter divorce, but my single-mindedness cannot risk any
distractions from the only reason for my being in this place at this time. I
am here only for my house, the house where my grandparents lived their
entire adult lives, where my mother was born and raised and later returned to raise my brother and me, where I returned after my mother's
death to remarry and raise my own daughter, the house that is no longer
mine.

I had planned my trip north only to visit my daughter, Chloe, who
chose to stay in Massachusetts though I had relocated to North Carolina.
For the past several weeks, that's what I had told everyone: "I'm going
north to spend time with my daughter." Sometimes I would add, "Oh,
and I might swing by my old house while I'm up there." A side trip to
my hometown would be only supplementary, a lark, a way to kill a bit of
time while Chloe worked in her tattoo studio about forty five miles away.
After all, there was no real need to go to North Brookfield. Or perhaps, if
time permitted, I would drive there only to check on the cemetery, to
make sure that the family plots at St. Joseph's were being kept up. If I ran
out of time though and didn't get to town during this trip, no big deal.
These were the lies I had told my friends, my daughter, and even myself.
The reality, however, was that the house had summoned me, and I had to
respond.

The nightmares that had plagued me since childhood had magi-
cally stopped the previous year, once I signed over the house. No more
sickly greenish lights seeped from my mother's attic to chase me down
the stairs and out the back door. No more sizzling embers landed on her
roof, spontaneously igniting and spreading, blackening shingles and
crackling into second story rooms as I helplessly watched from the sidewalk. I no longer dreamed that inexplicable evil; instead, I dreamed of

driving into town, always at night, the nearly empty house solid and unlocked and (though no longer mine) waiting for me, as I clandestinely
returned to retrieve some item from my childhood, usually a long gone,
long forgotten toy, its memory dredged up by my subconscious.

One especially vivid dream featured Annie's Singer treadle sewing
machine, left to Jay, along with most of the antiques, according to my
mother's Will. Oddly, in the dream, the Singer did not sit upstairs in its
once customary spot in my mother's sewing room but surprised me from
a shadowy corner in the otherwise empty dining room where, with dream
-strength, I hoisted it by myself, cabinet and all, somehow fitting it into
the trunk of Isabelle, my new Volkswagen. All of my dream-items no
longer exist in reality yet remained within reach of my subconscious to
be spirited away in my car.

Only one dream-trip sent me back for an item from my recent
past: a box of leftover Bruce hardwood flooring from when I'd renovated the Other Side, the space where Annie had once had her dry goods
store, turning it into the master bedroom. When loading the moving truck
that drizzly day in May, I'd decided I had neither room nor need for the
extra flooring and so had stored it up in the rafters of my dad's garage.
When I returned for it in my dream, however, the box was gone, oddly
the only dream-item I sneaked back to reclaim that was not still there
waiting for me.

Somewhat puzzled but relieved that the original nightmares had
stopped, I shrugged off what I called these new "packing and loading"
dreams as simply my subconscious coming to terms with the closing of
the North Brookfield chapter of my life. Until one dream changed my
perspective.

This closest thing to my earlier nightmares began the same as the
other packing and loading dreams except this time my quest took me upstairs instead of just to the garage or first floor of the house. As I started
back down the stairs, my arms full of miscellaneous dust-gatherers, I
heard the sewing room door creak open behind me (the attic just beyond),
a sound so familiar to me - mundane in reality but horrifying in my night-

mares because it usually signaled that whatever it is or was that lived in the attic among the murky green would be slithering out and headed directly for me. The old panic tightened my throat, but instead of bolting down the stairs (as I had in past nightmares), I determinedly maintained my pace, not wanting to drop any of the precious items for which I'd returned. Surprisingly, the air did not thicken and turn smoky-green; instead I felt myself being gently yet firmly pulled back up the stairs, as if by a giant magnet at the top. Against my will, my feet began their slow-motion backward climb, my head never turning, my gaze never wavering from the front door below me. Once at the top of the stairs, I was held fast, flat against the wall for just a few seconds, then released. I calmly resumed my descent, only to feel the house's force pull me back, hold me to the wall, then release me. Again and again, I tried to leave, but the house refused to let me go, and I understood through this dream, that the force drawing me back was no unnamed unseen attic monster; this force was the house itself, its essence, its soul, and it was calling to me the only way it knew how. Although I had already said goodbye, it was letting me know that we had unfinished business.

As I take the second left up School Street onto Forest Street I try to calm my breathing. After a glance through my rearview mirror at the empty road behind me, I ease my foot off the accelerator and slow the car to barely a crawl, wishing I could slow my pounding heart as easily. All along Route 9, I'd been fine, through Spencer, through East Brookfield. The late afternoon sun was shining through Isabelle's sun roof, Tom Petty was rocking on the CD player, and I continued to downplay the significance of this trip by focusing on tomorrow's early birthday present from Chloe: a new tattoo she'd just designed for me. I bore right at the fork, heading towards town, and passed the bowling alley. Just before the town line, by the boarded-up antique barn where the road turns bumpy and rutted, the palpitations began, and the memories flooded in, breaking through my façade of indifference: memories not of my childhood but of adult decisions made, legal papers signed, plans finalized, tears shed.

There was the day I finally faced up to being unable to afford the expense and upkeep of a one hundred and forty year old house in a town where utilities and taxes were steadily rising and, before I lost my resolve, called the realtor to take the listing. As professional and matter-of-fact as I tried to be over the phone, I burst into tears the second we ended the call.

On All Hallows Eve, about a month later, full of guilt and remorse over putting my mother's legacy on the market and having earlier that day gone to the cemetery to enlist her spiritual guidance, I lit a candle, cast the circle, and shuffled then cut the Tarot deck and asked her to speak to me through the cards, vowing to abide by the result. My mother had never once hesitated to put her children's needs ahead of her own, and though she had passionately loved and cared for her home, I knew that her concern would be only for my welfare and ultimate happiness. Half expecting the Four of Coins (protecting one's possessions), I instead turned over the Hanged Man, the card that advises sacrificing something for one's own good, immediately followed by the Eight of Rods, the "take action now" card. I had no doubt that my mother had not only just given her consent for me to part with the house but was advising me to move on to something better, and again I cried.

And finally, months later, when, having failed to sell the house and unable to afford two mortgages, I made the trip back to sign over the deed to the bank "in lieu of foreclosure," to pick up the remaining odds and ends in the garage and attic, and to say what I thought would be goodbye to the house.

"It's for the best," my family's attorney assured me, extending the bank papers across his mahogany office desk, then patting my hand, his smile kindly, his eyes sympathetic behind gold-rimmed glasses. Blaise had long ago guided my mother through a land dispute and a few years later had drawn up her Will, sitting by her hospital bed and holding her hand as she weakly explained her intentions. He had advised me through the handling of her estate and represented me in my divorce from Bob.

"Your mother would not want you burdened by her house," he said, handing me a pen. "She would want you to move on."

I nodded, sobbed, and signed.

Just minutes after leaving Blaise's office, as I made my way from room to room of my house one last time, I saw not the many cosmetic changes that I had made during my adult life there but, instead, each room as I remembered it from my childhood, and more tears fell as I mourned all that I had lost: my childhood, my parents, my past, all gone forever now that the last piece that held it all together was no longer mine – the legacy passed from my grandmother, Annie; to my mother, Pauline; to me and that I had hoped someday to pass down to Chloe. Although my mother had released me from my obligation to the house on All Hallows Eve, I still felt as if I was abandoning my responsibility and even the house itself, and I felt its disapproval as I neared the door. Key in hand and guilt choking my throat, I reached up to stroke its moldings, as I had so many times before.

"I'm sorry," I said out loud, "but someone else will love you," doubting the truth of my words even as they left my lips. So much bad karma over so many years had been stored up in that house that evidently even prospective buyers could feel it. And why should the house believe me anyway? Hadn't I previously promised always to love and take care of it? As I stood in the doorway, I envisioned it sitting empty and un-loved, deteriorating until eventually claimed by the elements, and for just a second considered reentering to open the gas lines to the kitchen and parlor stoves, mercy-killing by incineration seeming more compassionate than the slow, lingering death I foresaw.

Nearly a year later, I am virtually idling up Forest Street, shiver-ing despite the summer heat, hands gripping the steering wheel and cold sweat rolling down my back, my throat and chest tight with the fear of not knowing how I will react upon once again seeing the house, hating being here but feeling its magnet pull me closer.

My prediction for the house, death by desertion, has proven inac-curate. A young couple bought it from the bank only a couple of months before my trip. Although I had not wanted the house to languish, the idea of new owners – strangers – moving freely about MY house while I am restricted to only a sidewalk view adds to my anxiety and the sick feeling in the pit of my stomach. Perhaps I had fleetingly considered burning it down only so that no one else could have it. I wonder, not for the first time, why the house still beckoned. Shouldn't the story be over, the book closed? Yet that last dream in which the house pulled me back up the stairs and held me fast had occurred after I'd heard news of the sale.

My Volkswagen rolls up Forest Street, past the Senior Center, formerly the Knights of Columbus Hall; past the old American Legion Hall, recently converted to a duplex; past an apartment building the first floor of which used to be Morrison's Café. Hart's Café, now "Still Hart's Café," will be coming up on my left. I consider pulling over, parking, and walking the last half block to my house, so that I can slowly drink in its every detail but remain nearly paralyzed behind the wheel still aimed straight ahead at the intersection of North Common and Forest Streets.

Seconds later, there it is: the albatross on which I had spent thousands of hours and dollars; the star of countless nightmares of fires and hauntings throughout both childhood and adulthood; the place where I had planned, dreamed, loved and cried; and I feel…nothing. I do not fall apart as I'd feared. No lightning bolt shoots out of the sky, and the world does not end. To my astonishment, I suddenly realize that, if I feel anything at all, it is only a mild curiosity.

A quick look as I roll through the intersection reveals that little has changed. An overgrown shrub has been removed, and the remaining shrubs are neatly trimmed. Pots of annuals hang from the farmer's porch Mike Sanford had rebuilt for me using pictures in Annie's album as a guide, and an American flag waves from the peak. Additional multi-colored annuals bloom in the space between the porch lattice and the sidewalk. I slowly continue past the side yard, noticing that the old crabapple tree is no longer scraping its branches against the new roof and will no longer drop its bitter inedible fruit all over the driveway, and I briefly wonder why its absence does not sadden me. For years I fought its impending death from whatever disease weakens and kills crabapple trees, mostly because it was a Mother's Day gift I'd bought as a teenager, and, true to form, I'd been unwilling to let it go. My mother hadn't even really liked the tree, which, other than its all too brief blossoming period in early spring, turned out to be a nuisance, especially when, as it grew, its roots threatened the house's foundation. Good riddance, I now decide.

An SUV and a pickup truck are in the driveway, and I can hear male voices coming from inside my dad's garage. I continue up the street, picking up the pace a bit, and turn around where Willow Street meets the end of Forest, waving to the Fat Tree as I pass. Doubling back, I park the car at the edge of the back yard, and, hidden by the privet hedges, contemplate my next move.

Inspiration strikes, and I reach for my cell phone to call Lissa, who lives just across the street. "Come out of your house," I say to her hello and hang up. Leaving my car to walk back toward the house, I edge towards the road as Lissa's front door opens. As soon as she sees me, we start running to each other. The hug barely ends and conversation has not even begun when I jerk my head towards my dad's garage and say, "Introduce me."

Tall and lean, with dark curly hair sticking out of his Red Sox cap, Bart offers a friendly smile and apologizes for the oil-stained hand he holds out for me to shake. Behind him, in the open garage, squats an old pickup with its hood up, and various engine parts litter the concrete floor. His wife, he explains, is shopping and will surely be disappointed to have missed meeting the house's former owner. I am only half aware that Lissa has begun relating an abridged version of my family's owner-ship; I'm too busy trying to see as much as can be seen from my vantage point while trying not to appear nosy.

Then I jump in. Has he, by any chance, noticed the 1969 penny forever preserved right there in the concrete, placed there by my father to commemorate the garage's completion? Dad designed and built the struc-ture mostly by himself, the sounds of sawing and hammering (as well as the alternate cursing and laughing when my brother Jay was there to help) echoing through the neighborhood well past dark during many late summer nights. I then point to the back door and begin to tell Nate how my grandfather cut that doorway, that the house had had no back entrance in 1920 when it became part of my family history, but a glance at his face indicates that he is listening only out of politeness. Deciding not to bore him further, I ask if he has any questions for me. He brightens. The roof looks new; is it? And do I know how many layers of shingles there are? And when was the insulation blown in? How old are the replacement windows? I answer each question, understanding that only these issues would be of concern to a young couple having just bought their first house. As we speak, I frequently glance at the house, no longer focusing on the little changes to its exterior, but instead unsuccessfully trying to figure out why I have been summoned, why I am HERE.

Wait, what? Something about the hot water heater, but in my reverie I missed it. Evidently, the hot water heater I'd bought, so new that it still wore its price tag, mysteriously exploded in the Other Side one day not two weeks after the mortgage papers had been signed and, while no one was at home, spewed scalding water all over the new Bruce hardwood floor. Fortunately, Bart had found the box of extra flooring I'd left behind in the garage. Worse, though, was that by the time the explosion was discovered, sparks were shooting out from the new circuit box Jimmy Angel had installed for me just behind the hot water heater, and connections were sizzling, scaring the young couple into calling the fire department and necessitating electrical repair work before power could be restored. Much longer and there would have surely been a fire.

Stunned, I stare at the house. Defiance at being abandoned? A test for the new owners? "That's not the way to get people to love you," I silently admonish it, but part of me shamelessly admires its…arrogance? Audacity? Sheer orneriness? Barely suppressing a smile, I turn to find Lissa looking directly at me. Fair-skinned, blue-eyed, strawberry blond Lissa, with the map of Ireland on her face (as my great-aunt Lizzie would say), who has been like a sister to me for many years, so "fey" that she had often been able to read my mind, is surely reading it now. We exchange a knowing smile.

I can see that Bart's "project truck" is demanding his attention, so

I wrap up the pleasantries by assuring him that any further questions he might have can be forwarded to me through Lissa. We again shake hands, and he heads back into the garage. I spend the next hour drinking wine with Lissa and her mother, alternately catching up and reminiscing, while periodically glancing through their kitchen window at the house, still puzzled by its silence and wondering if I will ever get the answer for which I've come.

Later, at St. Joseph's Cemetery, I speak aloud to my parents while I pull stray weeds from their plots, feeling a bit guilty (as I always do) that I direct most of my attention to my mother. Because I'd I lost my father at sixteen, we'd never developed more than a parent-child relationship, and a tenuous one at that. I'd also been unable to forgive him for his emotional abandonment of both me and my mother. She and I, in contrast, had been as close as a mother and daughter could be, closer than Chloe and I will probably ever be, and had in many ways been more like confidants than parent and child.

Raucous cawing breaks my reverie as a murder of crows flies overhead toward Bell Hill. The sun will be setting soon, but I decide to drive by the house once again in my search for an answer, this time approaching it directly from North Common Street.

I hear the happy shouts of a ballgame in progress as I round the corner of Grove Street and cruise past the Common, and I can't help sneaking a glance at my ex-husband's house where I'd been babysat as a child by his mother, Della Mallon. Old habits die hard.

Just before the stop sign at the intersection of North Common and Forest, I again sit, engine idling, as I gaze at the house that is no longer mine.

"What?!" I silently urge it.

Two hanging bird feeders, one on either end of the farmer's porch, gently sway in the summer breeze, and a bright blue wind chime tinkles. A couple of lights glow from inside; perhaps Bart's wife has returned.

I notice a detail I missed during my earlier pass: hanging from the front door, behind which ascend the stairs that lead to my former bedroom at one end and the attic room at the other, hangs a small wooden sign that reads "Johnson," concrete evidence of Bart and Denise Johnson, the new owners, staking their claim, marking their territory, signifying their commitment. And then I hear it, actually feel the rumble as the house speaks its message: "See, I don't need you anymore," and I finally understand that it was not enough just to hear of the sale; in order to be truly free of its psychological hold over me, the house needed to show me that it is being loved and cared for. At this moment, I know there will be no more nightmares. After fifty years of being tied to this house and this town, I am finally being released. I smile as I turn the car down Forest Street.

On impulse, I drive out of North Brookfield the back way, through the apple orchard. Tucked into one corner, in a clearing among the trees, is a playground next to the "Country Store." Having spent many hours there during my youth and knowing that it will be deserted at this time of day, I park my Volkswagen and head for the swings. One lone crow seems to be watching from the nearest tree as higher and higher I soar, and each time I pump my legs, my heart lightens until I seem almost weightless, all tension completely gone from my body and mind. I am no longer the child of my parents, held emotionally captive by the town of North Brookfield.

As I stretch my feet up and out towards the clouds, the crow flies off and my head fills with happy thoughts of the house waiting for me – not the 1870 modified Cape with the wrap-around farmer's porch, but my white "Arts and Crafts" style cottage set back off the road and flanked by Carolina pines.

Acknowledgements

I would like to thank Susan Tekulve, Dan Wakefield, and Richard Tillinghast, who read this book when it was a work in progress, for their advice and encouragement.

Thanks also to my husband, Scott, for his emotional support and to my daughter, Chloe, for reading, rereading, and listening to me read this manuscript in its entirety.

Thanks to dear friends: Betsy Murphy, Nancy Chapman, Lissa Pratt, Andrea Kirk. and M.J. Simms-Maddox for their help and suggestions.

Finally, my thanks to all of those people, alive and deceased, who shared their memories and impressions with me, including my sister, Karen; my brother, Bruce; cousins Flory, Marion, and Billy; my Aunt Ruth; and, most of all, my mother, Pauline.

The Photographs

www.ingramcontent.com/pod-product-compliance
Lightning Source LLC
Chambersburg PA
CBHW031500270326
41930CB00006B/180